D1483216

'Two young West African soldiers shipped halfway across the world in 1943 to fight for the British in Burma find themselves abandoned – wounded, starving and sick – in the unmapped jungle of the Arakan. Their astonishing adventures are reconstructed here in gripping detail… A real-life thriller with sobering implications for the British reader – but I found it impossible to put down.'

Hilary Spurling
author of *Burying the Bones*

'Barnaby Phillips has uncovered a tale which touches the world in every sense. The story is a deceptively simple one, of a lanky boy who runs away from his dusty Nigerian village to join the British Army and is left for dead thousands of miles from home in the Burmese jungle. The miraculous sheltering and survival of Isaac Fadoyebo not only make an irresistible human drama. They also illustrate the terrifying global swirl of the conflict. Told with warmth and colour, this account of a forgotten soldier in a forgotten army in a forgotten war will not itself be easily forgotten.'

Ferdinand Mount
author of *The New Few*

ANOTHER MAN'S WAR

The Story of a Burma Boy in
Britain's Forgotten African Army

BARNABY PHILLIPS

ONEWORLD

A Oneworld Book

First published in North America, Great Britain & Australia by
Oneworld Publications, 2014
Copyright © Barnaby Phillips 2014

The moral right of Barnaby Phillips to be identified as the Author of
this work has been asserted by him in accordance with the Copyright,
Designs and Patents Act 1988

ISBN 978-1-78074-522-0
Ebook ISBN 978-1-78074-523-7

Note on the Text
In 1989, Burma's military government changed the name of the
country to Myanmar, and at the same time the capital Rangoon became
Yangon. I have used the original names throughout this book, for the
sake of consistency, as the greater part of it concerns the years around
the Second World War. No offence is intended.

Typesetting and eBook design by Tetragon, London
Map artwork copyright by Critiqua
Printed and bound in Great Britain by
TJ International Ltd, Padstow, Cornwall

Oneworld Publications
10 Bloomsbury Street, London WC1B 3SR, England

Stay up to date with the latest books,
special offers, and exclusive content from
Oneworld with our monthly newsletter

Sign up on our website
www.oneworld-publications.com

CONTENTS

To my parents

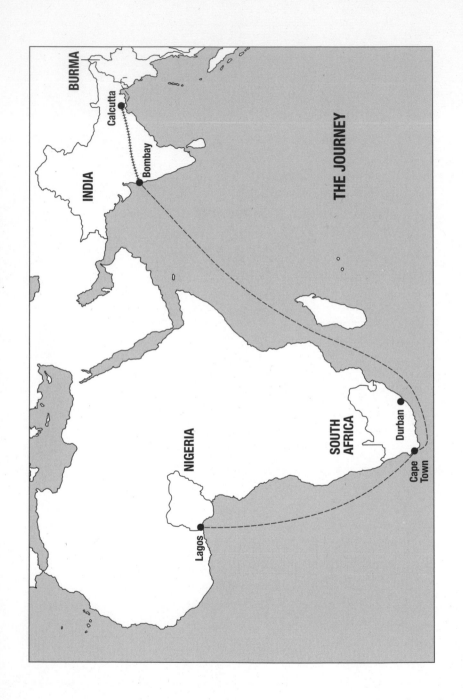

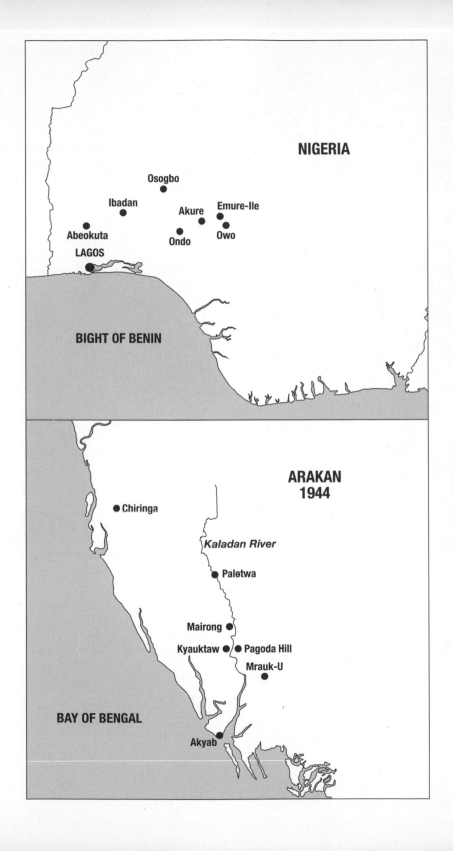

NIGERIA

Osogbo

Ibadan   Akure   Emure-Ile

Abeokuta   Ondo   Owo

LAGOS

BIGHT OF BENIN

ARAKAN
1944

Chiringa

Kaladan River

Paletwa

Mairong

Kyauktaw   Pagoda Hill

Mrauk-U

BAY OF BENGAL

Akyab

PROLOGUE

2 March 1944
Burma

Isaac Fadoyebo would always remember the Kaladan as a wide and calm river, as silent as a graveyard. They had been drifting down it for four days. Trees lined the banks and monkeys played in the branches that reached above them. They were some ninety soldiers, British officers and their West African men, equipment heaped precariously high on the little fleet of bamboo rafts. Most of the West Africans could not swim. When Lance Corporal Felix Okoro fell in a couple of days previously, he had drowned. His body had washed up on the far bank the following morning, and, by the time the burial party reached him, vultures had already started to tear away at the flesh. It had been a horrible accident, Isaac thought, although not one that had created a feeling of impending disaster. He had woken that morning with no sense of foreboding. He didn't know that, for the rest of his long life, he would always think in terms of before and after this day.

The officers and men were taking breakfast together around a campfire. A simple affair of bread and tea, washed down with plenty of sugar, but no milk. This would be their last day on the river. That afternoon they hoped to arrive at the town of Kyauktaw, which the 81st Division had captured only the week before. They were a medical unit, trying to keep up with the advance. At Kyauktaw, they'd been told, they would be setting up a small field hospital for the division, because the Japanese were expected to put up more of a fight to the south. There would be casualties, and they would be responsible for them.

None of the men on the riverbank that morning could have been described as battle-hardened. The officers were doctors, almost all from Scotland. They were volunteers, and most had only signed up after war was declared. The West Africans were from Nigeria and Sierra Leone, and had joined the Army in the last couple of years. They'd been trained in first aid and nursing, but given only the most rudimentary of fighting skills. The few that carried guns probably hoped they'd never have to use them. Their unit's name precisely determined their role in the great British Army's attempt to recapture Burma: they were the 29th Casualty Clearing Station (CCS), and they belonged to the 6th West African Brigade, part of the 81st Division of the Royal West African Frontier Force.

It sounded grand, put like that, but the truth was that the 29th CCS was an odd assortment of men of variable quality. When they'd crossed the border from India, they'd heard artillery, and seen British planes strafing enemy positions on distant hills. On one occasion, they'd even treated some injured Japanese soldiers who had been captured by the frontline soldiers. But that was weeks ago now. There were some who'd begun to hope quietly that the Japanese had pulled out of the Kaladan Valley altogether.

The men dawdled. Most were wearing only vests and shorts. Many were barefoot. If they were going to spend another day back on the rafts, they asked, why bother to put boots on? Some ambled down to the water, to wash their faces. Others wandered off in the direction of the nearby village, a line of bamboo and thatch huts strung along the riverbank. When they'd arrived the previous evening, they were relieved to see that it was an Indian settlement. *Indians*, that's what they called the Muslims, because that's what they looked like. They could be trusted; the officers had drummed this into the men before they'd set out, and it was turning out to be true. It was the others, the Arakanese Buddhists, or Burmese as they called them, who were slippery. Why, they even looked Japanese. The Africans asked the Muslims what name they gave to their village. 'Mairong,' they replied.

The commanding officer, Major Robert Murphy, looked at his watch. Half-past seven, time to load up the rafts. The mist over the river had burnt away, revealing the outline of the trees on the far side. He wondered if he should tell the men to make less noise. He didn't like this complacency. Looking down the sloping muddy bank, he saw Isaac sipping his tea and chatting to Company Sergeant Major Archibong Bassey Duke, a fellow Nigerian. There are two young men who seem to be enjoying this adventure, thought the Major.

That morning, Bassey Duke was warming to one of his favourite themes: life after the war. When it was all over, he told Isaac, they'd return home with some money to spend, and some stories to tell. Bassey Duke was a giant of a man. He wore blue shorts and a white vest, and would have been easily visible from the far side of the river. It was the end of the dry season, so the opposite bank was only a hundred or so yards away. Behind it, the sun was rising over the steep hills, the dark jungle still in shadow.

Bassey Duke jerked and spun, and only then did Isaac hear the shots. He watched his friend fall to the ground, still clutching his red enamel mug. Tea spilled from it and trickled down the bank. There were flashes of light in the jungle on the opposite side of the river. Bullets buzzed past Isaac's head. Like angry wasps, he thought. He fell face down into the reeds. His heart thumped against the cold ground. They were in a terrible position, exposed on the steep, slippery bank. Machine guns had opened up now. How many? One, at least, probably two. He caught a glimpse of Major Murphy stumbling past, walking like a drunk. That was strange. From higher up on the bank, he could hear screaming. Then he saw that Major Murphy's head was covered in blood. The shooting stopped. Someone nearby was gasping in a quiet voice. 'Take me, O God, take me, O God.' It sounded like Private David Essien, but Isaac could not be sure. He tried to crawl towards the voice, but as soon as he moved the shooting resumed. More angry wasps spun through the air. The Japanese had Isaac in their sights, and bullets ripped through the reeds around him.

When the shooting stopped a second time, Isaac reached out with his left hand for Essien, who was no longer gasping. It was strange how still Essien was, how cold he felt, for Isaac could see no blood on his uniform. Isaac tried to crawl up the bank, but one of his legs did not seem to be working properly. He looked down and saw that his khaki trousers were soaked with blood. So was his shirt. He closed his eyes and said to himself, 'Is this me? Is this really me, boy?' He saw his father Joshua, sombre and pained, sitting on the veranda of the family house in the village, pleading with him to run away from the Army before it was too late. Good advice, he thought now, but at the time he had shrugged his father away. 'I am in trouble, I am in deep, deep trouble.' His leg had started to ache, sending spasms right through his body. Tears rolled down his cheeks. Tears of fear or pain? He didn't know. He was sure of only one thing: he was going to die.

Many hours must have passed, because the next thing he can remember is that the sun was low in the sky, and a kind white face was looking down at him. A miracle. It was Captain Brown, who seemed to be unhurt. He was smiling, and still trying to talk like one of the soldiers. 'Ebo, my boy, you are down o!' Ebo, the affectionate name the Captain always used for Isaac because, so he explained, Fadoyebo was too long to pronounce. The others must have all run away, but the Captain had stayed, or maybe even come back, to try to help the injured. As far as Isaac could see, Captain Brown did not even have a scratch on him. Isaac reached feebly out towards his officer. 'I'm thirsty, so thirsty,' he said.

The Captain went away, and Isaac could see he was fetching a flask of tea from one of the bamboo rafts that were still tied up on the riverbank. He came back and urged Isaac to sit up, take a sip. He was talking fast, telling Isaac that Major Murphy was badly hurt, he'd been shot in the head, and that he'd been dressing his wounds.

It sounded like Captain Brown didn't think Major Murphy would make it. Now he wanted to take a look at Isaac. He took a knife to Isaac's trousers, and carefully cut them open, to reveal a bloody mess of a right leg. The Captain was saying something about bullets and a fractured femur, and how he was going to put together an improvised splint. Isaac struggled to raise his head to drink the tea, when he saw the Japanese soldiers running up the bank towards them, bayonets pointed at Captain Brown.

They had crossed the river.

The Captain turned around in surprise and jumped to his feet. He remonstrated with the Japanese. 'I am Captain Richard Brown, a medical officer,' he said. He did not even reach for the pistol at his waist.

His words made no difference. The Japanese surrounded him, and led him away. For some time after they'd disappeared from his view, Isaac could still hear the Captain, protesting.

Isaac watched other Japanese soldiers as they tore through the equipment on the rafts. One of them carried the flag of the rising sun. Then they turned to the dead bodies – there seemed to be two or three near Isaac – and took guns, ammunition, even clothes. They seemed desperate, taking whatever they could get their hands on. Only after they'd finished their plundering did they show any interest in him.

They spoke so quickly he couldn't understand. But they repeated a phrase again and again: 'English people, English people,' they seemed to be saying. Were they asking him whether there were any other officers? Did they want to know where the survivors were hiding? Now they were gesturing for him to stand up. One of them pointed a rifle at his head. They were saying something else, it must have been 'Get up, get up,' but Isaac could not even sit. He wondered at the idiocy of it all. Did they think that, if he could get up, he would still be lying here?

He knew what was coming. The Japanese, take a prisoner? A white man, like Captain Brown, perhaps, but a black man? No chance. That was not how they did things. He closed his eyes and waited to be shot.

PART I

SACRIFICE

1

ONE BIG MAN

IIIIIIIIIIIIIIIIIIIIIIIIIIIIIIIIIIIIIIIIIIIIIIIIIIIIIIIIIIIIIIIIIIIIIIIIIIIIIIIIIIIIIIIIIIIIIIIIIIIIIIIIIIIIIIIIIIIIIIIIII

All they knew was that one big man was quarrelling over God-knows-what with another big man in the whiteman's land, somewhere far away…One of them was called Hitler. No one knew the name of the other, although it was rumoured that he was related to the District Officer.

Jolasanmi Olaleye Falore,
The Life and Times of Moses Oni Ayeko-Falore

IIIIIIIIIIIIIIIIIIIIIIIIIIIIIIIIIIIIIIIIIIIIIIIIIIIIIIIIIIIIIIIIIIIIIIIIIIIIIIIIIIIIIIIIIIIIIIIIIIIIIIIIIIIIIIIIIIIIIIIIII

December 1941
Owo, Nigeria

Isaac Fadoyebo's journey to the Burmese jungle began here, by the gates of the palace of the *Olowo*, in December 1941. An olive-green army lorry groaned and slid up the sandy streets to the meeting place under the palace walls in the small hilltop town of Owo, in the British Colony and Protectorate of Nigeria. Market women, squatting on the ground beside their little piles of beans or soap or palm oil, or black coils of smoked fish, looked up. An excited crowd gathered and swelled around the vehicle. From a gramophone came the distant, tinny voice of Winston Churchill.

Everybody in Owo knew about the war. For two years now, they'd seen the posters all over town. Some depicted stern and merciless German soldiers shooting a group of defenceless Africans lined up against a wall. Others showed the same Germans, wearing big black boots, whipping the Africans who laboured for them. The Germans displayed no emotion, but the Africans were depicted as terrified. 'Hitler has already said that ALL AFRICANS MUST BE SLAVES FOR GERMANS!' the posters screamed in red letters.

People had looked at these posters in morbid fascination. It was true that everyone now called it 'Hitler's War'. That the Nazis were 'wicked people', and that Hitler was behaving like a wild beast, was beyond dispute. Well, almost. One woman in the market had been overheard saying that this Hitler must be a *real* man, if all of Europe was so afraid of him. The woman was shouted down. Not only at the market, but also at church, most people agreed that, if Britain fell to this man Hitler, they would come under '*Ja'man*' control, and that would be a bad thing.

Some even argued that what Hitler really wanted was Nigeria itself. They said, 'He knows all about our gold, our precious stones, our cocoa and our groundnuts, and now he wants to take them.' This seemed to fit with another rumour that a trader had heard in Lagos, that Their Majesties the King and Queen had fled there from London, and were now living in Government House. They went for short walks along the Marina after dark, apparently, taking some care not to be recognised.

It was hard to know what to make of it all, or of the way the colonial government was becoming ever more insistent in its appeals for contributions towards the war effort. The *Oba*, or king, of the mighty city of Benin had let it be known he was donating ten pounds a month from his salary. Lesser chiefs said they would give whatever they could afford. The district officer was urging farmers to grow more palm oil and rubber. One school, in the nearby town of Ondo, had scraped together some shillings and pennies to send to London, specifically to help those poor children who had been made homeless in the bombing. At the local school, the pupils had composed their own rude ditty about Hitler:

Adolf Hitler ma ṣẹ o
Ani ko ma ṣẹ, ani ko dara, o ranri
Abẹ ọ titi iwọ ṣẹ tirẹ o
Maṣe, maṣe olo o ṣẹ
O dẹ buṣe
O tẹ na

Adolf Hitler, don't do it.
We asked you not to do it, we told you it's not good,
But you were obstinate.
We begged you for a long time, but you did what you wanted to do.
Don't do it, don't do it, but you said you would
And now it's all over, you're disgraced.

So it was on this December day that the smartly dressed man took up his position by the *Olowo*'s palace, and began his speech. He was talking about what Hitler might do to Africans, but that wasn't all. He was urging the men who'd gathered round him to sign up and fight. Not just for Owo, but for Nigeria, the British Empire and King George. At that, someone in the crowd cheered, and Isaac's curiosity got the better of him.

He was barely sixteen, but he was an imposing boy, already almost six feet tall, and he knew his own mind. He pushed his way through, closer to the lorry, so he could better hear what the recruiting officer was saying. Nigerians faced a stark choice, said the officer: to live under British justice, 'the finest system in the world' he called it, or to be slaves under Hitler. It was a hot day, and the officer knew he would not have his audience's attention for long if he only stuck to rhetoric. People needed to hear practicalities. Join up, he said, because the pay is good, the uniforms are dashing, and, when the war is over, you will be first in line for all the good jobs, maybe even in government service. The officer kept his message simple, as he'd been told to do, and he was rewarded with murmurs of approval.

It was in faraway London that Churchill's government fretted over the bigger picture. The African colonies were a vital source of raw materials – food and rubber and gold. The Royal Navy relied on the ports along the African coast – Freetown, Lagos, Cape Town and Mombasa – as refuelling stations and bases so that Britain could keep control of the Cape and Suez shipping routes. Britain needed an African army, a large one, to protect these colonies. These were matters of global strategy that a crowd in a country town like Owo could not be expected to understand. The recruiting officer himself probably struggled with some of it.

Hitler didn't really feature at all, at least not directly in sub-Saharan Africa. The threat in East Africa had originally come from the Italians, whose African territories bordered the British colony of Kenya; in West Africa, it came from the Vichy French, whose territories sat between and above the four British colonies spaced along the coast. To complicate things further, the recent news from the Far East, of a Japanese attack on Malaya, suggested an ominous new danger to British interests in the Indian Ocean. However, it was Hitler who everyone had heard of, and for that reason British officers in Nigeria felt it was best to keep the focus on him. And so the message that Isaac got that day was maybe somewhat simplified, yet it contained one fundamental truth: in the dark days of December 1941, Britain needed Isaac Fadoyebo, and thousands of other Africans like him, to defend its Empire.

Not so long ago, the land around Owo had been covered in forests of towering trunks and buttressed roots, thick with tangled creepers and vines. There were elephants, buffalos, leopards and chimpanzees. The first road-builders, in the early years of the twentieth century, had to put up red signs that read 'Elephant Pass. Beware'. When Isaac Folayan Fadoyebo was born, in December 1925, those forests were still largely intact, although the loggers and their teams were methodically select- ing and cutting down the greatest trees, shooting out the game as they went. There were many who said the old way of life was disappearing.

Isaac's birthday, to be precise, was 5 December 1925. Not many families recorded dates then in the small village of Emure-Ile, but Isaac's father Alago was an unusual man. Some twenty years earlier, Alago had been a small boy in the village, when the first schools opened in Owo, which was the nearest town, a few miles away. Most parents were suspicious of these schools. Send children away when they need to be taught how to plant yams and look after goats? What if, at the end of it all, they don't want to come back and farm? In the end, Alago's mother and father only let him go because they feared he was too lazy for the farm. When they took him to the fields, he sat crying while his brothers did all the work. He was 'a good for nothing boy', so what was there to lose, they thought.

So off Alago went, to Owo, to try to enrol at the new government school. He didn't have a birth certificate – nobody did – but the teachers had their own crude method of assessing whether a little boy or girl was old enough to start lessons. All the children were asked to stretch their left arm over the top of their head, and see if they could reach as far as their right ear. Then, they had to repeat the exercise with their right arm and left ear. On this basis, Alago was enrolled. He was the first child from the village of Emure-Ile to get a modern education, a distinction he carried proudly for the rest of his life.

The British had established control over Lagos, on the coast some two hundred miles away, in the 1850s and '60s. The British professed noble ideals, but they were prepared to use ruthless methods. Royal Navy ships had shelled Lagos in 1851, after the *Oba* refused to stop trading in slaves. A sailor on board one of the British ships said, 'the town burnt famously all night'. A colonial official would write many years later that the burning of the Portuguese *barracoons* was 'the final act in the long struggle to suppress an infamous traffic that had brought profit to many and credit to none'. However, the Victorians' anti-slavery fervour did nothing to stifle the British appetite for imperial expansion, nor their growing conviction of racial superiority. If anything, quite the opposite. Slavery, they had decided, was sinful, but it was also an impediment to progress: the British Empire had a duty to promote free labour and commerce instead. Thus, it pursued enrichment and took over new territories, confident in the morality of such actions. In 1894, the Liberal MP Wilfred Lawson said in the House of Commons that 'formerly we stole Africans from Africa, and now we stole Africa from Africans'.

By the closing years of the nineteenth century, the British were remorselessly extending their influence into the hilly and forested interior, into the heartland of the Yoruba people. In 1897, they sent a punitive expedition to the neighbouring kingdom of Benin, some seventy-five miles to the south of Owo, to seek revenge for the killing of several British soldiers. The *Oba* tried to ward off the invasion with many human sacrifices, but this seemed to have little effect on the advancing enemy, nor his maxim guns and seven pounders. The British were horrified by what they found in Benin – pits filled with bodies, piles of human heads – and they burnt the city to the ground. But first they helped themselves to its treasures: the executioner's swords with silver handles, the ivory leopard carved from the tusks of five elephants, and the thousands of bronze sculptures. All these were carted back to London, while the *Oba* was sent into exile in distant Calabar. With the fall of Benin, the British were now masters of a vast area that they would soon declare was Southern Nigeria. Not long afterwards, missionaries and civil servants, exuding an air of brusque confidence, began arriving in towns and villages the length of Yorubaland and beyond. To say the British brought change to these unsuspecting communities scarcely does justice to the jarring rupture their arrival announced.

The British had also crushed the last resistance in the very different territory to the north. In 1903, British soldiers captured the ancient cities of Kano and Sokoto, the capital of what had once been a great Fulani empire. Despite these violent beginnings, British officials quickly came to feel very much at home in what they called Northern Nigeria. They loved the open, dry landscape, the small isolated rises of kopjes on the plains, which stretched all the way to the edge of the great Sahara. It was perfect horse-country, good for hunting, and reminded some imperial old hands of northern India. The British found the North's lingua franca, Hausa, both pleasing and relatively easy to learn, whereas in Southern Nigeria they complained that the 'pidgin' was a demeaning and debased version of English. And in the autocratic emirs of the North, the British saw noble and courteous aristocrats – kindred spirits, they liked to think, with their own ruling class. A cosy and mutually advantageous relationship developed between the emirs and colonial officials, sealed on the polo field. The emirs were allowed to stay in their palaces and enjoy their revenues, provided they heeded the discreet advice proffered by the British. In time, British officials came to speak of the 'Holy North', a place where empire building was a romantic pursuit.

In 1914, the British amalgamated the territories of Northern and Southern Nigeria, their very different peoples brought together in a single protectorate. It was a fateful decision. The North already lagged far behind the South in education and economic development, and in the subsequent decades that gap would only grow. But for all 'Nigerians', as they were now called, the world was being turned upside down by the power of new imported beliefs and technologies.

In 1897, the same year that Benin was sacked, the first British person was seen in Owo. The local king there, the *Olowo*, had a more acute sense of which way the wind was blowing and understood the need to come to some sort of accommodation with the newcomers. The British governor in Lagos had recently described the practice of human sacrifice as 'detestable, abhorrent, disgraceful, cruel and revolting'. The *Olowo* freed his slaves and declared an end to human sacrifice, and the British allowed him to stay in his sprawling palace, with its many shrines, and to keep all his wives.

However, Owo would be transformed by the arrival of the British. First, the missionaries gave out bibles, and built a church. Next came the administrators. The district officer – *Aṣoju Ọba Ilu Oyinbo*, or 'Agent of the King of the Land of the White People' to give the literal translation of the Yoruba version of his title – positioned his house on a hill just to the north-west of the town. This, the people were told, was the 'Reservation', where neither loitering nor noise was allowed after 6pm. Next to the Reservation was the barracks, the *Bareke*, soon crowded with clerks, soldiers, prison warders and interpreters as the new government took root.

By 1903, Owo had two schools, a courtroom and a post office, and, by 1906, an upwardly mobile trader or clerk could go to the post office and make a phone call to Benin, or even Lagos. In the market, the traders now preferred the silver shilling coin bearing the bearded king's head to the old cowrie shells. Some of the more prosperous families had a sewing machine, perhaps a bicycle, and had replaced their palm-thatched roofs with the corrugated iron, or 'pan', that was already fashionable on the coast and in the bigger towns.

People in Owo thought the district officer had some very odd habits – he was said to dine alone in a special white coat, served by his steward, who also wore white but with a red sash – but they grudgingly admitted that he also made himself useful. He had ordered that a clean stream be dammed, so that piped water flowed into two large concrete tanks. The women and children queued up by these every morning and evening, waiting to fill the empty kerosene tins that they carried on their heads.

This was the Owo that Alago arrived in when he started at the government primary school. He was taught English, and how to read and write. He also learnt about Christianity, and converted to this new religion. He changed his name to Joshua, which was how he would be known for the rest of his life. However, school was not always a happy experience. When Joshua failed to learn the difference between 'steal' and 'steel', a master beat him severely with a cane. Covered in blisters, he refused to return the following day. His school days were over. He took a job as a clerk in a timber company, but his parents urged him to return to Emure-Ile, so that he could get married. He agreed, and, to his delight, discovered that his few years of education and formal employment commanded some respect in the village.

In his absence, Christianity had arrived in Emure-Ile, brought by the traders who moved from town to town. A group of converts met each Sunday in the house of a village elder. In 1913, with the encouragement of a British priest in Owo, they built a small Anglican church, with mud walls and a thatched roof. They called it 'Our Saviours'. Joshua was appointed 'scribe', a position that brought modest remuneration but some prestige, and one that he would hold until his death. His young bride, Isaac's mother, had been christened Lydia, but she always preferred to be called by the Yoruba name her parents had first given her, Ogunmuyonwa. She had received no education, and she would never learn to read or write.

Emure-Ile in the 1920s was a place of red-dust streets and a few rows of rectangular mud houses, with modest courtyards, shaded by mango trees. The people grew yams and maize in the surrounding fields, hacked and burnt out of the great forest. In more recent years, many had started to plant cocoa trees, as traders returning from further west brought stories that this new crop could bring wealth. The nights in the village were dark and quiet, illuminated by a handful of paraffin lamps and countless stars. But, when the moon was full, the villagers gathered in front of their houses to hear women sing and perform plays, sometimes accompanied by the metallic rhythms of the *oteye*, a simple instrument comprised of a metal rod, which makes a rasping sound when scraped by a smaller stick.

People in Emure-Ile had adapted to the arrival of Christianity in their pragmatic way. Adopting new beliefs did not mean discarding old ones, and the pantheon of Yoruba gods retained a powerful hold over the villagers. Joshua's modest position in the Anglican Church did not stop him from acquiring six more wives. He was good-looking, tall and slim, and his womanising ways sometimes got him into trouble. There were brawls in the village, and a court case. On one occasion, a local chief, the *El-Emure*, was so upset with Joshua that he put a curse on him, saying he 'would not reap what he sowed'. Ogunmuyonwa gave birth to five boys, but they all died in infancy. So, when she became pregnant again, she decided to travel to a neighbouring village to have the delivery there, beyond the reach of any curse. In later years, she would always say she'd made a wise choice, because this time the precious boy, Isaac, survived.

On the day of Isaac's birth, Ogunmuyonwa's mother, Aleke, went to see a fortune-teller, to see what portended for him. 'This boy will be a soldier, and will raise his family up and shine a light on them,' the fortune-teller said, and advised that Isaac's arrival be celebrated with the slaughtering of a goat, shared among everyone in Emure-Ile. Joshua would eventually have ten children, but Isaac, as the eldest surviving son, was always a favourite.

Isaac's first lessons took place besides the Anglican church in Emure-Ile, where the pastor gathered the younger children together and taught them basic literacy. Soon, Joshua and Ogunmuyonwa were in bitter disagreement over whether Isaac should go on to primary school. Joshua had seen enough to know that a new society was taking shape, and that to 'go school' was the key to economic and social success. Ogunmuyonwa thought in the old way and struggled to see beyond the confines of the village. A boy, she said, was a useful pair of extra hands on the farm. It took the special pleading of an uncle for her to give way. Sometime in the early 1930s, after Joshua had saved up enough money, Isaac went to stay with relatives in Owo, and enrolled at St George's Anglican School. He was not yet ten years old.

Discipline was harsh at St George's. The children were caned and flogged. Their teachers were African, but British inspectors would pass by on regular visits. Each time this happened, the headmaster would produce the brown leather book he kept in his desk, and the inspector wrote down his observations in a beautiful flowing hand. This was always done with great solemnity. Sometimes, to the dismay of the teachers, the British officials could be terse in their comments. On 13 September 1936, the Acting Chief Inspector of Education for the Southern Provinces, L.W. Wakeman wrote, 'it is to be hoped that a little pressure will be brought to bear upon parents to leave the children in school for the full infant course'. The education officer for the province, G. Waterfield, regretted that the school had 'a good African band, but the Yoruba school boy does not seem to judge the music so much by the sounds produced as by the rich glitter of the brass on the more expensive powerful instruments imported from abroad'.

Anthony Enahoro was growing up in Owo at the same time as Isaac. He was the son of the headmaster at the government school, just up the road from St George's, and he remembered that the school inspectors were treated like demi-gods, their visits awaited with great anticipation; 'flowers were trimmed, paths cleaned, sanitary blocks washed out, the garden was weeded, rotten fruit picked off the trees in the orchard, uniforms...washed and ironed afresh and the school band played God Save the King and Rule, Britannia to near perfection'. But not, apparently, near enough to the satisfaction of G. Waterfield.

Isaac and his classmates didn't have exercise books, instead writing their lessons on small wooden slates with pieces of chalk. The teachers taught in English, and imposed fines of half a penny on any child caught speaking Yoruba. Isaac, who had already picked up some English by reading his father's collection of books at home, was never fined, and was always near the top of the class. He learnt not only the Englishman's language, but also his history and geography. Likewise, Enahoro wrote of his Owo schooldays that he became 'as familiar with the famous sites of London as with the streets of Owo. The measure of one's education...was one's degree of familiarity with the English language, English culture and English life, of which I came to know far more in my boyhood than I knew of parts of Nigeria outside my own.' The children in Owo sang English songs, and learnt about heroic white explorers who discovered lands inhabited by barbarous and black natives.

On Empire Day, at the end of May each year, Isaac competed in the high jump and pole vault. He had inherited his father's strong, athletic body. The celebrations were especially elaborate in 1937, to mark the coronation of George VI, the colonial masters' new king.

At least once a week, Isaac's favourite younger sister Adedeji would meet him at the school gate after classes ended in the early afternoon. She often went to the forest to pick leaves for wrapping pounded yam, which she had discovered could be sold in Owo market for a few pennies. She shared her small earnings with her brother. Isaac would show his gratitude by accompanying her halfway home to Emure-Ile. The two children walked barefoot through the forest groves, and then the open patches of yam and cassava lined with banana trees and palms. Flocks of hornbills and plantain-eaters glided overhead. Then, every Friday afternoon, Isaac would walk the entire journey to Emure-Ile, to spend the weekend in the village with his mother and father, and young brother and sisters, before returning to Owo on Sunday. They were happy days.

School opened Isaac's eyes. He started to imagine a wider world, one that stretched far beyond the fields on the edges of Emure-Ile and Owo. The first motorcar had arrived in Owo in 1927, and, when Isaac started at St George's, there were still only four in the entire town. They were owned by the town's elite: a rich businessman, an agent of the John Holt trading company, the district officer (of course) and the *Olowo*, who insisted that a bugler march in front of his Model T Ford whenever he was taken for a drive. But by the mid-1930s vehicles passed through Owo on a regular basis. Travelling salesmen arrived, hawking little packages of quinine and castor oil, which, they said, could cure every ailment known to man.

The more entrepreneurial people in Owo were also beginning to take advantage of new opportunities, some even going as far as Lagos. The distant city had a romantic allure. Trams ran through the streets, it was said, and two- and three-storey buildings were powered by electricity. There were any number of *Oyinbos*, or white people, in Lagos, and great ships docked at Apapa wharf. 'The Liverpool of West Africa', some of the *Oyinbos* had been heard to call it. A 1924 guidebook for British businessmen described it as 'the most modern and civilised town amongst the English possessions on the West African Coast…where one can indulge in almost every kind of sport, including horse-racing and polo'. But, for the humble trader from the interior, the attraction of Lagos was not polo, but the opportunity to make a few pennies, selling traditional cloth and bush-meat.

From Owo, the journey took more than twenty-four hours. Travellers would hitch rides on the back of the timber lorries, which jolted slowly along a sandy track under the dark-green forest canopy all the way to the town of Osogbo, some seventy miles to the north-west. There, after arriving in the evening, exhausted and coated in dust, they would wait for the morning train to Lagos, struggling to catch some sleep on the station platform during the long night. The train was reliable but slow, proceeding as it did at a dignified pace through the hills and towns, through the thick bush and cocoa trees and oil-palms of Yorubaland, stopping frequently at small stations, each one an impromptu market, before finally arriving in the capital late in the afternoon.

It must have been the traders who brought the newspapers back from Lagos. In the pages of the *Daily Comet*, Owo's teachers read about the Italian invasion of Abyssinia, and wondered why the British were not doing anything to help the brave Abyssinians. The teachers were dismayed to learn that Europeans were dropping bombs, even poisonous gas, on their fellow Africans. They launched a 'Help Abyssinia Fund'. Even in this sleepy town, deep in the backwaters of a West African colony, the rise of fascism in Europe caused agitation. They were small ripples, only felt in a tight circle, but they were ripples nonetheless.

The city was where Isaac had set his heart on. If not Lagos, he thought, at least Ibadan, which already had a reputation as a centre of reading and learning. He'd heard of the prestigious secondary schools: King's College Lagos, Government College Ibadan, and so on. Each was self-consciously modelled on English public schools and designed by the British to produce a local elite who would absorb the values of fair play, discipline and selflessness; perhaps some of these pupils might go on to play a role in running the colony. King's College had even taken to calling itself, with just a touch of grandeur, 'The Eton of Nigeria', and announced it was committed to producing not just fine cricketers but also 'gentlemen of polite learning and a liberal education'. The pupils at King's College wore blazers in class, and a boater or cricket cap and tie whenever they stepped 'beyond the gates' and out into the streets of Lagos.

Isaac understood very well that entry to one of these schools would transform his prospects in life. And he felt he stood a good chance of gaining admission. Older boys from Owo who'd taken the entrance exams in Ibadan brought back the question papers, which the teachers would then copy up on the blackboard. Isaac typically scored 95 percent. He was sure he had the brains. The only obstacle was money.

Isaac argued his case passionately with Joshua, but to no avail. His father had already made up his mind. He had been paying Isaac's school fees for several years, and saw no need to carry on. He wanted a return on his investment, and he wanted his favourite son closer to hand. Besides, he could sense resentment brewing in his large family. Every day, working on the farm, Joshua worried about whether the other children were jealous of the sacrifices he had made for Isaac. Secondary school in Lagos or Ibadan would cost a lot more than the primary school in Owo. The boy's demands were impossible.

The problem was that father and son saw things so differently. For Isaac, a primary school education had been merely the beginning of a long journey. For Joshua, it was an end in itself. Isaac's education at St George's was enough to secure a local job at a respectable salary. Joshua told Isaac he should sit exams for the position of 'pupil teacher' in the Anglican missionary schools. This job paid fifteen shillings a month, which was, as far as he knew, as much as anyone in Emure-Ile had ever earned. Reluctantly, Isaac did as he was told. He enrolled for the pupil teacher exams. His sense of pique was only heightened when, to his surprise and embarrassment, he finished just outside the top ten percent, and was not offered a position straight away.

He was a young man in a hurry, not used to failure, and full of pride and frustration. He was sure of one thing: he had no time to sit in the village of Emure-Ile and rot his life away. He began looking for ways to escape.

The Army propaganda team rolled into Owo a few days after Isaac received the disappointing news about his exams. Standing by the palace of the *Olowo*, he had listened intently to what the recruiting officer had to say. The following morning, he waited until Joshua and Ogunmuyonwa had gone to the fields and then approached his favourite sister, Adedeji. He asked whether he could borrow some money, explaining that he had a meeting with friends in Akure, the provincial capital, and said that he would pay her back. It was a strange request, because, as far as Adedeji knew, Isaac had no friends there. Still, she suspected nothing, and gave Isaac a couple of shillings.

Isaac set out for the road and got on a lorry that was passing through Akure, but he did not get off there. He stayed on board as the lorry continued west, all the way to the town of Abeokuta. There, he signed up with the Royal West African Frontier Force, swearing an oath of loyalty to King and Empire with a Bible pressed to his forehead. He had become a British soldier.

When the news of Isaac's deception reached Emure-Ile, Joshua wept bitter tears. He was sure it would end in misfortune. This war, he said, it has already gone on for two years. Where will it take my son?

2

LET THIS BAYONET DRINK MY BLOOD

||||||||||||||||||||||||||||||||||||||||||||||||||||||||||||||||||||||||||||||||||||||||||||||||||||||||||||||||||||||||||||||

If I am disloyal or show fear in battle,
let this bayonet drink my blood.

British Army swearing-in oath for African followers of
traditional religions; taken while kissing a bayonet

||||||||||||||||||||||||||||||||||||||||||||||||||||||||||||||||||||||||||||||||||||||||||||||||||||||||||||||||||||||||||||||

1942
West Africa

John Hamilton was an ambitious and clever young man. The son of a London policeman, he had won a scholarship to Christ's Hospital School and then Balliol College, Oxford. The political atmosphere at Oxford University in the late 1930s was highly charged, a heady cocktail of disgust with the older generation, fear of the threat of fascism and growing dread of what would have to be done to stop it. Hamilton joined the Communists, he said, 'largely because no other party at that time seemed to have any serious intention of opposing Hitler'. He enlisted just three days after Britain declared war on Germany in September 1939. After officer training, followed by a frustrating hiatus kicking his heels in barracks, Hamilton was surprised to be told he was going to West Africa, a place he knew nothing about. The Army gave him a khaki uniform and inoculated him against yellow fever, but provided little information on what he would be doing in Africa. He was, however, told to buy a topee hat from the renowned tropical kit specialists Humphrey and Crook, on Haymarket.

In 1942, he travelled by boat from Liverpool to Britain's smallest African colony, the Gambia, on the very western tip of the continent. As the boat approached the coast, Hamilton could see a line of single-storey whitewashed buildings under the palm trees, mud huts roofed with thatch and an old slaving fort. The long white beaches were pounded by Atlantic surf. This was Bathurst, the capital of the Gambia. Hamilton was far from the action he wanted to see, and yet he would learn that even this imperial outpost could not escape the Second World War.

In peacetime, the Gambia's tiny military had amounted to 150 local men and a handful of British officers, little more than a lightly armed gendarmerie to deal with internal security. Now the British were expanding this force some thirty times, to more than 4,000 men. One night, shortly after Hamilton arrived in the Gambia, the governor ordered a clean-sweep of all the 'corner-boys' who loitered on street corners. Four hundred were rounded up in MacCarthy Square, put on lorries, and driven to the barracks. The following morning, Hamilton spent a few hot and busy hours enlisting them as soldiers. The reluctant recruits, all Muslims, swore their loyalty to King and Empire on the Holy Koran, but the press-gang was not a success. Within weeks, three-quarters of the men had run away, taking with them the most coveted items of clothing and equipment. It was a salutary lesson. Volunteers, Hamilton concluded, would certainly make better soldiers.

Hamilton was as much bemused witness as active participant, but what he experienced in Bathurst was just one small act in the great recruitment drive that was happening all across Britain's African colonies. In towns and villages, from the Gambia on the Atlantic to Kenya's warm coast on the Indian Ocean, the Army was hurriedly trying to build up its fighting forces.

Until the early 1930s, the British Army in Africa, excluding white-run South Africa, had numbered a paltry 15,000 men. By the end of the war in 1945, some 500,000 Africans had worn the British uniform. Some, like the corner-boys of Bathurst, had been forced into joining. And it wasn't only in the Gambia that the British used coercion, or even trickery, to get Africans to join a fight of which they had little understanding and defend an Empire for which they might have little affection. A British officer in the West African colony of Sierra Leone remembered an African sergeant asking a new recruit whether he was prepared to serve for the duration of the war. 'What war?' came the answer. A thirteen-year-old boy from Nyasaland left a pathetic account of white missionaries going from classroom to classroom, pulling out any schoolboy who looked old enough to go off to war. Before he knew it, the boy himself had been signed up to the King's African Rifles. A young man from Tanganyika was picked up on the streets of Kampala, in neighbouring Uganda. He was thrown in jail, and the next day he and many others were put on a train, 'packed...like firewood', before eventually arriving at an enlistment centre in Kenya. One British lieutenant in Nigeria was taken aback to discover his entire platoon were former inmates of Kano jail, handed over to the Army at the emir's instruction. There was a general assumption, officers in West Africa recalled, that war provided local chiefs with a useful opportunity to get rid of their undesirables.

Coercion was not the whole story. As the fiasco in Bathurst showed, it wasn't in Britain's interests to field an army of reluctant conscripts. Volunteers, the British authorities believed, were less likely to desert, and would be more reliable when the fighting started. And volunteers there were, aplenty. Not that the distinction between those who joined the Army willingly and those who felt compelled to do so was necessarily obvious. The British system of indirect rule, practised with the co-operation of emirs and chiefs, could be used to exert formidable social pressure. In an eastern region of the Gold Coast, women mocked men who refused to sign up with the derogatory term *kosa-ankobifour* ('those who refuse to go to war'). However, there were also signs that many of the men enlisted with genuine enthusiasm. A British officer recruiting in the north of the Gold Coast was encouraged that 'vast numbers of men came forward prepared to serve anywhere for the duration of the war'.

Robert Kakembo, who signed up for the Army in the British protectorate of Uganda, was one of them. In his 1944 pamphlet on his experiences in the Army, he recalled, 'The recruiting officers worked from early in the morning to well beyond dusk. They saw all sorts of people, varying in education and intelligence and standard of living, from ex-students…down to half-naked men, all eager to help.' Kakembo's pamphlet, entitled 'An African Soldier Speaks', was seen as so subversive by the British that they initially only allowed the release of a few hundred copies, with a warning stamped on the front page: 'Confidential, Not for Publication or Circulation'. Yet Kakembo was not much of a dissident: his main argument was that the majority of African soldiers had not signed up to fight for King George VI or to defend the Empire, but to help the Europeans they had come across in their own lives, perhaps 'a certain kindly lady missionary or a good District Commissioner whose wife plays with their children'. But there were also African soldiers, he says, who could see a bigger picture. They'd heard about Nazi theories on race, sometimes even read extracts from *Mein Kampf*, where Hitler had described black people as 'semi-apes'. As a result, they were ready to fight 'that accursed man's ideals and save themselves and their children from cruelty and permanent bondage'.

It's an attractive idea; an ideological commitment to the fight against fascism, born out of an understanding of what victory for Hitler and Mussolini might mean for black Africans. Esther Salawu, who was at boarding school in Nigeria during the war, said four of her uncles volunteered to join the Army. 'We thought that the Germans then wanted to rule the world and didn't like black people,' she said. 'And it was true. So people eagerly joined. Everybody was "up" to finish this thing.'

In Sierra Leone, John Henry Smythe volunteered as soon as the war broke out. Born into the Creole elite, a descendant of freed slaves who had been transported by the British from North America to Africa, Smythe read *Mein Kampf* at school, and Hitler's philosophies had shocked him. 'It was a book which would put any black man's back up and it put mine up. I grew up with hate for this man and his cronies and was pleased when I had the opportunity to fight against him.' Smythe became the first black officer in the RAF, flying bombing missions over Germany. In 1943, his plane was shot down, and he was brutally interrogated by the SS. He spent the final eighteen months of the war in a prison camp on the Baltic coast.

And then there was Isaac Fadoyebo, whose motivation for signing up was both more obvious and, in its way, more banal. Isaac became a British soldier because it seemed the best job available to him at the time. In this, he was surely typical of the majority of recruits. He'd seen the British propaganda in Nigeria and he had listened carefully to what the recruitment officer had to say on that December day in Owo. He'd not been impressed by all the talk of loyalty and patriotism, and he certainly wasn't joining the Army for the sake of anybody else. Even the oath to King and Empire meant little to him. But if, as the recruitment officer had said, the Army offered the chance for a young African man to better himself, well, that was another thing entirely.

The officer had promised that soldiers were to be paid one shilling a day. That was a head-spinning amount of money, twice what Isaac would earn if he took his father's advice and became a teacher. And there were tangible enticements. Soldiers were given smart uniforms, sturdy boots and regular meals. Isaac had heard that some were being taught to drive, to do bookkeeping, even to operate radios. He'd caught glimpses of the modern world, but if he joined the Army he would have the chance to see much more. Becoming a soldier offered the prospect of travel, the chance of participating, if only in a walk-on role, in the historical events that were shaping the faraway places that he'd read about at school. Isaac had a spirit of adventure.

He had no idea where the Army might take him, but he'd enjoyed his geography lessons, and had pored over maps of Europe and America. He was young and there was much that he couldn't possibly know or understand. But he saw other men around him joining up, and he too decided to take his chance.

His primary school education marked Isaac out as an unusual recruit. He was literate, and that put him in an exclusive minority. A British officer in Isaac's brigade estimated that about one in every hundred African soldiers under his command could read and write. Nigeria was Britain's most populous African colony with a population of more than twenty million, a complex mosaic of dozens of ethnic groups, languages and different religions that had little in common. The British, just as they had in India and other African colonies, quickly developed firm theories as to which Nigerians were best suited for military service. Until the 1930s, recruitment had taken place almost exclusively in the North. Here the British were pleased to discover that their close relationship with the emirs ensured a steady supply of well-built fighting men. Northern Nigerian soldiers had served with distinction in the First World War, fighting in the German colonies of Cameroon and Tanganyika. When John Hamilton eventually met Hausa soldiers from Northern Nigeria, his assessment was typical of the British officer class: 'even if not particularly sophisticated in thought and word…[they] were cheerful and willing, seldom complained and had very good physique'.

At the beginning of the Second World War, the British again turned to Northern Nigeria for the bulk of their recruits. The Hausa, it was agreed, made loyal and dependable soldiers. Southerners, on the other hand, were too 'savvy', thanks to their access to some education. They were potential mischief-makers, too clever by half. But the sheer size of the force required from Africa, as well as the changing nature of warfare, forced the British to take a different approach. Modern armies needed engineers, drivers, nurses, signallers and clerks. Clearly, some of these tasks required education. And so the recruitment drive was expanded to include Southern Nigeria.

When Isaac enlisted in Abeokuta, he was told he would be trained as a medical orderly. He was sent to a nearby military hospital where he was lectured on the basic principles of nursing. He was being taught how to administer first aid to wounded troops on the battlefront.

Britain's African soldiers were told they were defending freedom against fascism, but there was never any doubt that the Army would be comprised of white officers in charge of black men. As recently as 1938, Army regulations had stipulated that an officer who held a King's commission had to be 'of pure European descent'. This condition was dropped soon after the beginning of the war. Nonetheless, when the first West African, Seth Anthony from the Gold Coast, was made an officer in 1942, his appointment caused a sensation. Anthony rose to the rank of major by the end of the war, but he never forgot that some of the Rhodesian and South African officers in his own battalion never addressed a single word to him in all those years. He remained a lonely black face in the officers' mess; only one other West African in the entire Army had been made an officer by 1945. The vast majority of British soldiers simply could not imagine, or countenance, receiving orders from a black man. Many Africans were promoted to the non-commissioned ranks of corporal and sergeant, but they were quick to notice the difference between their pay packets and those of white colleagues of theoretically equal standing whom they had to address as 'Sir'.

Isaac had never questioned the racial underpinnings of Empire before, and it did not occur to him do so now, even when he was being asked to risk his life for it. The British officers that he came across impressed him with their education. Many had been to Oxford and Cambridge. He respected them for their knowledge, and, by and large, their humane treatment of the men who served under them. But there was also a minority who carried a haughty air of racial superiority. Isaac and his fellow recruits grumbled that these officers looked down on them, considering them, as he put it, 'as little better than black monkeys from the jungle'. A particular sergeant major, a notorious bully who was later transferred back to Britain, loved to taunt Isaac as he passed by on his way to the prayer meetings that had been arranged by a devout officer. He would laugh, and ask in a loud and mocking voice, 'Praying? Praying?! You think that prayers are going to save you from a bullet?!' Isaac had an education, and he was a volunteer, but the sergeant major held all his African soldiers in contempt.

The combined force of the four British West African colonies, known as the Royal West African Frontier Force, had only numbered some 5,000 men in 1930, spread across the four colonies of Nigeria, the Gold Coast, Sierra Leone and the Gambia. West Africa had the reputation of being something of a military backwater. A posting on 'the Coast' brought with it the risk of disease, so officers were discouraged from bringing their wives, and young children were prohibited. The staff at Humphrey and Crook would ensure that the young men heading out on the Elder Dempster ships got all the elaborate kit they would need for Africa, from a tin hipbath to polo gear. They were also happy to arrange for copies of the *Daily Telegraph* and *Horse and Hound* to be sent on. 'Everything had to be portable in 60 lb loads, in order to be carried on carrier heads,' recalled one officer.

Indeed, one of the pre-war highlights of service for officers in West Africa were lengthy expeditions through remote frontier lands, accompanied by trains of porters carrying an array of personal possessions. The officers had ample time for shooting game and leisure. In Northern Nigeria, polo became an obsession, as it had been for colonial administrators and emirs for a generation. Many Army officers kept several ponies so that they could play at least three days a week. An officer who served in the Gold Coast in the 1930s remembers, 'we took an enormous amount of exercise, either golf, cricket or polo and evening consumption of alcohol was considerable – half a bottle of gin or whisky per person was not considered excessive, but whisky was occasionally consumed at breakfast from a teapot as camouflage to deceive higher authority.' Morning parades were followed by long siestas. Sunday lunches of groundnut stew were washed down with so much gin that officers frequently retired to bed by teatime.

It was an idyll, of sorts, but with the advent of the Second World War the Army was forced into a painful period of expansion and adaptation. Some of the new British officers were hurriedly enlisted 'Coasters' – the traders, administrators and policemen who already lived in West Africa. These men, at least, knew something of the languages and customs of the region, and many had some sympathy with, and interest in, the Africans who served under them. There were also white Rhodesian volunteers sent to West Africa, typically as non-commissioned officers. Tough men, undoubtedly, but they brought with them the ugly racial attitudes of the South. John Hamilton was surprised to find that his Rhodesian company commander referred to all Africans as 'bloody Kaffirs'. Another British officer, in the Gold Coast, also found the Rhodesians' attitude a bit 'off', although he soon noticed that their contempt for 'silly munts' did not preclude them striking up close friendships with local women.

Hundreds of officers, like John Hamilton, were also arriving from Britain itself, with orders to command men with whom they could barely communicate. They disembarked at Bathurst, Freetown, Accra or Lagos, then travelled on by train or road to a hastily constructed training camp. It was a shock for many. There were officers who confessed they'd never even seen a black person before landing on the West African coast. They had to adjust to the humid and energy-sapping climate, prickly heat rashes, the bitter taste of quinine, water shortages and any number of venomous creatures. Still, there were consolations to these punishments. Queues of Africans formed outside camps as soon as word spread that a British officer had arrived. They were vying for the position of 'boy', a sort of batman who ensured an officer's clothes were clean and neatly pressed, his shaving water always warm, and his pink gin mixed just right.

The Army provided a special booklet, 'Meet the West African Soldier', to help officers fresh off the boat understand the men who were suddenly in their charge. Respect and loyalty, the booklet said, had to be earned; swearing, shouting or hitting an African soldier was not acceptable. Racist abuse was a definite no. Officers were advised to spend a good deal of time listening to their soldiers' problems, learning their customs, ensuring they were well fed – and making them laugh. Familiarity, however, should only be taken so far; it was best to 'avoid too easy fraternisation with the African for he, like you, is suspicious of those who attempt to make friends among people not of their own colour'. The officers might have been disheartened to read that an 'African cannot reason things out for himself, and is not mechanically minded…Every simple little thing that is self-evident to us must be explained and demonstrated', but at least they were forewarned. They were perhaps more encouraged to learn that, where the African 'has not been spoiled by living in large coastal towns, he has an instinctive respect for position and authority'.

One British sergeant, Arthur Moss, arriving on the Gold Coast at the beginning of 1943, found a stifling culture of dreary racism among his colleagues. 'We were one army firmly divided by colour,' he wrote with regret in his old age. In the sergeants' mess each night, he heard the talk of idle, lying and thieving 'wogs'. Moss was suspected of having liberal views and was himself labelled a 'white wog', a sobriquet he thought 'applied more in pity and amusement than in contempt'. Whenever the white officers gathered to watch a film outdoors, their Africans soldiers had to make do with the reverse image, seen from behind the screen.

Moss felt attitudes improved over time, and mutual respect built up between the British and Africans. But prejudices endured. As a military convoy set sail for India in late 1944, one ship was held up off the coast of Freetown when an alert lookout shouted, 'Man Overboard!' 'One bloody African', a British engineer grumbled in his diary, 'why couldn't they have let him stay in the water instead of sending a destroyer to pick him up?'

There were rich experiences to enjoy in West Africa, if a British newcomer was only willing to look for them. On a Sunday morning outside Freetown, a group of junior officers, among them a man called Fred Clarke, were lured by music towards a clearing in the forest, where they found a simple church, decorated with a bamboo cross. The men slipped inside and joined rows and rows of Africans dressed in all their finery. One officer, a talented musician, volunteered to play the organ, while the others joined in the singing of hymns. As the harmonies rose and the mutual smiles widened, Clarke, a former postal worker from Taunton, said that 'the men and women who had lived all their lives in that jungle clearing realised that the white men who came from England, Australia and Canada were singing the same songs that they knew'. It was an unexpected but wonderful moment of mutual recognition. Also on a Sunday morning, a young Catholic officer, Hugh Lawrence, cycled into Accra, capital of the Gold Coast, in search of the cathedral. He was astonished to find a packed congregation singing the entire mass in Latin with great enthusiasm, at a time when many in Europe were complaining that they could no longer understand the liturgy.

Good officers, of course, knew that their success, perhaps one day their very lives, would depend on commanding the respect and affection of their men. Language was often the key, and in Nigeria the majority of soldiers spoke Hausa, and no English. A British captain, Charles Carfrae, found himself in the northern garrison town of Kaduna, a place that, he felt, 'echoed Rawalpindi and Dar-es-Salaam, Rangoon and Colombo' in its neat bungalows, boozy parties and other staple ingredients of imperial life. There were 'petty snobberies and assumptions of gentility, the talk of Home, the clothes no longer quite in fashion', and the same handful of old records, played again and again at the European Club's Saturday-night dances. It was a suffocating atmosphere. But Carfrae was more interested in the men he was drilling on the parade ground and whom he would one day lead into battle. They were tall and, to his eyes, mysterious, with their jet-black skin, fine physiques, lines down their cheeks and closely shaven heads. He quickly realised that 'without some knowledge of Hausa one had no hope of becoming an influential commander', and so he knuckled down to months of hard study. On lengthy marches through the surrounding bush and hills, Carfrae forged a bond with his men. He was unusual. In the hot and drowsy afternoons, he would sit the soldiers down in the shade of a tree and attempt to explain, in his halting Hausa, the wider progress and ramifications of the war. Often, he would notice his men gently dozing off during these lessons, exhausted from their drills. He continued just the same, for the benefit of the few who remained alert.

Today, Carfrae's attempts come across as well intentioned, but paternalistic. But, as one officer stationed in Sierra Leone reflected years later, 'we regarded the troops as our children, while they, fed, clothed, housed and paid by the army, were content with the regularity of army life.' In this, he had taken to heart the advice of the 'Meet the West African Soldier' booklet, which explained that officers had to play the role of 'father and mother' to their men. In his old age, the Catholic officer Hugh Lawrence saw things a little more cynically. 'I'd been sent to pick up cannon fodder for the Empire in West Africa,' he said. 'But after all, there was no conscription, most joined the army because they wanted to...and a lot of them were not averse to fighting either.'

Isaac's horizons began to broaden in his first weeks of training. Abeokuta, just fifty miles north of Lagos, made Owo seem dull and provincial. It boasted more schools, more churches, and more commerce than Owo, and even had a bookshop, with a chalkboard outside, advertising *Baker and Bourne's Algebra*, *Shakespeare for Secondary Schools* and *Longmans Latin*. Isaac felt intimidated in that bookshop; he had no money for books, and no understanding of Shakespeare or Latin. In fact, he often felt inferior in Abeokuta. Many of the town's elite were Creoles, who had migrated from Sierra Leone. *Saros*, the Nigerians called them. They had names like Macaulay, Coker and Crowther, and they dressed and spoke like Europeans. Some even preferred European food. Their houses had pan roofs and were built of brick and stone. In comparison, Isaac felt like an *ara-oko*, a country-boy. He envied the *Saros'* class and sophistication, but even the British were impressed by Abeokuta society. When the local king, or *Alake*, arrived at the barracks in a large car, the officers had admired his flawless English and his robes of spotless white silk with gold clasps on the sleeves. His crown, one visitor noted, was equally impressive, something between a bishop's mitre and a duke's coronet. The *Alake* stood on a leopard skin, which in turn was laid on top of a small Persian carpet. A stern policeman had the specific task of carrying the skin and the carpet, while an official umbrella carrier ensured His Majesty always remained in the shade. As the *Alake* passed by, local people prostrated themselves on the ground. 'For to them he is more important than King George VI,' wrote a British soldier to his wife back home in England, evidently surprised by this discovery.

In the military hospital, Isaac was busy, helping the doctors treat soldiers for malaria and any number of sexually transmitted diseases. He also saw many sufferers of the dreaded Guinea Worm, a parasite that grows inside its victim, and eventually emerges through a blister in the skin, causing an excruciating burning sensation. Isaac watched as the doctor carefully wrapped the worm – long, thin and white, resembling a wriggling piece of cooked spaghetti – round a stick, so as to extract it faster. The patient often screamed in agony.

When Isaac wasn't in the hospital, he was invariably in the barracks. The British officers slept in wooden huts with thatched roofs, but the 'African Lines' were comprised of rows of simple communal tents. The 'Cookhouse' was not much more than a grass roof on poles, but at least the food that was boiled up in its great steaming vats was edible enough. The cooks served it up twice a day, piles of mashed cassava called *eba*, over which they poured a stew of meat and vegetables.

On Sunday afternoons, Isaac escaped from his soldier's life, hitching a ride on an army lorry to the town centre. From there, he climbed the steep path up the Olumo Rock, the great granite inselberg that rises over the town. He clambered past the entrances to several caves, too frightened to stop and see the shrines inside. From the top of Olumo, he saw the silver band of the Ogun River running through the red roofs before disappearing into the dark green of the forests beyond. On clear days, he imagined he could see as far as Lagos, as far as the Atlantic Ocean. Briefly, he had time to dream, to wonder where this adventure would take him, before he had to hurry back to barracks.

Officers had more freedom than their men. There was a cinema in Abeokuta, run by a Lebanese man, who dutifully played 'God Save The King' at the end of each evening. The British noted his loyalty, although they were invariably left feeling like awkward dummies, standing rigid as the Nigerians filed around them and out into the night while the anthem was still playing. Then there was the European Club, where an officer described one bleak evening as 'the usual dreary drinking session…a certain amount of singing, one or two brawls, and bodies quietly folding up in corners'. For the more adventurous, there was a far more joyful option: local society dances, where Creoles in immaculate tails and evening jackets mixed on the dance floor with Yoruba chiefs in magnificent robes of indigo, canary and jade. A gramophone blared foxtrot and boogie-woogie, and Africans jitterbugged and did the conga. Then the band would take over. The musicians, dressed in flowing white robes, played their drums and guitars with such pulsating rhythms that the British officers could not resist. Briefly, they were carried away in oblivious enjoyment, and, for once, the sense of escape was not fuelled by drink.

In Lagos, there were still more temptations for those British officers who could get down to the city for a day or two. There were boat trips across the harbour to Tarkwa Bay, its protected waters perfect for swimming, with little thatch cabins on the beach for shade. Officers gathered on the roof of the Bristol Hotel at sunset to enjoy the cool breeze off the lagoon. They drank beer and admired the view over the eucalyptus and palms of the Marina to the docks at Apapa. Then, later in the evening, in back streets that stank of animal droppings and sewage, some of those officers would file sheepishly into a dingy brothel, where they were warmly greeted by heavily painted madams, and presented with a choice of taciturn girls. 'You

need jig-a-jig? Come see my sistah, is she good for you?' the madam
would ask. And, although the movement of ships in wartime was in
theory 'Top Secret', many noticed a strange thing: it was the madams
who had the best intelligence on the imminent arrival of the Royal
Navy convoys, better even than the Harbour Master. But, as the war
dragged on, and more American ships refuelled at Lagos, the ladies
of the night reached their own judgement on who made the best
customers, captured in cutting verse:

> *Me-no likee English sold-ier,*
> *Yank-ee soldier come ashore;*
> *Yank-ee soldier plenty mon-ey,*
> *Me-no jigajig for you no more.*

The Army could be cruel, and unfair, as many African soldiers were
discovering. A British major in the Gold Coast remembered what he
called 'an unfortunate phase', when it was commonplace for new
recruits to be 'hit or beaten for apparent stupidity and idleness'. He
attributed this to the sheer frustration of trying to teach the unedu-
cated. Corporal punishment, known as 'Six for Arse', was widespread.
Typically, it was administered by African sergeants or corporals, but
some British officers joined in.

In his old age, Albert Carpenter liked to sit in his well-tended
Hertfordshire garden, and think about the past. He wrote adventure
novels set in West Africa during colonial times, and played Mozart
and Paganini on his classical guitar. He was a tall, handsome man,
a little stooped, with silver hair and a moustache. In 1942, he was a
young sergeant major in a remote bush camp in Northern Nigeria, an
Islington boy suddenly tasked with getting a motley group of African
recruits ready for war. He led forced route marches through the bush,
and came face to face with lions and hippopotamus.

At first, spirits were high; many of Carpenter's men, after all, had
walked for days from distant villages so that they could join the Army.
But he was worried about one soldier in his platoon, the driver, James

Abuji, who spoke a little English, and whom he gradually came to see as a poisonous influence. Abuji, he learnt, was extorting money from other soldiers, intimidating them by boasting of his *juju*, or black magic prowess. Carpenter decided that Abuji was a threat to morale and needed to be dealt with. In the heat of the midday sun, he had the men tie Abuji, spread-eagled, to the metal roof of an army truck. Then he placed the bleeding carcasses of chickens around him. Vultures soon appeared in the sky, and, when they swooped down to the truck to tear at the chicken flesh, their talons passed within inches of Abuji's face. Abuji screamed with terror. When he was eventually untied, by now delirious with thirst, he fell weeping on the ground. Then Albert ordered the rest of the platoon to urinate on him, taunting him as they did so. 'You want water, Abuji? We come, we give,' they said.

Abuji had been made a laughing stock, and hatred festered inside him. He waited two years to take his revenge. In the confusion and noise of a jungle battle in Burma, he rushed towards Carpenter with a grenade, yanking the pin out with his teeth. Another Nigerian solider, Musa Pankshin, saw what was happening, and wrestled Abuji into a ditch. The grenade exploded, killing both Abuji and Musa. Of all his experiences during the war, this was the one Carpenter thought about the most in his old age. 'I probably did overdo it, looking back over the years,' he said with a shake of his head as if to convince himself that he'd done nothing wrong. 'He was a dangerous man, that one, and he was destroying my men one by one. Something had to be done. No, I don't regret it.'

When Isaac was transferred from Abeokuta to Enugu, in eastern Nigeria, to an Infantry Training Centre, he had his own taste of how uncomfortable military life could really be. He was no longer spending his days with nurses, doctors and laboratory technicians in a hospital, or his Sundays scrambling over the Olumo Rock. Instead, he was drilled under a scorching sun, from dawn until dusk. Quick steps, slow steps, eyes right, eyes left, for hour after hour. And when he wasn't being drilled, he was sent on gruelling exercises. The men were ordered to swing themselves along suspended rope ladders, sprint across fields with heavy packs on their backs, and crawl through oil drums, taking care to avoid the metal spikes and broken glass that had been strewn inside them.

Isaac had little contact with British officers, but the African sergeants and corporals in his unit were ruthless. Their English did not seem to extend beyond a few words of abuse. One sergeant major at Enugu, known by the soldiers as *Werewere* – 'Quick, quick' in Yoruba – had an especially vindictive streak. The men said he was tougher than thunder. He could hurl abuse, or *flog for mouf*, with the worst of them, but he liked to use his fists as well. He was a hulking man, with blood-shot eyes, and he seemed to reserve a particular hatred for any recruit with a semblance of education. His favourite punishment was to make an errant soldier dig his own grave, bare-handed, in a nearby cemetery. That way, Werewere used to laugh, the burial would be nice and easy, should the feeble recruit not survive the training course.

For Isaac, the drill and fitness training was a chastening experience but one that taught him valuable lessons. For the first time in his life, he had ventured outside the Yoruba lands of southwest Nigeria. He was mixing with Hausas from the North, Tivs from the Middle Belt, and Igbos from the East, picking up words from all their languages. He met Muslims, other kinds of Christians and followers of traditional beliefs. Isaac was beginning to understand the diversity and complex-ity of this territory the British had so hastily constructed. '*Ṣe o ri bi ti wọn ti gbin obi n'ile Hausa? Abi ti wọn tin sin maalu n'ile Yoruba?*' asked a Yoruba recruit whom Isaac met in Enugu. 'Have you seen where they plant kola nut in the North? Or where they rear cattle in the South?' His point was that each of the different peoples of Nigeria gratefully consumed what others could produce.

The Hausa soldiers nicknamed Isaac *Dogonyaro*, or tall youth. His schooling attracted opprobrium, but it also brought advantages. For a modest fee, he could help his fellow soldiers by writing handsome letters home on their behalf. 'Dear Wife', the letters might begin, and they would often be signed off with a final flourish: 'I hope this finds you swimming in the ocean of good health'.

There was another benefit to those months in Enugu, one that Isaac would only appreciate with hindsight. He was being toughened up, in mind and body, being taught to obey orders, but also to endure hardship. He could not have imagined the ordeal that lay ahead, but one day he would surprise himself by looking back with something approaching gratitude towards the bullying sergeants whom he had once cursed so bitterly.

After six months in Enugu, Isaac travelled by train to Lagos with hundreds of other recruits. They saw nothing of the city he had heard so much about, but were taken straight to the wharf at Apapa. They were ushered onto a troopship, and taken to their cramped compartments down below. Only now did Isaac learn where they were going: to Freetown, Sierra Leone, more than a thousand miles along the West African coast. But nobody told him what they would be doing in Sierra Leone, or how long he would be there. He was a tiny cog in the vast machine that was the British Army, a machine that rarely accounted for its workings to the hundreds of thousands of little moving pieces trapped inside it. If Isaac had been in any doubt about this beforehand, he now understood it plainly. Better, he philosophised, to accept the machine's mysterious ways and allow it to take him where it decided to go. In fact, he was excited. As the ship pulled away from the wharf, the soldiers rushed back up to the deck and waved goodbye to the people on the quay below. Isaac looked down from that ship and felt a sudden thrill: he was leaving Nigeria for the first time.

The journey up the coast lasted several days. Everything was new: the crashing of the waves against the hull, the dolphins and strange fish with wings that leapt out of the sea and flashed in the sunlight, the jellyfish swaying just beneath the surface, the tang of salt in the air, the cool breeze that made standing on the decks so refreshing. Between nine and ten o'clock in the morning, there was 'boat parade', when everyone assembled, wearing lifejackets, at a designated emergency position and awaited inspection by a senior officer. They did the drill again and again, until Isaac could do it with his eyes shut. 'You put the jacket over your head like this,' the officer said, miming the actions with his hands, 'you tie one knot here, one knot here, you pull this cord here, and you jump. And then you pray.'

One morning, they came into Freetown harbour, sailing past King Tom Point, and came to dock in the bay. Green mountains trailed away to the south in a series of great folds. It was time to disembark. They travelled on a railway up into the mountains, crossing ravines and passing waterfalls, before eventually arriving in a village tucked into one of the valleys. It was a place of flaming hibiscus and banana trees, bright-blue houses, Victorian lace curtains and old wooden churches. The village was called Regent.

It was here that Isaac was finally assigned to his medical unit: the 29th Casualty Clearing Station. Most of its one hundred men were Sierra Leoneans, but he and several other Nigerians had been drafted in to bring it up to strength. The commanding officer, Major Moynagh, explained the purpose of a CCS. It was a sort of mobile military hospital, where the sick and wounded who came in from the front were assessed, given emergency treatment and then evacuated to a general hospital further back down the lines. The Major had twelve British officers working under him, all medical doctors, including some surgeons. Most of the Africans would work as nursing orderlies and operating theatre assistants.

Major Moynagh was a mild and pious man. He organised prayers every morning, which Isaac dutifully attended. Several of the officers urged the Major to be strict with the Africans when they stepped out of line, but he always replied that justice should be tempered with mercy. Isaac and the other Africans joked that the Major was like a vicar without a vicarage, a man who would have been happier in the clergy than in an army.

The 29th CCS was working in a military hospital in Regent, treating British and African soldiers who were sick or had been injured in jungle training exercises. On his days off, Isaac and his friends from the unit would travel down to Freetown. The familiar Yoruba names on the shop fronts – Ayodele, Abimbola, Taiwo – made them feel at home. But the Creoles that brushed past them on Freetown's pavements appeared, if anything, even more refined and intimidating than the ones Isaac had admired in Abeokuta. They were called *Krios* here, 'sabby boys'. Some had studied medicine and law in England and they spoke loudly in what Isaac imagined to be an Oxford accent. Their wives had fantastic names like Venus Bonaparte Smith and Kissy Black Jones. Not everything was familiar.

A few weeks later, Major Moynagh called the 29th CCS together, and told them that they would be travelling back down the coast to Nigeria. The night before they left, the men staged a concert in the Major's honour. They had composed a special song for him, '*Major Moynagh wa o, ọmọ ọlọla, ọpẹ; Iba f'alaga oni o, iba o*' – 'We thank our dear Major Moynagh of noble birth; We doff our hats for the chairman of today's occasion.'

The next day, the wives and families of many of the Sierra Leonean soldiers came to the barracks to say goodbye to their men. The women cried and wailed, and one beat the ground with her fists. The soldiers tried to reassure their families: they were only moving to another part of West Africa; they were not going to the war. Some, no doubt, believed what they were saying. But others, even as they did their best to comfort their loved ones, must have suspected that Nigeria would not be their final destination.

The Royal West African Frontier Force was now a valuable asset to the British Army. Many of its units had been training for more than a year. At some point, surely, the politicians and generals in London would look at bringing it into the fray. Rumours, shared by officers and soldiers alike, swept through the ranks in those first weeks of 1943. The suspicion grew that they were not going to be sitting on the sidelines much longer. The focus of the war was changing.

The German invasion of Britain that had seemed imminent in 1940 was now considered to be a remote possibility. From the summer of 1941, following Hitler's attack on the Soviet Union, the crucial battles in Europe were being fought on the Eastern Front. Initially, the Germans had made sweeping advances, but they could not crush the Soviets, and by late 1942 they were on the verge of surrender at the Battle of Stalingrad. The tide had also turned in North Africa, where, in November 1942, the British defeated the German army at El Alamein, raising the prospect of an Allied invasion of southern Europe. Britain's African colonies, apparently so vulnerable at the start of the war, appeared much more secure. The Italians were defeated in Abyssinia and Somaliland. The Vichy threat to West Africa, the original impetus behind the expansion of forces in the British colonies there, had never materialised. And, after the Allied landings in Algeria and Morocco, the French West African territories had capitulated. Thousands of Africans had already served in the British Army as labour and pioneer units during the campaigns in North Africa and the Middle East, but, at the end of 1942, for the first time, it became possible for Britain's generals to contemplate using African soldiers further afield. Their eyes turned to the one theatre of war where the outlook was still extremely bleak.

The Japanese had attacked Pearl Harbor and invaded British Malaya in December 1941, just a few days before Isaac had enlisted. In the following weeks, they had swept down the Malayan peninsula towards Singapore. British strategy in the Far East was based on the assumption that Singapore, with its huge garrison and naval base, was an 'impregnable fortress' that guaranteed protection to the surrounding colonies and Australia to the south.

However, the British had been far too complacent. Their propaganda portrayed Japanese soldiers as small, buck-toothed men, with slitty eyes and glasses – untrustworthy, but no match for their British counterparts. The British military attaché in Tokyo complained that 'our chaps place the Japs somewhere between the Italians and the Afghans', and his warnings about Japanese military competence fell on deaf ears. When the Governor of Singapore, Sir Shenton Thomas, was told about the Japanese landings on the north-east coast of Malaya, he is alleged to have said, 'Well, I suppose you'll shove the little men off.'

The truth was that the Japanese infantry was highly trained, able to march long distances with heavy loads, surprisingly mobile in dense jungle and formidable in battle. Belatedly, the British were confronted with the folly of their prejudices, but they were in no position to respond. They had more troops, but their morale was low, their equipment poor and their leadership unimaginative. Furthermore, British aeroplanes were obsolete, and, with no control of the skies, British ships were hopelessly vulnerable. Singapore surrendered on 15 February 1942. Some 100,000 British troops, most of whom were actually Indians and Australians, were taken prisoner. They would endure appalling conditions during their long captivity. It was the greatest defeat ever suffered by the British Empire. A Japanese soldier remembered the giddy sense of disbelief of the victorious army. 'The Japanese did not expect that a stronger and richer country like Great Britain would be conquered so easily,' he wrote. 'The Japanese felt they were the Shining South. All the fears and worries at the outbreak of the war disappeared. Now Japan had the south in her hands…pretty soon Japan would be on top of the world.' Suddenly, these 'little men' appeared to be invincible.

The next prize for the Japanese, another British colony, lay to the north-west. Burma had oil, rubber, tin and rice – all resources the Japanese coveted. Northern Burma was also a vital supply route for the Chinese, longstanding enemies of the Japanese, who were receiving American weapons from British India. The Japanese wanted to cut this route, which they believed would tilt the war in China in Japan's favour. They had bombed the Burmese capital, Rangoon, in December 1941, killing hundreds of people, many of whom had innocently stepped outside to watch what they thought was an air display. The Japanese advanced rapidly on the city, which the British abandoned in early March 1942.

British generals had learnt some lessons from the debacle in Malaya, but their men were still no match for the Japanese in jungle fighting. The British Army fell back to the Indian frontier. Its units were largely intact but utterly demoralised. If the myth of white supremacy was the confidence trick that kept the Empire going, in South-East Asia it had been all but shattered in the space of just a few disastrous months. In this moment of crisis, the British had proved themselves incapable of defending those they ruled over. They had cut and run. Britain's dependants, those who served the Empire as policemen, clerks and domestic servants, were abandoned and betrayed. The Japanese were poised, should they wish, to launch an invasion of India itself, the jewel of a badly dented imperial crown.

In Delhi, General Archibald Wavell, the Commander-in-Chief of the British Army in India, was acutely worried that he did not have enough soldiers to defend India, let alone recapture territory in Burma and Malaya. And so he cast his eyes over the Empire for a source of fighting men. On 9 December 1942, he wrote to the War Office in London, saying, 'I have been considering use of African troops for operations in Burma or Eastwards. Advantage of West African troops is that they are used to jungle and to moving with Porter transport which would be invaluable in certain parts of Burma and Malaya.' African troops, including West Africans, had fought well in Abyssinia, he said, and should be able to 'compete' with the Japanese.

The suggestion went down well in London. A senior civil servant wrote that it would 'be in accordance with the general Colonial Office policy of associating Colonial peoples actively in the war'. The final decision to send both East and West African soldiers to India was taken at a Chiefs of Staff Committee meeting in London on 30 December. The generals concurred that there was now no realistic threat of invasion to Britain's West African territories. They also noted the West Africans' supposed familiarity with jungle conditions and immunity from malaria. And so approval was given. The Chief of the

Imperial General Staff, Sir Alan Brooke, agreed 'that these resources released from West Africa would be most useful'.

Isaac and his colleagues sailed back to Lagos at the beginning of 1943. From the capital, they travelled to a camp called Ede, near Osogbo. By this time, some of his officers had made their own deductions, based on the state of the war, that they would soon be going to Burma to fight the Japanese. A British attempt at a counterattack there, launched at the end of 1942 in the coastal region of Arakan, was running into difficulties.

In January 1943, the War Office in London formally notified West African HQ that it would need two divisions to serve in Burma. This amounted to some 56,000 soldiers from the West African colonies alone, perhaps more when supporting units were included. Time was not on Britain's side. The African army needed to be trained quickly, if, as the War Office demanded, the first of these two divisions was to embark for Burma by the middle of the year.

A British brigadier called together the officers at Isaac's camp. 'I cannot tell you where you are going to go, gentlemen,' he said, trying to strike an upbeat note, 'but I can tell you this. You are very lucky people. You are going to fight the Japanese.'

Some of the officers were privately dismayed by the brigadier's words. A largely untested West African force was being sent to fight the hitherto invincible Japanese. It was a daunting prospect. Trevor Clark, a young lieutenant, who was fresh out of Oxford and had been in Africa only a few weeks, felt that he knew little about his men or his fellow officers, and that their training had been basic at best. He worried that they would be 'the virtually naked led by the largely clueless', and no match for the Japanese.

The generals' theory, expounded in Delhi and London, that Africans were 'used to jungle' and would therefore be good jungle fighters was based on equal measures of ignorance and optimism. Trevor Clark ruefully remarked that he might as well have been defined as a street fighter because he 'had been brought up in cities'.

In fact, the majority of African recruits, not least from Nigeria, which would provide the greatest number of troops, came from dry savannah and semi-desert areas. But John Hamilton, who ended up fighting alongside Clark in Burma with the Gambian battalion, did believe that West Africans 'jungle-reared or not…had senses more acute than those of Europeans, sharper hearing, quicker eyes and more far-sighted'.

Meanwhile, Isaac and his friends talked excitedly of joining the Allied armies in North Africa, for an eventual push into Italy or France. This, after all, was the war front the recruitment officers had described when they scoured the villages looking for young men. And they were sure they would be travelling soon. Their conviction only hardened when they were suddenly granted a month's leave, and advised to go home and see their families.

For the first time since he had run away to join the Army, Isaac was on his way to Emure-Ile. He was greeted in the village with delight and relief by his parents; it seemed that some relatives had worried that he might already be dead. Instead, Isaac found himself to be something of a local hero. He had tales to share. He knew the workings of the great British Army from the inside; he'd seen the sea and travelled on a ship all the way to Sierra Leone.

After three weeks at home, Isaac was called into his father's bedroom late one evening. Joshua sat in the dark room, with a candle on the bare table in front of him. He had heard the stories that Nigerian soldiers would soon be shipped abroad, and this worried him. The British were going to send his eldest son far away, to an unknown place, to fight a war the meaning of which he still did not understand, let alone care for. No other boy from Emure-Ile had enlisted. What was his son playing at?

Never mind, thought Joshua, he did not wish to berate the boy. For he was about to make him an offer that he was confident would be accepted. Joshua explained that he'd saved enough money to pay for a secondary education, should Isaac gain admission to a good grammar school. Isaac was speechless. He'd always wanted to complete his education, but, faced with his father's offer, he realised that he had changed in the time he'd been away from home. He felt the pull of a new loyalty, one that he had scarcely been aware of before, to the officers and colleagues that he'd been training with for more than a year now. Soon, he believed, they would be setting off together on a great adventure. He sensed the shame and disgrace that would come from deserting the Army almost on the eve of their departure. He'd be branded a coward, and would spend months in prison if he was caught. No reputable school would want to admit him after that.

'Me, not go back to the Army, to my unit, to desert?' he said. Isaac surprised himself with how he was talking to his father. His voice grew louder. 'I'm not going to desert. I'm going with my unit!'

A few days later, Isaac left Emure-Ile to go back to his barracks. Joshua, deeply saddened, did not go to the edge of the village to say goodbye.

3

A CALABASH IN THE WIND

Since the day we left Lagos, we saw nothing but long stretches of water like the wide world, we saw no living creatures except ourselves on the steamship. Although the ships were such big ships, they were tossed about like a piece of calabash in the wind of the water.

Letter from a Nigerian soldier
on board a troopship

July 1943
Lagos

In the early hours of 10 July 1943, Allied landing craft ploughed through heavy seas towards the beaches of Sicily. In the skies above, American paratroopers and British gliders from the 8th Army were blown badly off course by the strong winds, and many landed miles away from their intended destinations. But, for all the confusion, the Allied invasion of Italy had begun, and the initial resistance by German and Italian troops was not as fierce as Eisenhower and his generals had feared.

That same morning, in Lagos harbour, another chapter of the Second World War was opening. It was a damp grey day and a convoy of six troopships and four destroyers cut through the leaden waters of the lagoon and out towards the sea. The men on the troopships would take part not in the war against fascism in Europe, but the one to defend the British Empire in Asia. They were the very first West African troops to set sail for Burma.

The Royal West African Frontier Force's 81st Division comprised some 28,000 men. To move them around the African coast and across the Indian Ocean was an enormous operation, involving three additional convoys and several weeks. As Isaac and his colleagues set off that Saturday, there were no military bands on the Apapa docks playing jaunty tunes, no reporters or photographers to capture the scene, no cheering crowds waving little Union Jacks. They were slipping out, unannounced and uncelebrated, after a couple of nights in a transit camp by a swamp on the edge of the city.

When they had left for Sierra Leone a few months earlier, the soldiers on board Isaac's ship were boisterous and full of bluster. This time, they were quiet and pensive. Everyone understood that this was a journey of a different magnitude. Many lingered on the decks, gazing sadly back at the shore. The cathedral, the red-brick secretariat, the square white façade of the governor's mansion and the other handsome buildings along Lagos Marina were growing smaller and smaller by the minute. They glided past the mouth of Five Cowrie Creek, and the mangrove swamps of Victoria Island, and the little fishing villages where men squatted by canoes, mending their nets. Maybe the 'fish mammies', the stout ladies who sat under the palms sorting through the catch, looked up and saw the ships go by. If so, they must have wondered where all those young men were being sent, and how many would come back. Then the convoy was past the mole, with its barbed-wire cover and the little machine-gun post at its end, and into open water. Already Lagos had all but disappeared, the coastline a vanishing smudge of green on the horizon. There was no turning back now.

During their final days in Nigeria, the pace of training at the camp in Ede had quickened. More troops poured in, not just from Sierra Leone but also from the Gambia and the Gold Coast. They slept in long marquees, their bunk beds closely packed. The Sierra Leoneans, unhappy at the absence of their preferred staple, rice, complained of 'belly palaver' as they struggled to adapt to *garri*, the Nigerian cassava flour. The rain came down in buckets. The bullfrogs kept up a ferocious chorus throughout the night, and the recruits were up before dawn, setting off on a series of route marches wearing full battle dress. The infantrymen spent days on the rifle range, being taught to clean and fire their weapons. The soldiers spent their precious few off-duty hours in nearby Osogbo. British officers turned a blind eye to the trucks that came back from town carrying women as well as men. The officers themselves were known to spend evenings in Osogbo's Syrian Club, enjoying beer and chicken, before retiring behind a curtain, where there was said to be dancing, sometimes more.

The men of the 29th CCS ran for hours through forests and up steep hills, carrying mock casualties on stretchers. They practised putting up and taking down their bulky ward tents, and assembling the portable operating theatre. They packed, and unpacked, their medical equipment, until the officers were satisfied that every man knew his own little role to perfection, and that every action was being done as fast as possible. To the disappointment of many in the unit, the gentle Major Moynagh was removed from the command. He was a much-loved officer, though it was also true that Isaac and the others had wondered whether he really had the qualities to lead men into war. His replacement, Major Robert Murphy, was more remote.

The 29th CCS now belonged to the hurriedly assembled 81st Division, formally proclaimed in March 1943. The 81st Division would be the first of two West African divisions to go to Burma. It would be joined by the 82nd Division in late 1944.

The 81st was put under the command of a forty-nine-year-old veteran of the First World War, Major General Christopher Woolner. John Hamilton wrote that Woolner was 'known to his peers as "Kit", to the Europeans of 81 Division as "Father" and to the Africans as "Pappa"'. He had a reputation for being a stern disciplinarian, trim and smartly dressed and always clean-shaven. Woolner had clear blue eyes, and could deliver a cold stare of disapproval to soldiers and officers alike when he felt they had fallen short of his exacting standards.

General Woolner had spent five years in West Africa before his appointment, but, if he appeared well qualified for his new position, in private he had many doubts and worries. He was concerned that his troops had had little time for jungle training, that they did not have enough equipment, and that his divisional headquarters was short of experienced officers. He fretted that many of his officers had only arrived from Britain just in time to embark for Burma, while large numbers of the African recruits had been drafted in 'at the last moment to replace men found unfit on mobilization'. On 19 March 1943, he prepared a secret training policy document for his officers. He warned them that the Japanese soldier 'really does fight to the last man and the last round', and that the 81st Division needed to think of the jungle not as a hindrance, but as 'a friendly cloak, that enables us to close with our enemy and kill him'.

Woolner chose a black spider on a yellow background as the divisional badge, and one of these was sown onto each soldier's uniform. The spider represented *Ananse*, from Ashanti mythology. It was a cunning animal spirit that could change form, and used its wits to achieve apparently impossible feats and overcome larger enemies. He hoped that his men would take his choice to heart.

'Prepare for six weeks at sea' was all Major Murphy told the men of the 29th CCS. This was not going to be another short run up the coast. When the men were issued with warm clothes, the mystery deepened. Some argued that this proved that they were going to Europe, to fight the Nazis. Others, who'd overheard talk in the officers' mess, had a more intriguing and more accurate explanation. Everyone would need to keep warm, they said, because they would be travelling around Africa's cold, southern Cape. From there, they would sail to India, and then march to a country called Burma. *Boma*, some of the Africans pronounced it. Few of them had ever heard of it before.

They had no official confirmation of their destination, even after boarding the ship at Lagos. The officers knew it had become received wisdom, however, that the ship was going to India, and they had not denied the rumour. In the days before their departure, one British officer remembered a Sierra Leonean soldier asking the more critical question that lurked at the back of everyone's mind: 'Sir. Which time dis war done finish?' Perhaps some of the men noticed an unfortunate omen as their ships moved away from the docks that July morning. A Royal Navy destroyer was coming into Lagos harbour, carrying the survivors of a torpedoed ship, gathered in weary, blanketed huddles on the decks. The soldiers' war had just begun.

At the docks, Isaac's ship, the *Staffordshire*, had towered above the men as they waited to board, but now, out in the blue expanse of the Bight of Benin, it seemed small and vulnerable. Isaac could just make out the silhouettes of the other troopships in the convoy, spread out over several miles in front and behind the *Staffordshire*, as well as the Navy destroyers sailing by their side. The *Staffordshire* was soon dipping and lurching in the white-capped waves, and by the early afternoon many of the soldiers were overcome with nausea. The decks were full of miserable, frightened men, staggering to the railings, and emptying their guts over the side of the ship. One soldier was heard suggesting that seasickness could be cured by eating raw chilli, but most simply prayed for deliverance, to Muslim, Christian and other, older gods. As the day wore on, a few men even said they wished they'd taken the advice of friends or family, and deserted just before they'd left Lagos. But there was no more land to be seen now, only an ocean without end.

Conditions on board the *Staffordshire* were basic. The officers had shared cabins. Trevor Clark, who was on the *Staffordshire*, remembered how his Gambian platoon came up to admire his four-berth cabin, so fine they called it 'a house'. The Africans, for their part, slept in their hundreds in the dark hold, not in beds, but in rows and rows of hammocks. The first nights were stifling, and the men stripped down to loin-cloths or shorts. Were any of the British officers who saw that gloomy hold of near-naked black bodies struck by an uncomfortable similarity with the past? Africans had been taken from this same coast before, and packed onto ships for an unknown destination. Only this time the Africans would be fighting for the white men, not labouring to produce their wealth. Many of the men pleaded to be allowed to sleep on the deck, and, when the captain agreed, Isaac and the others took it in turns over subsequent nights. They all preferred to be out in the open. After dark, they peered over the ship's railings and marvelled at the filigree lines of phosphorescence in the bow waves. Then they laid out their blankets, and fell asleep beneath a vast tableau of stars.

If accommodation was wanting, at least the food was plentiful. General Woolner had ensured there were fifty days' worth of rations on board all the convoy's ships, more than enough for the journey. There was rice and beans, as well as *garri* and meat, and the occasional apple.

It was a journey of many discoveries, both great and small. Some of the soldiers who came from more remote communities had never seen, let alone used, a flush toilet before. Shortly after leaving Lagos, an African sergeant approached his puzzled British counterpart to say that his men were worried that the wells on the ship were nearly empty, and the water inside them tasted salty. Eventually, a British soldier had to arrange a practical demonstration of lavatory use, complete with hand gestures, which seemed to dispel the confusion.

Another revelation was the ship's crew. They were white men, plainly, yet they wore dirty overalls, laboured with their hands, and were even observed to give passing Africans a friendly slap on the back. Most West Africans had never seen, let alone experienced, anything like this. They had always known the white man as a remote figure, part of the small ruling class. He was a missionary, a civil servant or a military officer. He assumed, and wielded, authority, and he invariably lived in a large house surrounded by servants. He had his own club, where he socialised with other whites. If he was sometimes admired for his knowledge and apparent incorruptibility, he was also resented for his austerity and attitude of superiority. But these sailors, with their strange Cockney, Liverpudlian and Glaswegian accents, assumed no airs. They were quick to share both jokes and cigarettes with their African passengers. There may have been a few

Africans on the *Staffordshire* who reached a startling conclusion; for the first time in their lives, they were meeting white men who were less educated than they were. And at mealtimes some of the African soldiers could not resist peering through the saloon windows, for the thrill of seeing white stewards waiting on the officers.

As the convoy approached Cape Town, the seas grew more turbulent. On 21 July, just after breakfast, someone caught a first sight of Table Mountain. Hundreds of men rushed to the port side of the *Staffordshire*, which began to list. The mountain was draped in its cloth of silver cloud, but the city was laid out in bright sunshine beneath. The more distant jagged peaks of the Hottentots Hollands were capped in snow. The air was cold and fresh, the light had a piercing clarity. The soldiers could see seals plunging off the rocks of Robben Island, into water, they said, as dark as the indigo of *aro*. Was this really Africa? A place that looked so fine, said one Nigerian, that 'dis place ebe Englan, nobbe Blackman country'.

They spent four days in Cape Town harbour, as the convoy took on food, fresh water, fuel and other supplies. The British officers were given a warm reception onshore. Cape Town's whites queued up at the quayside in their cars to take their visitors on sightseeing trips of the surrounding countryside, into the Winelands and forests of umbrella pines at the foot of Table Mountain. They invited the officers to their homes for dinners and parties. Months later, sheltering from the rain in the jungles of Burma, the officers would remember picnics in the Kirstenbosch botanical gardens, dinners at the Mount Nelson Hotel, alluring women at Delmonico's nightclub, and wonder if it had all really happened.

For the African troops, the Cape was seductive, and yet also cold-hearted. Most, like Isaac, were not even allowed off the ships. Eventually, some of the men were given permission to go ashore, but the local authorities received them only grudgingly. After much negotiation, they were allowed to march in the outer suburbs, but were ordered to leave their weapons on the ship. One lady, seeing a British captain with his African men, asked, 'But you don't arm these monkeys, do you?' The captain replied that they were, in fact, frontline troops, at which the woman walked away, wondering aloud what the Empire was coming to.

They were the first West African convoy to land at Cape Town. Some of the ships that came in later weeks were given a slightly warmer reception. A Nigerian soldier remembered parading through the streets, marching to the beat of the drums, the enthusiastic crowds cheering wildly. He saw trams, and tarred roads, and splendid houses. It was only later, back on board the ship, that he and his fellow soldiers wondered why they'd seen so few black faces on the streets of Cape Town.

Durban, further east on South Africa's Indian Ocean coast, was generally friendlier to the passing West Africans. Here, too, the officers had a wonderful time. The white residents, of overwhelmingly British descent, embraced them with open arms. Captain Charles Carfrae would remember being 'spoilt almost to death for ten days of eating, drinking and lovemaking. In retrospect Durban appears as a golden city, a southern paradise, the stuff of sensuous dreams: and I for one have never forgotten its delights'. This was a city of 'well-lit and well-stocked shops and lovely weather', a salutary contrast with the grim conditions in wartime Britain. Another contrast that the British officers noticed, however, was the difference between their well-built West African soldiers, and 'the undernourished and ill dressed native blacks'.

One contingent of West Africans was allowed to wander around Durban under the supervision of a British officer. They soon found themselves being chased out of a 'Whites Only' public toilet, and then got into a vigorous argument in the Woolworths department store over the price of oranges. Employing the skills they used at home, they could not understand why the girl behind the counter refused to be drawn into negotiations over the price. A crowd gathered to see what was happening. The misunderstanding was resolved when an older white woman intervened and bought oranges for all the soldiers. As the troopships sailed away from Durban, Africa slipped out of view. It was too much for one soldier from the Gold Coast. He stared at the receding coastline, and was heard to cry, 'I cannot leave my homeland.' Then he leapt overboard. The ship did not stop, and so the Gold Coast Regiment recorded its first casualty since setting out for the war.

When Isaac's ship entered the warm, calmer waters of the Indian Ocean, a British officer noted that the sea was 'like a huge sheet of glass, across which our convoy chugged like stately swans'. The days began to merge into one another. Every morning after breakfast, a Catholic priest held a well-attended prayer session on the deck, always starting with a rendition of 'Onward Christian Soldiers'. Never mind that many of the soldiers were Muslims; they joined the hymn-singing with gusto. The officers arranged boxing tournaments on the deck. In the heat of the afternoon, some of the African soldiers who had been to school gave literacy lessons to their colleagues, using primary school books that one of the British officers had bought in Cape Town. 'One would see them huddled in small groups here and there, studies in concentration as they painstakingly wrote down three letter words with a grimy stub of pencil,' he wrote.

Otherwise, the men had nothing more to do than sit and talk and talk. The Gambians on the *Staffordshire* spoke in Mandingo and Wolof. The Sierra Leoneans spoke in *Krio*. And the Nigerians spoke in Hausa, Igbo and Tiv, although a handful, including Isaac, spoke in Yoruba. Everyone found those who shared their tongue, and did their best to communicate with the rest. They talked about where they'd come from, and they tried to imagine where they were going. Sometimes they would sing. These great ships, said a Yoruba man from Ekiti, were gliding across the endless sea like the vulture glides through the sky.

E i lọ dẹẹ E i lọ dẹẹ
Ogongo baba ẹiyẹ
E i lọ dẹẹ

It's gliding away, it's gliding away
The vulture, the king of birds
Is gliding away.

The Sierra Leoneans answered with a song of their own:

When shall I see ma home?
When shall I see ma native land?
I shall never forget ma home,
Home again, home again.
When shall I see ma home?
When shall I see ma native land?
I shall never forget ma home.

Sometimes the Africans would talk about death and the possibility that they would not come home, or the changes that would take place while they were away. One Igbo man put it bluntly: 'No be say all people where de for house na him go de when we come back o. Whe our fathers, whe our fathers father De no die?' – 'Don't think everyone we left at home will be there when we come back. Where are our fathers, and our father's father? Did they not die?'

According to a British officer on Isaac's convoy, 'as the weather grew warmer, the drums beat, and the Africans danced'. It was a way to break up the tedium. The officers arranged their own evening entertainment. They gathered in the crowded, hot lounge, its windows blacked out for safety reasons, and cheered on amateur dramatics and cabarets gamely performed by their peers and the ship's crew.

Richard Terrell was a lieutenant who travelled in the same convoy as Isaac, an LSE graduate who'd already noticed that some of his fellow officers disapproved of his leftish views. He gave lectures to the Africans, not only about the war, but also about geography, different civilisations, and the relationship between the earth, the moon and the solar system. Terrell had plenty of experience of lecturing bored British soldiers who, he said, invariably 'sat glumly waiting to be dismissed'. The Africans, in contrast, saw any chance of self-improvement as 'a real treat'. Terrell found himself trying to answer innumerable questions, as the men thrust their hands in the air, eager to catch his attention and learn more. When Charles Carfrae made the same crossing two months later, he too gave lectures, although these were more narrowly focused on the battles that he feared were to come. The Japanese he said 'are the King of England's enemies, and yours too. If they are not defeated, they will enslave many – perhaps even yourselves.' He found the Nigerians scornful of this possibility, and confident that the Japanese in Burma would prove no more dangerous a foe than the Italians in Abyssinia had been at the beginning of the war. 'This unclouded confidence disturbed me,' confessed Carfrae.

There was a daily boat parade on the *Staffordshire*, not only to keep the men busy, but also to remind them of the very real dangers that lurked beneath the waves. The convoy steered a zigzagging movement through the ocean, led by a Navy destroyer at the front. This was intended to throw enemy submarines off course, although it also caused confusion among some of the Africans, especially after many days without any sight of land. An officer on Isaac's ship recalled one of the Gambians saying to him, 'One thing doubt me, sah. I watch the small scout boat yonder for a long time. Now he go look this side, now he go look that side, but he never able for find proper road. I think we all lost.'

The threat from the Japanese may have felt improbable on those calm days and balmy nights in the Indian Ocean, but the lookouts were on twenty-four-hour alert for the dreaded sight of a periscope poking out of the water. One night, the men were woken abruptly by the wail of the siren. In wordless fear, they hurriedly put on their lifejackets, stumbled onto the deck and got to their stations. This was the scenario they had trained for, again and again. The destroyers were scanning the surrounding ocean with powerful lights, trying to find the suspected submarine, occasionally firing into the blackness. Amid the melee and the noise, Isaac could see the tension on the faces of the British officers. He tried to imagine what the explosion of a torpedo would feel like; the violent rocking of the ship that would follow, the panic on the decks and the cold water gushing up from the hold until it enveloped him. Then the shooting stopped and the siren fell silent. The men waited on deck for another half-hour, before someone shouted, 'Stand down!' and they all went back to the hold.

A few months later, disaster did strike another British troopship in the Indian Ocean, this one carrying East African soldiers to Ceylon. On 12 February 1944, the *Khedive Ismail*, with 1,511 people on board, was sailing in bright sunshine through placid waters near the Maldives, when it was hit by torpedoes fired from a Japanese submarine. There were two enormous explosions. The *Khedive Ismail* went down in just two minutes. Its passengers made frantic efforts to escape, but the vast majority were trapped inside; 1,297 people drowned. Of the 996 East African soldiers and British officers on board, only 143 survived. It was one of the worst sea disasters of the Second World War. A sailor on board a Royal Navy destroyer who helped pull survivors out of the water remembered that the Africans 'were utterly bewildered by the whole episode. Many were experiencing their first trip at sea and most of them had probably never even heard of submarines.' The sailor offered the exhausted Africans milk and sugar with their tea. A junior officer intervened, arguing that they should not get used to such comforts, given the hardships that lay ahead.

As a medical orderly, Isaac assisted in the running of the clinic on the *Staffordshire*. In the damp and crowded conditions of the troopship, especially in the colder seas off the Cape, the British were worried that disease could spread quickly. They were especially concerned about meningitis, pneumonia and other chest infections. On Charles Carfrae's ship, there were several fatalities, 'the sufferers became frightened, abandoned hope, closed their eyes and quietly died'. Another British officer on the same convoy as Carfrae said Nigerian soldiers were 'dying almost like flies', apparently convinced they were the victims of witchcraft, as a result of being cursed by enemies back home. During the port call at Durban, they 'took them all off and put them in a transit camp and medicated them – what medication there is for witchcraft I don't know – but at any rate they were alright after that'.

The *Staffordshire*, for its part, recorded only a single fatality during the journey to India. It was announced one morning at boat parade, and that afternoon, at two o'clock, Isaac and all the other soldiers and sailors on board lined the decks and stood at attention. The body of the young African soldier had been sewn in canvas with lead weights, and then wrapped in the Union Jack. It was placed on a platform slide amidships. As the *Staffordshire*'s engines came to a halt, the ship's captain led the men in prayers, and everyone doffed their hats. Then the captain pulled a rope that released the body down the slide and off the side of the ship. It landed in the ocean with a dull splash before sinking out of view in the deep water. A full ten minutes passed before the engines of the *Staffordshire* hummed back into life, and the ship moved gently forward once more.

As the convoy approached its destination, the air grew clammy and humid, the skies greyer. The monsoon rains were still falling, not with the violent intensity and thunderstorms and wind gusts of previous weeks, but with a dismal constancy. On 14 August, a soggy day of low skies, they reached Bombay. Thousands of West African soldiers in khaki uniforms filed off the ships, onto the quayside next to the Gateway to India. They made for an exotic sight, and Indians gathered to stare. The Africans stared back. Isaac absorbed it all: the rickshaw pullers forcing their way through the crowd, the officers waving papers above their heads, shouting to make themselves heard, and the rows of women crouched over little charcoal stoves, offering up fried snacks. He was only seventeen, but he had come far from the red dusts and thatched huts of his village. He might have been a mere *ara-oko*, but he had travelled across the world, and arrived in a strange new land.

4

THE GENERALS ARE MET

|||||||||||||||||||||||||||||||||||||||||||||||||||||||||||||||||||||||||||||||||||||||||||||||||||||||||||||||||||||||

The Generals are met. The scene is Delhi
Upon the wall a map of Arakan
And thus the C in C; 'Oh Woolner, rehelly
Where shall I put your soldiers African?'
And Woolner spoke; 'I've heard it's hot and smelly
Unfit for Sepoys in the Kaladan'
'Then that's the place, I will not keep you longer:
Oh, Colonel! Send a sweeper for my tonga'

Captain David M. Cookson,
De Bello Kaladano: An Unfinished Epic

|||||||||||||||||||||||||||||||||||||||||||||||||||||||||||||||||||||||||||||||||||||||||||||||||||||||||||||||||||||||

August 1943
Bombay

Throughout the weeks at sea, the West Africans had tried to imagine this famous city of Bombay, but now that they had finally arrived they were not impressed by what they saw. The labourers in *dhotis* who unloaded the ships on the docks were thin and lethargic, and the emaciated beggars who gathered round the West Africans imploring, '*Baksheesh, sahib, baksheesh,*' had desperation in their eyes. Beggars were almost unheard of in West Africa. Even the Lagos boys, the ones who came from the tough and crowded backstreets of Olowogbowo and Isale Eko, had never seen anything like this. They wondered what sort of place it was, this India, which they were supposed to defend. 'Are these people India people? Then we fine past them' – 'Are these really Indians? Then we are better than them,' they said.

The Africans marched through the cleared streets, from the docks to the Gothic glory of the Victoria Terminus, while the crowds watched on in silence. At the station, the soldiers boarded the trains waiting to take them past the bleak housing estates on the edge of Bombay into the interior, then up a forested escarpment, before coming to a stop at Nasik, on the Godavari River, where a single conical basalt hill rose from the plateau. It was a holy place, they learnt, with a temple two-thirds of the way up, which could be reached by climbing five hundred steps. The divinities of Shiva and Parvati, Rama and Sita, Ganesh, Vishnu and Krishna were carved into the local canyon walls. They were escorted to their camp, three miles away at Deolali, by a unit of horse-mounted Indian Engineers who played the bagpipes and wore magnificent uniforms of scarlet, blue and white. But the camp itself was only half built. Ragged labourers were still working on the roads, latrines and cookhouses. There was mud everywhere. The Africans saw women and children scavenging for food scraps from dustbins on the edge of the camp, and boys trying to sell tea through the fence, shout-ing, '*Garam cha, garam cha!*' Kites and crows circled above. The soldiers were assigned to bell-tents, each one housing six men, and on that first night they slept long and hard, despite the heavy rain that fell outside.

Isaac would spend over four months in India, before crossing into Burma. It took that long for the 81st Division to assemble its forces; the last convoy did not dock in Bombay until November 1943. General Woolner, who had flown to India with a handful of senior colleagues, wanted his men to use this prolonged pause to build up their fitness and do more jungle training, in conditions he hoped would replicate those they would encounter during the fighting to come. The 81st Division went for long marches in the Western Ghats, through deep gorges, and up and down hills and valleys of thick forest. The monsoons car-ried on late that year, and the soldiers spent their days toiling up steep slopes on muddy paths, carrying heavy loads, often in torrential rain.

The Africans also went for long runs before breakfast, cleared fields of rocks so they could play football, and shooed away the donkeys that wandered around camp with a proprietary air, defecating and urinating everywhere.

Isaac spent much of his time working in the military hospital at Deolali camp, with his colleagues from the 29th CCS. The doctors had named the various wards after their hometowns in Scotland: Glasgow, Edinburgh, Aberdeen. They treated the soldiers for skin diseases, malaria, food poisoning and hookworm.

When the days ended, the British officers and the African men gathered round their respective log fires, exhausted but relaxed, and talked. In the flickering light, black and white faces alike grew softer, more child-like. The sunsets at Deolali were magnificent, and, as the giant red ball of fire sunk below the hills, one officer was known to bring out his wind-up portable gramophone. The men crowded round to listen to Deanna Durbin or their favourite, Paul Robeson singing 'Ol' Man River'. On one heavenly night, a band from an Indian village far below emerged out of the growing darkness, played their strange instruments under the countless stars, then disappeared.

Some evenings, officers and men would wander into Nasik town. The officers gravitated to the gold- and silversmiths, where they bargained for jewellery. The Africans preferred to spend their few pennies at the tailors, commissioning jackets, trousers and new shoes. John Hamilton remembered that they asked for their new clothes to be 'starched and pressed, to the highest degree of smartness, with razor edged creases'. Richard Terrell enjoyed going to the cinema in Nasik, and would often see African soldiers there. Neither they, nor he, could understand the Hindi and Marathi movies, but they liked the music, and would recite the songs in camp later.

Not long after they settled into camp, a clerk from the Gold Coast offered to write letters on behalf of his illiterate colleagues. Although Burma and the Japanese were still a thousand miles to the north-east, a confused censor discovered that every letter composed by this clerk began with the words, 'With my rifle hot in my hands...'

There were other recurring themes in the Africans' letters: they were struck by how small Indian men were; how beautiful their women ('India woman like angel'); and how odd it was, to their eyes at least, that men and women dressed alike. The Indians seemed so frail, and the Africans wondered what ailment it was they suffered from, that made them spit what looked like blood onto the ground.

The West Africans arrived shortly before the local townspeople celebrated a Hindu festival. A swaying procession made its way gently up the steps to the temple near the top of the conical hill. There were bullocks with their horns painted red, the tips covered in brass, and gilded rings threaded through their noses; some donkeys were decorated in bright colours and draped with baubles and bells. The Africans watched, torn between awe and a feeling of superiority. They laughed at the way the Indians allowed their cows and bulls to wander at will through the towns and villages and sit in the middle of roads as if they owned them. Surely, they asked, 'Is it not madness to worship what is good to *chop*?' Yet the Africans could not help but feel the allure of this rich and novel culture. They were intrigued by this mysterious religion called Hinduism, which so few of them had heard of before landing in India. Caste, religion, diet and sacred animals – they had already seen and absorbed so much in their first weeks.

On 17 September 1943, an important visitor came to the camp. General William Slim, a veteran of the trenches and Gallipoli, was about to take command of Britain's 14th Army, which was ranged along India's frontier with Burma. He had a daunting double task: preventing a Japanese invasion of India and re-conquering Burma.

A charismatic, tough man who had risen through the ranks, General Slim inspired loyalty from the troops because of his obvious concern for their welfare, but he was taking over at a desperate time. The much-heralded Arakan offensive of early 1943 had ended in an ignominious retreat, and the commander of the British forces in Eastern India, General Noel Irwin, had been relieved of his command. He was departing under a cloud. At a meeting in Delhi, a few days after General Slim had visited Deolali, General Irwin painted a scathing picture of the British soldiers on the India–Burma border. Disease, he said, had ravaged them; for each battle casualty in hospital, there were 120 men suffering from tropical diseases. Unless this problem could be addressed, he warned, it would be 'useless to try and stage an offensive into Burma'. Moreover, General Irwin doubted that he could count on any of his frontline units to hold firm in the event of a Japanese advance into India.

General Slim was taking over an army of many races and backgrounds. Most of the men in the 'British' forces that would fight for him in Burma were, in fact, Indian, some three-fifths of a total force of more than 500,000 men. The British and African contingents each amounted to about 100,000 soldiers. Slim set out to restore morale among this diverse force. He attacked each of the challenges with thoroughness, putting as much emphasis on better hygiene, food and logistics as he did on ammunition supplies. Officers who failed to look after the health of their men were sacked. He made them more flexible in their tactics and better prepared for jungle fighting. He understood that Burma was often an after-thought for his political masters in London, and that he would not get all the resources and men he wanted. He would have to just get on, in Clement Atlee's words, 'with the scrapings of the barrel'.

Unlike many of the British commanders, Slim also managed to build a working relationship with Joe Stilwell, the American general who was leading a Chinese nationalist army in north-eastern Burma. Allies in the war against Japan, the awkward truth was that the British and Americans had fundamentally different objectives in the region. The British wanted to take back the colonial possessions that they had lost; the Americans wanted to reopen the supply route to the Chinese through northern Burma. Indeed, the Americans' main concern was to keep China in the war, so that it could provide air bases for the fighting in the Pacific and for an eventual attack on Japan itself. They had no interest in putting the British Empire back on its feet. And yet the British had become reliant on American logistical support, and especially American aircraft. Slim believed that Allied superiority in the air could prove of huge significance, even in the apparently unpromising terrain of the Burmese jungle. 'Vinegar Joe' Stilwell was an abrasive character, but Slim handled him with skill and tact.

Slim knew that 1944 would be decisive. The Japanese feared that the tide of war had turned in favour of the Americans in the Pacific, and saw the British Army as the weak link of the forces opposing them. Some Japanese generals argued that a successful attack on India could swing momentum back their way. India, after all, was in ferment, with Gandhi in jail and Britain struggling to contain the nationalist 'Quit India' Movement. The Japanese included in their ranks the 'Indian National Army', men who dreamt of overthrowing the Raj and achieving independence by force of arms, many of whom were defectors from the British Army. The Japanese hoped an invasion of India would spark off a popular anti-British uprising, just as it had done in Burma.

Slim spent four days at Deolali with the 81st Division. He wanted to take a good look at the West African soldiers whom he knew would play a crucial part in the fighting in the months to come. He was an aggressive and bold commander, and had no intention of sitting back and waiting for the Japanese to strike first. He had his own plans, for an offensive into Burma in the first weeks of 1944, and the 81st Division was to play an important role.

As he addressed the officers, he took off his battered slouch Gurkha hat and said, 'I want you to take a good look at this ugly mug, because it's the one that is going to be buggering you all about before long.' The burly, grey-haired man with the broad nose, jutting jaw and twinkling eyes – the man that a British Army magazine said looked like a 'well-to-do West Country farmer' – won the officers' support. Perhaps he would be able to lead them where General Irwin had failed.

Slim also watched the Africans in training, and was impressed by them. He liked their discipline and smart appearance, and thought that they were 'more obviously at home in the jungle than any troops I had yet seen'. But he was concerned that the African units relied on large numbers of porters to carry supplies. These long lines of men, he thought, could prove vulnerable to Japanese ambush in the jungle. He also worried about the British officers; that there were too many in the West African units, and that some of them had been drafted willy-nilly, without any real enthusiasm or understanding of their men. This could stifle the initiative of the Africans themselves.

The waiting was nearly over. In mid-November, when the last units of the 81st Division arrived in India, Isaac and the others at Deolali began packing up in preparation for the long journey to the Burmese frontier. They travelled by train across the sub-continent. It took them five days and nights to reach Calcutta. Isaac slept on board, enduring uncomfortable nights on the train's hard wooden benches. When the British officers wanted tea, which was frequently, they'd pull the emergency cord, and the driver would bring the train to a grudging, grinding stop. Then the *charwallahs* would trudge down the tracks to the front of the train, and pour steaming hot water from the engine boiler's relief valve into great metal urns of tea and sugar. The officers dunked their hard ration biscuits in the tea, and the train moved on.

Beggars thronged them at every station, thrusting their sores and deformities towards the carriage windows in hope of some pity. Their thin brown fingers reached up pleadingly, and strong black fists passed down cigarettes and coins. Through the window, Isaac watched Indian women, bent over the brown river where they washed their clothes and scrubbed their pots with sand, look up at him as the train rolled by. Their naked children splashed happily around them. Then the train sped up. A glimpse of a village, of a cow standing in the shade and a man pulling a handcart, and it was gone.

Maybe the Africans wondered if this war meant anything to the people in these villages, trapped in their land of poverty. But their fate, just like that of the poor villagers, was being shaped by forces beyond their control. For they were part of the war machine, rushing towards an unknown destination.

★

J.O. Ariyo was one of the Nigerian soldiers who made that train journey across India. Amid all that was new and different, he was also struck by the similarities with his own country. He saw great diversity in India and Nigeria – a multitude of languages and tribes – but also distrust and divisions between the different groups. In both India and Nigeria, he observed, there are taller and fairer people in the North, and shorter, darker people in the South. And the British had conquered the respective territories in a similar fashion. The process was begun by trading companies, interested in profit, and only later did Imperial administrators and soldiers arrive. They created vast new countries where none had existed. Nigerians and Indians might resist the British, he said, but thus far internal divisions had undermined their struggles.

In Calcutta, the Africans would see the greatest wonders and darkest horrors of colonial rule. The officers organised excursions through the city for their men, and the West Africans feasted their eyes – Calcutta, where 'seeing is believing', wrote Lance Corporal Israel Agwu. It was Agwu's first time in a real city, and the 'buses, cars and personal traffics was too much complicating to me'. He rode a lift to the top of a 'conspicuous and lofty building'. He saw the 'dim, solemn and terrible' interiors of the British Raj, and the statues on the *Maidan* of 'great men on horses backs standing in memory of their braveries'. At Alipore Zoo, he marvelled at the giraffes, lions and parrots. With characteristic Nigerian pragmatism, he thought it would be no exaggeration to say, 'a rhinoceros can last the whole of five GTC [general transport companies] a fortnight meal'. Then there were the cinemas. 'Oh!...how I drew my breath'. It was, as Lance Corporal Sunday Waame wrote, a real 'European cinema, where people of all nationalities seemed to mix', and the seating, lights, decoration and comfort were 'beyond description'. They watched a newsreel, about Britain's 8th Army, which was now advancing up the Italian mainland. Calcutta's shops were stocked with the finest linens and fashionable ladies' hats. People thronged to the racecourse with its elegant grandstand. The West Africans had their heads turned by restaurants that were 'spick and span'. The most glamorous of these was Firpo's, where British officers danced waltzes on the famous sprung floor and drank iced coffee while being fanned by *punkawallahs*.

The Africans admired the 'many Chinese ladys and Black Americans and also another descendents people', their eyes opened to a more cosmopolitan world than they had ever seen before. Fierce-looking Sikhs manoeuvred their taxis round bicycle rickshaws and *tongas*. On the pavements, Bengalis in their white shirts and *dhotis* jostled past the British, Indian, African and American soldiers. Some of the Africans set off to look for their own entertainment. A British woman working at the Red Cross Welfare Office was surprised when five smartly dressed West African soldiers walked in and said, 'Please Miss, this be welfare? We want some fine women please.'

Isaac, too, was given a Calcutta tour, along with several colleagues. They were led by a dental surgeon, Captain Harrison, and they enjoyed the cinema, and what the men judged to be 'a first-class meal' in an expensive restaurant. They took their first ride in an electric tram – 'you can imagine my pleasure and delight', one wrote – and were dazzled by the noise and energy on the streets and the speed with which the cars hurtled by. Calcutta was not just the largest city in India, but also one of the great ports of the British Empire, perhaps twenty times the size of Lagos. Isaac had come for adventure, and he felt he had found it.

However, it was another Nigerian soldier, Corporal Agbaje, who made the most telling observation. For all Calcutta's wealth, he wrote, 'the most important thing that I saw, its that the Beggars are too much than the richest men in the town'. The West African soldiers had arrived in Calcutta in the midst of the Bengal famine of 1943, a catastrophe created by the combination of natural disasters, military defeats and administrative incompetence. At least one and a half million people died in Bengal, perhaps many more, before the British authorities, callous but also distracted by the challenges of the war, began to respond. In the weeks before Isaac got there, thousands of starving people had made their way from the countryside into Calcutta in the hope of finding help in the city. By then, Archibald

Wavell, newly promoted to Viceroy of India, had appreciated the seriousness of the situation. At the end of October, he visited Calcutta and wrote in his private journal that he'd seen 'widespread distress and suffering...obviously we have to get an immediate grip or it may get out of hand altogether'.

From the moment they had disembarked in Bombay, the Africans had been both horrified and intrigued by India's poverty. Now, death was staring them in the face. In the gutters of Chowringhee, on the traffic islands and in the shadow of the Victoria Monument, mothers held dead babies in their arms, or babies tried to suckle from the breasts of dead mothers. On street corners, human scavengers emptied rubbish bins, searching for anything they could eat. If they discovered a dead cat, they celebrated their luck. 'The feelings of our Africans were not easy to judge,' said Trevor Clark, who'd also arrived in Calcutta at the end of November, with the Gambia battalion.

In fact, the sight of people starving to death on a busy street made a vivid impression on Isaac. He was confused and frightened. He'd never seen anything like it in Nigeria, where anybody, no matter how poor and hungry, could always go back to the village to farm. Yet here people were dying in plain view, their dull eyes staring upwards, the outline of their ribs obvious against their taut, thin skin. And all this on the streets of a great city, as the crowds rushed past, everyone absorbed in their own urgent business. British officers with the West Africans confessed that, during their stay in Calcutta in those last weeks of 1943, they became hardened to the sight of emaciated children, and to stepping over recumbent figures on pavements and gutters, who might, or might not be, alive. Some of the Nigerian soldiers came up with their own name for this city where wealth and suffering rubbed shoulders: *Ka-iku-ta*, which in Yoruba means 'count all the dead and sell them'. They gave their tins of bully beef to the beggars, but the gesture was usually in vain. The Hindus would not touch the forbidden meat.

Viceroy Wavell had decided the starving needed to be moved out of Calcutta and into camps, and that the Army should give whatever assistance it could in the effort. Some West African soldiers were kept busy loading corpses on trucks and taking them to mass lime pits. But the British had brought the Africans to India to fight the Japanese, and the war was getting closer by the day. Calcutta was within range of the Japanese air force, a fact brought abruptly home to Isaac on 5 December, the day he was taken sightseeing by Captain Harrison. He and some fellow soldiers were in the city centre when the air-raid siren went off. They were confused, but they took their cue from the Indians who were running for cover all around them. Calcutta had been bombed before, and the locals at least seemed to know what to do. Traffic came to a standstill. Isaac dived into a ditch by a restaurant, his face pressed into the stinking mud, as the Japanese bombs fell far away, at the docks. It was, he suddenly realised, his eighteenth birthday. For the first time, he felt he had an idea of what war might be.

In the hot and sunny days of December 1943, thousands of West African soldiers were loaded onto troopships on the banks of the Hooghly. They were moving on from Calcutta. They sailed past fleets of *dhows*, into the mangrove swamps of the Ganges Delta, and then across the top of the Bay of Bengal, before docking at Chittagong, a vital port for the British as they brought in reinforcements for the frontier with Burma, some sixty miles to the south. There, as Isaac relaxed outside new billets, he saw British fighter-planes pursuing Japanese planes in the clear evening sky above them. Two of the Japanese planes seemed to be glinting in the sun, but they were in fact on fire, and soon tumbled to the ground in flames. A third plane was trailing thick black smoke from its wing. Then it too started to spiral downwards. Like a leaf falling from a tree, thought Isaac. It crashed only a mile away from where he stood. Without thinking, he and his colleagues ran towards the spot where it had come down, laughing and breathless with excitement. But, when they found the wreckage, they froze to a halt. There was twisted metal and ammunition scattered around. A tree was in flames. Just beyond, they could see the partially burnt bodies of two Japanese airmen. Roasted human flesh, Isaac could not help notice, smelled just like goat meat.

At Chittagong, the West Africans exchanged their khaki uniforms for olive-green battle dress, green jumpers and long rubber capes. And it was here that the commanding officer, Major Robert Murphy, called together all the men of the 29th CCS – the British officers, the Sierra Leoneans and the Nigerians. Major Murphy was a handsome man, with a neatly trimmed moustache; his sisters liked to tease him by saying that he looked like the film star Robert Taylor. He came from Greenock, a grey shipbuilding town on the banks of the River Clyde. His parents, who called him Bobby, were devout Catholics. They had prayed that their only son would go into the priesthood, so were disappointed when he dropped out of the seminary. Instead, he'd gone to Glasgow University, where he graduated in 1936, but he had put his promising medical career on hold at the beginning of the war. Robert Murphy had known little about Africa when he'd sailed out to the west coast in 1942, just as he knew little about Burma now. Still, he did his best to prepare his men for what to expect.

The 29th CCS would soon be crossing the frontier, said Major Murphy, in support of the frontline troops who would be fighting the Japanese. They would provide medical and surgical facilities for some two hundred casualties at a time. He told them they would be close to the fighting, but slightly behind the advance. They would be marching through jungle, at risk of ambush from a fanatical enemy who would prefer to die on the battlefield than be taken prisoner. There was a place in Japanese heaven, Major Murphy explained, that was specifically reserved for those gallant soldiers killed defending the land of their ancestors. No wonder the Japanese were such dogged fighters. Later, Isaac and the other Nigerians would refer to them as *Ajapani*. It was a pun from Yoruba, meaning 'the ones who fight to kill'.

If anyone in the unit was captured, warned Murphy, he should only provide the Japanese with his name, rank and service number. Under no circumstances should he reveal any information about troop movements, or even the identity of his unit. British officers, meanwhile, were asked to hand over all their personal diaries, letters and photographs, so that they would have nothing on them that might provide intelligence to the enemy. Murphy's language was direct and clear, and the men listened in hushed silence.

They wrote letters home, and then packed up and marched through the swampy Bengali countryside, dotted with villages, until they came to a railway. They clambered on board a train once more, and rode the thirty miles to the end of the line, to a place called Dohazari. On the horizon, they could see blue mountains covered in a thin film of mist. They marked the border between India and Burma, the direction they were heading in.

The mountains stretched away to the north, much further than the men could see. The British and Japanese armies were facing each other along this range, some six hundred miles in length, not in continuous lines, as one officer wrote, 'but in many small outposts and advanced bases that had been established in an immense expanse of tangled no-mans-land, where patrols of both sides wandered at will, emerging from the jungle to kill and destroy, and departing as silently as they had come'.

From Dohazari, the 29th CCS and other West African units were ferried on buses southwards, to the little town of Chiringa. The road was congested with other trucks carrying troops in the same direction, and cargo planes roared overhead. Isaac spent Christmas Day 1943 in Chiringa, where the 81st Division was setting up its headquarters. It was a rapidly growing bamboo town carved out of the forest. Dinner was corned beef and potato stew, followed by a pudding made from army biscuits and raisins. 'Happy Christmas!' bellowed one of the officers. His men grumbled back, 'Dis not a better Kismuss, no better *chop*, no better *coppah*; and we famble no dey sen we letters.' – 'This is not a good Christmas. No good food, no good money, and our families have not sent us letters.'

What was to come hung over everything. Ahead lay Burma, the jungle and the Japanese.

5

BLACK MEN HELD THE GATE

All Hail, you Africans, so often harried
By various commanders and their staffs:
What useless loads and heavy weights you carried
And yet were able to produce wry laughs,
In days when Delhi dithered, Kandy tarried
And things were left undone or done by halfs,
When Japs were pushing India to her fate,
The world found out that black men held the gate!

Captain David M. Cookson,
De Bello Kaladano: An Unfinished Epic

December 1943
The Arakan, Burma

It was some of the worst fighting country in the world, according to the British officers. General Slim had decided that the 81st Division should be part of the British offensive into the Arakan. Isaac and his fellow West Africans would be battling not just the Japanese, but also a landscape, a climate and even the vegetation.

The Arakan, today known as Rakhine, is a narrow strip of land, about four hundred miles in length, along the Bay of Bengal, in western Burma. It is cut off from the rest of Burma by a range of mountains called the Arakan Yomas, which helped to isolate the area's people, who developed a history and culture distinct from the rest of their countrymen. In southern Arakan, the land is open and largely flat – paddy fields, mangrove swamps and wide, serpentine rivers. But in the north, along the Indian border where the West Africans were entering the Arakan, it is very different – mountains and dense forest. 'This jungle is so thick that, when you are in the middle of it, you need a torch to see, although the sun may be high in the sky,' Isaac would say. 'We don't have jungle like this in black Africa.'

At night, even the light of a full moon could not penetrate the canopy. A soldier walking just a yard or two ahead of a colleague was swallowed up by the darkness. On the ridge tops, jungle gave way to bamboo, but this provided no relief. There was so little space between bamboo stems that the soldiers, trying to manoeuvre their way through, often had to turn sideways. Their heavy head loads or backpacks would invariably get snagged on the stems, making any movement extremely difficult. The only solution, they learnt, was to hack a path through with a machete. This made for slow and exhausting progress, but worse it was so noisy it could alert the enemy to their presence. The aroma of freshly cut bamboo also attracted swarms of bluish green flies, which would find their way to the men's exposed skin and deliver a nasty bite.

The mountain ranges of the northern Arakan rarely reach above two thousand feet but the ridges and peaks are razor-steep, packed together as tightly as nature allows and divided by countless narrow and deep valleys. The soldiers cursed them. Marching across this landscape, Trevor Clark predicted, 'we would be like microbes traversing corrugated cardboard'. On the ascents and descents, the tribesmen who lived in the hills recommended long walking sticks. 'Make a mistake, and you'll slip,' the officers warned their men, 'and fall all the way to the bottom of the hill.'

The hillsides are intersected with waterways, or *chaungs*, which cut deep grooves into the sandy soil. These made for yet another obstacle to overcome. Sometimes the only way for the men to advance was to walk along the beds of the *chaungs*. As they followed the tortuous routes down hillsides and valleys, clambering over slabs of sandstone, splashing through water, they were in constant fear of an ambush from the dense vegetation above.

For all these difficulties, the West Africans had arrived in the region at its most benign. It was the relatively cool, dry season, and the British generals were keen to take advantage of the conditions to get some hold on the land. Their window of opportunity would close in May, when the monsoon rains would begin once more, and any advance ran the risk of getting bogged down in mud and water. In the space of five months, from May until early October, as many as two hundred inches of rain could fall – about three times what the steamy coast of Nigeria receives in an entire year, making the Arakan one of the wettest places in the world. During the fighting of the previous two years, the British had learnt that in the monsoon season many paths became so slippery and muddy as to be almost unusable. The *chaungs* swelled into raging torrents. Mosquitoes and leeches feasted on the blood of the miserable, soaking combatants. But the trials of the monsoon lay far ahead. Isaac and his fellow soldiers had more immediate problems.

When the British lost control of Burma in May 1942, they had also retreated from the Arakan. General Irwin's ill-fated attempt to recapture the region later that year and in early 1943 had left the morale of the British and Indian troops at breaking point. A liaison officer who visited the British forces in the Arakan in May 1943 painted a pathetic picture. It was painfully clear, he said, that the men had not received the right training to fight in this sort of terrain, and that their officers had lost all faith in them. 'Our troops were either exhausted, "browned off" or both...both Indian and British troops did not have their hearts in the campaign. The former were obviously scared of the Jap and generally demoralized...the latter also fear the jungle, hate the country and see no object in fighting for it, and also have the strong feeling that they are taking part in a "forgotten" campaign in which no one in authority is taking any real interest,' he wrote.

One year later, under the command of General Slim, the British were preparing to try again. Whatever the difficulties of waging war in the Arakan, the territory had an enduring strategic importance. A successful offensive would not only remove the threat of a Japanese advance up the Bengali coast to Calcutta, but could also provide a launch pad for the British to make an eventual attack on the Burmese capital, Rangoon. In this regard, retaking the Arakan's main port, Akyab, was a key objective. Akyab could serve as a base for amphibious attacks further south along the coast. It also had an airfield, which would enable the British to supply the forces as they marched towards Rangoon, and to launch bombing raids on the capital.

A private, much less an African private, was told little of such grand strategy. Isaac could only assume that his division was going to push as far south into Japanese-occupied territory as they could, maybe all the way to Akyab – he had been told that taking the town was their aim. His British commanding officers were given many more details. They were informed that the main British–Indian force, also pushing southwards, would be trying to make headway against the Japanese forces that were positioned closer to the coastline. However, General Slim feared that the Japanese would be able to outmanoeuvre this advance. So the 81st Division would provide protection to its flank, by simultaneously fighting its way down the Kaladan Valley, about fifty miles further inland to the east. It was a sort of wide left hook. And the Kaladan River was in itself a useful prize. It emerged into the Bay of Bengal at Akyab, and for most of its length it was wide enough to accommodate steamers, making it a handy route for transporting men and materiel, as well as communications. If the West African division could take the valley, the Japanese might be forced to withdraw from the Arakan. That was the plan.

Establishing British control of the Kaladan Valley would not be easy. The West Africans were being ordered to cross an unforgiving landscape – no roads, no railways and, for the first stretch of their designated route, no navigable rivers either. They had no heavy machinery to clear away the jungle. How could they advance in these conditions, let alone fight and defeat the Japanese? General Kit Woolner was not being presented with a choice by his superiors – the 81st Division must move forward. An extraordinary physical effort was necessary. Using only picks, shovels, machetes and explosives, the men built a jeep track, some seventy-five miles long, through the wild jungle hills and ravines, all the way from Chiringa, India, down to the village of Satpaung, on the Kaladan River. In some sections, the track had to be cut into a cliff with a sheer drop of hundreds of feet. It took two months to build. The men called it 'West African Way'.

When the track was declared open on 17 January 1944, General Woolner hailed the 'enthusiasm and endurance' of his men, who had worked through sweltering days and slept outdoors on bitterly cold nights. But the effort had been costly. On a hot and still afternoon in late December 1943, a group of Gambian soldiers had stopped to drink water from an apparently clear stream. Forty-four would die of cholera in the days that followed.

Though the track would be abandoned with the start of the rains, it gave the 81st Division the opportunity to move its few artillery guns, as well as some jeeps, to the banks of the Kaladan. From there, they were transported downstream on barges, and eventually unloaded on the floodplain, further south, where more makeshift tracks would be built.

At this stage in the advance the 29th CCS was positioned some way behind the frontline troops, at the village of Mowdok, India, on the banks of the River Sangu. The commanding officer, Major Murphy, had been instructed to set up a makeshift hospital at Mowdok, in anticipation of the casualties that would be arriving from the Kaladan Valley. Isaac and his colleagues would look to the east, to the brooding green hills of Frontier Ridge. Beyond the trees silhouetted along the top of the ridge, just a few miles away lay the Arakan, and Burma. No wonder they called Mowdok 'the last village in India'. They felt restless, close to the war, yet isolated. They hoped for an order to advance, but they also feared it.

They did not have long to wait. Within a few weeks, the division's senior officers decided that the track to Mowdok was too steep. It would be impossible for jeeps to carry casualties back from the Kaladan Valley to the village. The 29th CCS needed to be closer to the fighting, if it was to be of any use. When Isaac and his colleagues received the order to move into the Kaladan Valley, they each put on a brave face. Nobody wanted to show fear, no matter what his secret thoughts might be.

They followed the route already taken by their colleagues in the 81st Division. Major Murphy oversaw the transport of the heavier medical equipment for the field hospital – the tents, blankets, generators, lamps, stretchers, operating instruments, glass bottles of chloroform, oxygen cylinders, steel bowls, even an X-ray machine – in a convoy of jeeps bumping along West African Way. The rest of the men travelled on a small river towards the Burmese border. They were paddled by Indians in *khistis*, wooden canoes, to a deserted village. It was evening when they arrived and set up their camp. In a hut, by the ashes of an old fire, Isaac picked up a small muslin bag and unwrapped it to find biscuits, sugar-ball sweets and tinned fish. Japanese rations. It seemed the enemy had left in a hurry.

The following morning, there was a surprise. A group of West African soldiers appeared with two Japanese prisoners that had been captured near the Kaladan River. Everybody crowded around to get a good look. Isaac had built up an image in his mind of what a Japanese solider would look like, but these two men did not conform to it. There was nothing formidable about them. They were obedient, pathetic even, in their ragged clothes, as they smiled and saluted their captors. When Isaac tended to their wounds, he noticed that their rifles were old. 'They were small men, their khaki uniforms and rubber-soled boots were scruffy, and they were living proof that, despite all the stories, some Japanese could and did surrender,' wrote one British officer. When the news was radioed back to the divisional headquarters, the senior officers could scarcely believe it. Japanese prisoners were a valuable source of information about the enemy's strength and intentions, but a very rare prize.

Later that morning, in the distance, the men of the 29th CCS thought they could hear the sound of artillery. Or was it thunder? No one was sure, but the Indian guides would not take them any further. Now, they would be forced to march through the hills. The men split into small groups, each one led by an officer with a map and a compass, and they headed east. Boots were laced tight, and heavy loads balanced on heads. They tramped and splashed along the *chaungs*, and their boots and socks were soon soaking wet. They sweated and panted up steep ridges. Each step was an effort on these climbs, the walking stick vigilantly planted to maintain balance, teeth gritted and eyes screwed tight to maintain concentration. After the first ascent, their thighs throbbed with pain. Eight miles a day was considered good progress in the Arakan. It must have been sometime on their first day of marching that they crossed into Burma.

Isaac had expected the going to be tough, and yet he'd never felt stronger. He carried his backpack, full of rations and clothes, as well as a forty-pound load of supplies on his head. His gaze never swerved from the path ahead, his head ever erect and steady, as they crossed the valleys and ridges. The lieutenant leading his group was helped by his 'boy', the personal servant tasked with carrying many of his possessions, but he still had to stop frequently to take compass readings and consult the map. These moments provided welcome respite from the gruelling trek. At the end of one especially long ascent, they paused and someone spied a piece of paper attached to a tree. A soldier from an earlier group had written: 'Congratulations! Rest and Thank God'. But they'd barely caught their breath when the lieutenant hurried them along. He had reports of Japanese in the area, and was anxious that they get to a protected camp before dusk. The nights in the hills were cold. Isaac slept in his clothes, with his blankets wrapped around his head as bats hovered and danced above.

There were also flashes of beauty and moments of calm. In the heavy morning mist that shrouded the valley, dew-covered vegetation caught the sun and sparkled like a field of diamonds. Emerald dragonflies and black-and-white butterflies flitted along the forest paths in front of them, seeming to guide their way. A sudden blaze of scarlet or electric blue would signal the flight of a forest bird. The birds were all but invisible when they sat in the canopy, but they could always be heard. Isaac came to recognise the song of one, an endless cascade of delirious notes; another resembled the tinkling of a small bell. Sometimes the men would find themselves on an elephant track, littered with great balls of droppings. A British officer in the Arakan reported that the West Africans often picked these up and carefully wrapped them in rags. Good *juju*, he was told.

The local tribesmen, small people with muscular bodies and few clothes, were known as the Kumi. They survived by fishing and growing rice on little patches of cleared land. When they'd exhausted the soil, they'd move on, building a new village of raised bamboo huts, or *bashas*, in a different location. The men wore their black hair long and carried a sharp knife, or *dah*, on the waist; the women had silver ornaments dangling from their ears, and the mothers among them went about their work with babies and baskets suspended on their backs from a broad band they looped across their foreheads. The elders spent their days smoking tobacco from long bamboo pipes, or *cheroots*. They looked up and, with wrinkled faces and squinting eyes, carefully watched the Africans march by. They seemed, in Isaac's eyes, desperately poor.

The Kumi were wary, ready to melt into the forest if one of the West African soldiers came too close. And indeed, they had learnt over the past two years that this war was nothing but trouble. Before the fighting had come, they had been able to move freely back and forth between India and Burma. They had sold tobacco and melons and bought cotton and metal hoes. Now, there was no trade. Worse, there was no safety. Give information to one army, they feared, and the other would soon take its revenge. Best to keep a distance from both. As Isaac and his colleagues travelled deeper into the Arakan, he saw that more and more of the Kumis' settlements were abandoned.

The soldiers carried 'dry rations' – tins of corned beef, sardines and fruit, as well as chocolate, biscuits and jam, and tea – but, three days into their march, they had to radio the Royal Air Force for fresh supplies. The pilots were flying C-47 Dakotas, which needed a drop zone with flat and open ground, so that they could circle, descend safely and jettison their cargo where it could be easily retrieved. The jungle hills could not have been less suitable for airdrops, and there were many frustrations. One day, Isaac's group made a rendezvous with other troops in the jungle, at a point where a drop was due to take place. They watched as the precious boxes tumbled from the Dakota, and then as their little parachutes – red for ammunition, white for food – got snagged in the tallest trees. A sudden breeze carried some of the supplies over a nearby ridge, into territory the officers feared was not safe. Sometimes, a bundle would lose its harness, or sacks of rice and flour, or coils of barbed wire, would be 'free dropped' without parachutes. Then, the soldiers ran to hide behind rocks and trees as the supplies came hurtling towards the ground. 'Not a few men, who have survived the worst that battle can produce, have been killed by a bag of rice or crate of bully beef,' wrote a British intelligence officer serving in the Arakan hills at that time.

In the first weeks, the food deliveries were few and far between. Isaac and the others grew accustomed to eating if and when food became available. Isaac would wolf down three days' worth of rations at once, everything mashed together in a ghastly-looking stew. It made for less to carry in the coming days. Thank God, then, for an officer, an old-time 'Coaster' who'd lived in Sierra Leone before the war, who'd arranged for the airdrops to include kola nuts. These gave them energy at the end of a long day's march, and kept hunger at bay.

The diet was monotonous. They all craved fresh fruit and vegetables. Invariably, they ate their food cold, because the officers would not allow fires. Smoke drifting up through the trees, one sergeant liked to say, 'will draw the Japanese artillery like angry wasps to a jam pot'. The men grumbled. Japanese artillery? They had only heard the faintest rumblings so far. The officers also made the men bury their empty tins, so as to leave no trace of their presence. At times, it seemed as though Isaac's officers had forgotten that an army marches on its stomach.

Over the months, the pilots and their crews perfected their techniques, and learnt to drop their loads with greater accuracy. They flew above the Burmese jungle in all weathers, sometimes as low as two hundred feet above the hill ridges. The Allies' dominance of the skies would be of vital importance to the 81st Division. The West Africans had no conventional ground lines of supply. Instead, like General Orde Wingate's Chindits, but on an even larger scale, they would be almost completely dependent on what was dropped from the sky.

On the ground, the West Africans had nothing more basic to rely on than their own strength and stamina. Dropping zones had to be cleared and marked, and the heavy loads that fell from the sky had to be collected and frequently carried through the jungle for several miles. This exhausting work was done by thousands of dedicated carriers, called auxiliary groups, who accompanied 81st Division's fighting men. These were the 'horde of unarmed porters' that General Slim had worried about. In practice, however, many were armed and did their share of fighting. But it was their sweat and toil that proved invaluable. Of all the different nationalities from which the British Army in Burma was drawn, only the West African, said John Hamilton, was 'capable of operating for months on end in the worst country in the world, without vehicles and without mules, and was alone able to carry all his warlike stores with him'.

One evening, Isaac was startled by a gunshot near the camp. It was Sergeant Archibong Bassey Duke, who had tracked down and killed a large monkey. Most of the Nigerians considered monkey meat a delicacy, and there was excitement in the camp. In a rare indulgence, the officers gave them permission to light a fire to cook it, using dry bamboo that burnt with a minimum of smoke. Isaac and the others swiftly skinned and roasted the animal, and greedily ate its pungent meat. The officers declined a portion, and several of the Sierra Leoneans also pushed their mess tins away in disgust. 'Men dey eat monkey all same man dey eat person,' they said, to guffaws of scorn from the Nigerians.

Later that same evening, the men received another treat. An officer distributed letters that had arrived in the latest airdrop. The soldiers crouched around the smouldering embers of the fire and read messages from loved ones at home. They learnt of births, bereavements, exams passed and promotions secured, and they were reminded that they were representing the honour of a village, a church or a town. 'I was so much happy to hear your tidings,' read one. 'My only advice that I can give you is that be humble and merciful to any one and more so to your senior officers...Be watchful and remember your prayers, let the Bible be your food that you eat...Let your conduct be good so that everybody may love you, high or low...Reply me as soon as possible, and give my best compliments to all your friends there...' Although he didn't know it, these were the last letters Isaac would receive for a long time. He would often berate himself for not having written replies while he had still had the chance.

Isaac was on lookout duty that night. Through the cold and lonely hours, he listened intently to the sounds of the jungle: the strange bark of the tuk-tu lizard, the rustle of rats in the undergrowth, the goodness-knew-what creature that sounded like a whistling kettle. Was it a bird? As the moon rose, he stared and stared at the strange shapes and shadows that were taking form around him. Sometimes they moved, for no obvious reason. He tried not to let his imagination run away with him. He prayed for dawn to arrive. His mind wandered back to Emure-Ile and Owo, to his father Joshua and his aunts and uncles. If he tried to write down in a letter everything that he had seen over these past few weeks, would he be able to bring it to life to those who were so impossibly far away?

Deeper in the Arakan, the combat units of the 81st Division were receiving their harrowing introduction to war. On 18 January 1944, the first West Africans had begun their descent into the Kaladan Valley itself. They soon ran into small groups of Japanese soldiers. For many, this was almost a relief. In his heart of hearts, General Woolner felt that his men were 'lamentably untrained and inexperienced…absolute beginners', but after so many months of travelling and anticipation, they were at last facing the moment of truth. The West Africans were ordered to move forward only on moonless nights. When a deer snorted from across a valley, or the tree frogs abruptly stopped their chorus, every soldier would halt dead. They tried to control their breathing and strained to hear something, anything, in the darkness. Then they blundered onwards, using a compass or following a waterway and resisting the temptation to take the more obvious option of an inviting track through felled bamboo, lest it should lead straight into an ambush.

There were two sounds the West Africans quickly learnt to dread. The first was the sudden *cough-cough* of the enemy machine gun, the one they called 'the woodpecker'. The other was the sharp whistle from the hillside above them, which meant an explosion of mortars would come seconds later, raining jagged pieces of metal shrapnel that shredded trees and flesh alike. There was no frontline in the Arakan jungle, and nowhere was safe. They never knew when they were being watched, and so they came to fear that the enemy was always there, his eyes following them, his finger tightening on the trigger. Usually, their fears were unfounded, but just occasionally they were not, and the Japanese were indeed waiting for them. 'He was an enemy you never saw, unless you managed to shoot him,' said Hugh Lawrence. The West Africans felt most vulnerable when they were forced to wade across a waist-deep *chaung*, their own rifles carried high above their heads as they waited for the *cough-cough* of the woodpecker. It was nerve-racking, pushing forward in a single file on slippery, narrow tracks, measuring the visibility ahead in yards. 'When we were lucky we ambushed them, when they were lucky they ambushed us,' said a Nigerian veteran, as he looked back on the war many decades later.

Soon after they arrived in the Kaladan Valley, Gambian soldiers were startled to see their officer, delirious from stomach wounds, being rushed past on a stretcher, crying for death to relieve him of his agony. A mortar landed in a *chaung* where an Army doctor was trying to treat the African wounded. Shrapnel cut the poor doctor to pieces. 'Can't somebody help me? I'm bleeding to death' were his last words. On another path a few days later, Nigerians came across the corpse of one their countrymen. 'He good man. He die, him body no smell,' said the gruff sergeant, as he walked on.

As the 81st Division passed through a series of abandoned villages, where many of the *bashas* were burnt to the ground, they realised that the enemy was retreating, but without significant losses. Rather, the Japanese were looking to stage attacks where it suited them best. 'They would let us move forward into a difficult position,' recalled a British officer at the front of the Kaladan advance, 'and then let us have it.' As soon as a firefight was over, the Japanese would disappear into the jungle, only to stage another attack a few miles further on. The soldiers at the front of a column could never let their guard down, but the Japanese would often allow them to pass by and then hit the middle or the rear of the group with all their force.

The British officers noticed something else. They were being shot at more than their men. The Japanese were targeting them, aiming to kill or wound a commander so as to throw whole units into confusion. The officers' whiteness, which brought automatic privilege over their men, was also a curse. They removed their badges, tried to grow thick beards, even covered their faces in black cream, in the hope it made them indistinguishable from the Africans. And each officer was provided with a vial of morphine, for instant pain relief should he need it.

The West Africans of the 81st Division were learning the hard lessons that thousands of British and Indian soldiers had learnt before them. The Japanese were bold and brave, and seemed to be able to march great distances through the jungle, even on a minimum of supplies.

They were skilful at digging deep, camouflaged bunkers – 'turning the hills into caves' was how the Africans put it when they later saw these positions. The Japanese built their bunkers with roofs of logs and tightly packed soil, which protected them from incoming artillery. They cleverly sited each one so as to give support to at least one other bunker. From inside, eight or ten men could fire machine guns. The Japanese air force was rarely seen over the Kaladan Valley these days, but the men on the ground fought on. British officers could, and often did, call in British or American planes to bomb and strafe the Japanese bunkers, but only the most accurate of fire would do serious damage. The Japanese were dug in. Besides, from the air, the jungle all looked the same. As the planes approached, nervous British officers and African soldiers would pray that their commanders had supplied the right co-ordinates, and that the pilots would not hit their own positions by mistake.

The Africans came to think of their enemies as masters of deception. A single Japanese soldier, tying ropes to the triggers of multiple guns, would create the illusion that he was part of a much larger force. The Japanese scattered cheap cameras and watches on the jungle paths, and then attached these to lethal explosives – booby traps for the unsuspecting. They put poison in tins of sardines and corned beef. They left the bodies of Africans in exposed places, waiting to fire on those who came to retrieve them.

Days of unrelenting tension were followed by nights of fear. Each evening, the Africans protected the perimeter of their makeshift camps with *panjis*, razor-sharp stakes of bamboo that jutted out of the ground at a 45-degree angle. They also dug trenches, narrow and two or three feet deep. They slept right by these trenches, guns by their sides, ready to roll straight in should they be woken by the sudden scream of a shell, or the gun-fire and shouts of rage as Japanese soldiers tried to storm their way into the camp.

Japanese 'jitter parties' would move through the night-time jungle screeching, barking and catcalling, in the hope that the African soldiers' nerves would crack and they would give away their positions by shooting into the darkness. They had long loved to mock the British, calling out in English, 'Hallo, Johnny, come out, Johnny!' If this didn't get a reply, they'd try, 'Come out, you white bastard!' Now they played the same games with the Africans. Nigerian soldiers were astonished to hear thickly accented but unmistakable Hausa being shouted in their direction. *'Bakin mutum…koma baya'* came voices through the darkness. 'Black men…go back!'

If forty-nine Japanese soldiers are killed, wrote a Nigerian who fought in Burma, the fiftieth will not surrender, even if he's injured. The last survivor in a Japanese bunker had a disconcerting habit of playing dead, only to spring to life once everyone had assumed the attack was over, shooting the off-guard British and Africans from close range. The ethos in the Japanese army was that to surrender was a disgrace and that anyone who was captured could never return to his homeland and his loved ones. To die for the Emperor was glorious. As the fighting wore on, it became apparent to the West Africans that those first two unimpressive Japanese captives, who had handed themselves over so willingly, were the exception. Many months would pass before British intelligence officers would have the opportunity to question another prisoner in the Arakan.

It was also in the nature of jungle warfare that very few captives were brought back to headquarters, by either side. The British and Africans were fighting with the Japanese at close quarters, on foot and sometimes several days' walk away from a safe base. There were few 'battles'; rather, there was a series of short, haphazard and often unanticipated skirmishes between small groups of infantrymen. After days of sweat and fear, the fighting might last for only a few frenzied seconds, each side lashing out at an enemy that could barely be seen through the undergrowth. The men hurled grenades at each other, and lunged with bayonets. Explosions and cries of pain and anger shattered the heavy silence of the jungle, if only for a few seconds.

In these circumstances, enemy prisoners, especially injured ones, were an unwelcome burden. What could be done with them? Reports of Japanese atrocities against wounded prisoners only increased the inclination of British and Africa soldiers to show no mercy. Captain Charles Carfrae struggled to convince his Nigerian soldiers not to kill three injured Japanese prisoners whom he hoped to send back for questioning. The Nigerians, he wrote, were 'at a loss to understand their commander's paradoxical wish to preserve the lives of foes'.

African veterans of the Burma campaign remembered a cruel enemy, but also their own terrible deeds. Marshall Kebby, a Nigerian soldier, said that, if he and his colleagues ever captured a Japanese soldier, they promptly executed him, as 'they didn't spare our people, we didn't spare them'. A former private with the Gold Coast regiment, Aziz Brimah, said that he heard horrific details of how the Japanese tortured their own prisoners. 'When we found the sort of thing they were doing, we don't spare them any longer. We shot them – we chopped their heads off. We don't allow our officers to see. We just eliminate them,' he said, adding that the Japanese prisoners often killed themselves anyway.

Victor Nunoo, from the Gold Coast, remembered fighting off his fear as he tried to identify bodies of fellow soldiers who were smashed or decomposed beyond recognition. 'Only way you can identify them is to pick their Army discs and their papers…you are trying to pick a disc from a dear friend, you can't bear to touch him. You can't but you have to,' he said. Others recalled rifling through the clothes of the bloated corpses of Japanese soldiers, looking for maps or letters that might help the intelligence officers.

Burma would leave its indelible mark on the Africans who served there, just as it did on the British, Indian and Japanese soldiers who were there. In this 'green hell', superstition and myths flourished. Many of the Africans who came back from Burma would tell a strange story of a female Japanese soldier who sat high in a palm tree for days on end, firing at anyone who approached her. She seemed to be invincible.

Victor Nunoo spoke of how some West Africans carried talismans or amulets that made them disappear when shot at. He said that two

African sergeant majors, members of secret societies back home, even had the ability to lift twenty or thirty people up, and move them to a different place altogether. 'The soldiers knew who had these powers and they liked to be in their company,' he said. British officers knew which of their African soldiers claimed special powers, and which ones carried small leather bags containing bones and mysterious powders and potions. They invariably felt it best not to interfere, so long as it made the men feel more confident.

Many of the men had brought these bags from Africa, and wore them round their wrists or ankles. They contained scraps of the Holy Koran, or powders purchased from a traditional healer in their home village. Victor Nunoo bought his talisman from an old man on his way through India. He didn't dare open it, and when he returned home to Africa he threw it away. Others made the mistake of keeping theirs, he said, and eventually they went mad.

All wars are dehumanising, and the Africans could no less escape the degrading power of this one than could their British officers or their Japanese foes. A Tanganyikan soldier, Musa Kiwhelo, fighting further north in Burma with the King's African Rifles said that his colleagues murdered Japanese captives in front of other prisoners, and would pretend to eat them. They would then allow some prisoners to escape, so as to spread the terrifying rumour that 'they were fighting against cannibals who particularly enjoyed eating Japanese flesh'. It was, Kiwhelo admitted, 'an inhuman trick', carried out without the knowledge of his officers.

By 1944, the British Army was at last getting the measure of the Japanese, and was more confident about fighting in the jungle. British officers started to recognise that, for all their courage, Japanese soldiers had shortcomings. The enemy's equipment was older and the Japanese supply lines were starting to fray beyond repair. Japanese officers, the British began to notice, lost their sense of initiative when things went wrong, persisting with an unsuccessful plan even when it was demonstrably failing.

The British forces were also strengthened and united by a fierce hatred of 'the Jap'. The writer George MacDonald Fraser, who fought in Burma as a young man, said he had the feeling 'that the Jap was farther down the human scale than the European'. Likewise, a British intelligence officer who served in the Arakan wrote about a successful ambush on a Japanese patrol, in which dozens were killed in just a few seconds of machine-gun fire and bomb blasts: 'This may seem quick work, but it's not quick enough. Assuming that no Japanese were born for the next ninety years and the present population were killed off at the rate of one a second, it would take all of that ninety years to see the end of the last Yellow Man.' This same man often dispensed with carrying extra ammunition in order to bring his most treasured volumes of poetry and literature with him into the jungle.

The West Africans fought for an army whose propaganda demonised the enemy as a kind of ruthless animal. They took their cue from the very top. General Slim described the Japanese as 'part of an insect horde with all its power and horror'. An officer with West African soldiers in the Kaladan Valley said that the hardships he and his men suffered were 'minute compared to the misery that would overwhelm the civilised world if the yellow scourge were allowed to spread its filthy tentacles'. General Slim would write after the war that, in Burma, 'quarter was neither asked, nor given'.

Occasionally, the propaganda would be challenged by a glimmer of humanity. One day, Charles Carfrae came across the body of a dead Japanese soldier. As usual, he went through the documents on the corpse, to see if there was anything of interest. He flicked through some photographs: a smiling girl with flowers in her hair; an old couple sitting stiffly on a bench; a young officer posing in a brand-new uniform, a sword hanging at his side. He had always thought of the Japanese as nothing but 'dangerous vermin whom it was our job to destroy...Now, faced with this pathetic evidence of our common humanity, forced to acknowledge that the gulf between us could not after all be fundamental, I felt as much cheated as moved.'

The Japanese had used propaganda to dehumanise their enemy, too. But the West Africans who arrived in the Arakan in early 1944 were a new foe, and they made quite an impression. A Tokyo radio broadcast talked of 'African cannibals led by European fanatics'. A Japanese diary found by the British in the Arakan had this assessment of the West African soldiers: 'Because of their beliefs they are not afraid to die, so even if their comrades have fallen they keep on advancing as if nothing had happened. They have an excellent physique and are very brave, so fighting against these soldiers is somewhat troublesome.'

Jack Osborne, a gentle man from the English Midlands who was a lieutenant in Burma commanding a unit comprised mostly of Nigerians, said his men made a formidable impact on the Japanese. 'They scared the Japs to begin with,' he said many years later, with a sparkle in his sunken and blurry eyes. 'When the Japs saw these hulking great blacks with filed teeth and slashed cheeks, they were pretty scared, as I must say too were some of the English white soldiers who were mixed up with them.' Japanese soldiers, interrogated after the end of the war by British intelligence officers, said 'the Japanese consider [the Africans] to be undoubtedly our best jungle fighters... The Africans were also admired for always contriving to rescue their dead and wounded after an action.'

In comparison with the troops already in the Kaladan Valley, Isaac and the men of the 29th CCS had had it easy. They had walked hard for days, and learnt to eat and drink whenever the opportunity allowed. They had blistered feet, and those who carried the heaviest loads had swollen necks. There had been some sleepless nights, as they struggled to attune themselves to the noises of the jungle. But of war, and of trying to track and kill the enemy while worrying that he is in fact creeping up behind you – of that, they had seen nothing. The British officers in their unit had been issued with pistols, and the non-commissioned officers, the sergeants and warrant officers had rifles. But the majority of the men were not armed. They were not, after all, in the Kaladan Valley to fight. They were there to tend to the wounded.

One afternoon, Isaac and his colleagues staggered over yet another ridge and came to a stop. Beneath them was a wide and shallow river, flowing gently through the hills towards the south: it was their first sight of the long-awaited Kaladan. A ragged cheer went up. They descended into the valley and followed the river's course, before arriving at a town of dilapidated wooden houses, weed-clogged gardens and fallen, twisted fences. The hospital and government building were in ruins, hit by British bombs, it seemed. Many walls were pockmarked with bullet holes and the gashes of shrapnel. Thousands of people must have lived here in peacetime, Isaac thought, but they had all vanished now.

The town was called Paletwa and here they were reunited with Major Murphy and the heavy medical equipment that had travelled by jeep convoy.

6

FULL OF LONELINESS

IIIIIIIIIIIIIIIIIIIIIIIIIIIIIIIIIIIIIIIIIIIIIIIIIIIIIIIIIIIIIIIIIIIIIIIIIIIIIIIIIIIIIIIIIIIIIIIIIIIIIIIIIIII

The jungle is eerie and troops are not 'At Home' in it. It is full of loneliness and surprises.

General Noel Irwin, 15 May 1943

IIIIIIIIIIIIIIIIIIIIIIIIIIIIIIIIIIIIIIIIIIIIIIIIIIIIIIIIIIIIIIIIIIIIIIIIIIIIIIIIIIIIIIIIIIIIIIIIIIIIIIIIIIII

February 1944
The Arakan, Burma

In the final days of February 1944, General Kit Woolner had good reason to feel satisfied. For all the 81st Division's struggles, for all the loss of men, it had pushed the Japanese back some seventy miles in a handful of weeks. It was not a huge distance, but it had been covered on foot, across the thick jungle. The West Africans had penetrated further south into Burma than any British Army troops had managed since the great retreat of 1942. Even more impressive, less than a year had passed since these recruits had been thrown together. If many in the British high command remained sceptical of their abilities, their achievements now spoke for themselves. The West Africans, General Slim acknowledged, had shown 'great dash in the attack'. General Philip Christison, the commander of the British Army in the Arakan, passed on a message of congratulations to Woolner.

As the West Africans moved down the Kaladan Valley, a ferocious battle was being fought about fifty miles to the west. Earlier in February, the Japanese had outflanked the much larger British force that was advancing closer to the coast. Yet again, the Japanese showed daring and courage, moving through the jungle at surprising speed. For several days, thousands of troops from the 7th Division, comprised of British and Indian men, were facing the worst. They had been pushed back into a small defensive 'box' – a flat, open area of about one mile square surrounded by hills and jungle – and forced to resort to hand-to-hand fighting in order to keep the Japanese at bay. Conditions inside the box were hellish. 'Flies in their thousands flew in and around the men,' wrote Anthony Irwin, a British officer who survived the battle, 'and nothing anyone could do could destroy them.' The reason was horrific: 'the whole area was turning into a graveyard of British, Indian and Jap dead and added to that were the mules and other animals whose bodies lay rotting on the *maidan*, out of reach of burial parties'. Despite the success of the 81st Division, it seemed as though the British were on the verge of yet another defeat in Burma.

The consequences would have been disastrous. Isaac and his colleagues in the Kaladan Valley would have been left dangerously isolated and exposed. The British would have been forced to put more men and resources into defending the Arakan frontier, in a desperate effort to prevent a Japanese advance into Bengal. The impact would also have been psychological. General Slim had struggled hard to dispel the idea that, when it came to jungle fighting, the Japanese were unbeatable. Another Japanese victory would have shattered the British morale that he had rebuilt so assiduously.

But the battle did not go as the Japanese had expected. The trapped men held their ground in the box for three bloody weeks, receiving ammunition, food and medicine, not to mention bottles of rum, from the reliable Dakota pilots. Then columns of Indian troops from the 5th Division fought their way through the Ngakyedauk Pass to join forces with the men in the box. On 24 February, the British broke the siege. Thousands of Japanese troops were killed, and the enemy pulled back to avoid even greater losses.

They called it the 'Battle of the Admin Box', a prosaic name that obscured its great significance. It was a turning point. At long last, the British had evidence that their planes, tanks and artillery were superior to those of the Japanese. Anthony Irwin wrote, 'It was a victory, not so much over the Japs but over our fears. For the first time in Burma we had stood and fought the Jap and the Jungle and beaten both.'

On the afternoon of the victory of the Admin Box, West African soldiers from the Gambian battalion of the 81st Division marched into the town of Kyauktaw, forty miles downstream from Paletwa, in the Kaladan Valley. The capture of Kyauktaw was a proud moment for Woolner's men. Before the war, the town had been a trading and administrative centre, a place of two-storied colonial edifices and broad avenues, where steamers from Akyab moored at busy jetties and loaded up with rice to take back downriver. The triumphant West Africans admired the corrugated iron pagodas and mosques – proof that they had captured a place of consequence.

Kyauktaw had fallen into decay in the two years of war, however. The temple courts were wrapped in weeds, the communal water tanks coated with bright-green algae and white lilies. Stray dogs roamed the streets. There were few other signs of life. The Japanese had retreated to the south, only a short time before and apparently in something of a panic. Among the first British officers to enter Kyauktaw was Richard Terrell. He found huts full of personal belongings, including handwritten letters from Japan, and beautiful sketches of the Burmese countryside. But there were no prisoners to be taken.

Discouragingly, most of Kyauktaw's native residents had also abandoned their homes and businesses. Those that remained met the invading Africans with sullen stares from their darkened doorways. 'They showed none of the joyous symptoms of newly liberated people,' admitted a captain in the Gambian unit. Perhaps they wanted to know which army really held the upper hand before they decided whom they should be cheering on.

By now, those West Africans at the front of the advance had left the hills and jungle behind. They were marching across the Kaladan's floodplain, a flat mosaic, about eight miles wide, of rice paddies adorned with palm trees, bamboo huts and water buffalo. It was still the dry season, and the river was languid. But the tides swept up across the flat expanse from the Bay of Bengal, some fifty miles to the south, with surprising speed, and then the river submerged the slimy mud banks and sand islands, before the waters fell once more.

On the floodplain, directly across the river from Kyauktaw, a single hill, about a mile long from north to south and covered in brush and jungle, rose sharply against the surrounding paddies and loomed over the town. 'An isolated whale-back hump' was how John Hamilton described it. A Buddhist temple had been built at its highest point, with a gilded pagoda roof that punctured the vegetation and glistened in the last sunshine of the day. The local people called it Pagoda Hill.

Immediately, the British officers appreciated that whoever held the hill would control not only Kyauktaw, but also the surrounding plain, for many miles. It was a vital strategic point to anyone hoping to take command of the Kaladan Valley. To their relief, the African soldiers that were ordered to capture Pagoda Hill met no opposition. The Japanese had chosen to melt away into the jungle instead.

Many of the villages around Kyauktaw were still inhabited. The people were subsistence farmers, and, if they had little by way of possessions, life did at least seem more comfortable here than up in the hills. There was plenty of rice, the buffalo looked content, even lazy, and flocks of chickens scurried around the *bashas*.

At first, each village was indistinguishable from the next, but the West Africans soon noticed that they were passing through two very distinctive kinds of settlements. In the Buddhist villages, the ones they called 'Burmese', the people were reserved. The British officers began to suspect that these villagers were passing on information about troop movements to the Japanese. Isaac would come to think of the Buddhists as 'brothers to the Japanese'. In other villages, they found people with brown skin and Bengali features. These 'Indians', as the West Africans called them, flashed broad smiles and cried out, '*Salaam aleikum*,' as the soldiers approached – they were Muslims.

'*Aleikum salaam,*' the West Africans would reply, heartened to hear a greeting they knew from home.

On the east bank of the Kaladan, a few miles to the north of Kyauktaw, British officers identified a suitable stretch of flat land for a camp. Over the next six days, hundreds of local farmers, paid in rupees and highly coveted parachute silk, cleared the land for an airstrip, so that the Dakota pilots could deliver more supplies. The first Dakota landed on 21 February. In the subsequent days and nights, there were dozens more flights as the division settled into position.

The planes brought equipment that could not be dropped from the air: heavier guns, folding boats, outboard motors and motorbikes. The British even flew in seventy-four bullocks that had been dyed jungle green, to be used as pack animals in the next stage of the advance. The position was secure, and it was now time to push on.

Back at Paletwa, Major Robert Murphy received his new orders for the 29th CCS. The bulk of his unit was to travel south by raft down the Kaladan River, in order to catch up with the 81st Division's fighting units. A smaller rear party, would follow some days later with the 29th CCS's heavier equipment.

On the evening of 26 February, the Major addressed his men. He told them that they would set out from Paletwa the following day, heading for Kyauktaw. They would aim to reach their destination by 1 March, paddling downstream at a speed of about ten miles a day. He might have been worried about how the many uncharted sand banks in the Kaladan River, as well as the upcoming tides, would slow their progress, but his plan was not overly ambitious. He knew his little flotilla of flat bamboo rafts laden high with medical equipment would be as good as defenceless on the Kaladan. But he, like his superior officers, was operating on the assumption that there were no Japanese stragglers left to the north of Kyauktaw. General Woolner himself had travelled by raft down the same stretch of river just a few days previously, with no incident.

It was another Scottish doctor, Captain Richard Brown, who read out the names of the soldiers who would be travelling the next day. Captain Brown was a wiry, small man with red hair, whose valiant efforts to speak West African pidgin had endeared him to the soldiers. He'd celebrated his thirty-ninth birthday during the march from India, and while the men called him *baba agba* – old man – they respected his prodigious appetite for hard work. Maybe that came from his upbringing, in a poor Presbyterian family in Aberdeen. His father George, a draper, had died of tuberculosis when Richard was just seven years old, leaving him and his sister in the care of his mother, Jeannie. But he'd managed to secure a place to read medicine at Aberdeen University, and had gone on to become a GP. Now, as he ran through the list, in the accent that his men sometimes struggled to follow, they listened closely. 'Company Sergeant Major Archibong Bassey Duke…Sergeant David Kargbo…Lance Corporal Daniel Adeniran', and so on, until he reached the end of the list, 'Private David Essien…Private Isaac Fadoyebo'.

They set out at dawn on 27 February. The men were glad to leave Paletwa behind. It was a forlorn place, they said, with bad spirits. When they punted off the riverbank, the shallow waters came alive with the disturbed flight of basking mudfish. They watched jet-black cormorants skim past, close to the river, and tribes of squawking green parakeets cross the canopy overhead, their flight direct and urgent. On an overhanging branch, a kingfisher perched rigidly still. But of human life, the men saw little. At least, at first.

Isaac shared his raft with Sergeant David Kargbo, a short man and a heavy smoker. He and Isaac had first met at the military hospital outside Freetown. David, a Temne from the northern part of Sierra Leone, had worked in the hospital as a clerk. They were friendly with each other, if also somewhat detached. It wasn't simply their differences in nationality that kept them from forming a closer bond. David was ten years older than Isaac, as well as being senior in rank. He knew about bookkeeping, and how to touch-type and write in shorthand, which gave him a certain status in the unit. Back home, he said, he had a fiancée, and he would be marrying her soon after he got back to Sierra Leone. Such talk made Isaac feel that he was, in comparison, a mere boy. Their conversation slowly dried up. They paddled away under the fierce sun, both men concentrating on keeping up with Major Murphy's raft.

In the evening, the men drew up by the bank, and tied their rafts to the trees. After a supper of corned beef, they laid canvas sheets on the ground and huddled under blankets, hoping to catch some sleep. They talked in whispers about what the next few weeks might bring.

This was among the last days of innocence for the men of the 29th CCS. That evening, some argued that it was futile to resist whatever fate had in store for them. 'If death should come, it will come, and, if it doesn't come, it won't come,' said Isaac. As the men debated their future, a strange thing happened: the British officers, who usually sat apart, talking among themselves, joined the conversation, sharing food, drink, cigarettes and intimate fears with the Africans. The days of marching and rafting through a hostile land had brought them together. The differences imposed by race and rank had eroded. Afterwards, the Africans wondered why this was. 'Maybe the closer we are to our graves, and to our Maker, the better we behave,' suggested Isaac. At this, some of the men murmured in agreement, but most were silent, lost in their own thoughts.

Other British and African soldiers who fought in Burma also experienced the falling away of barriers in the intensity of the jungle war. A Kenyan corporal, serving with the King's African Rifles on the Kalewa battlefront to the north of the Arakan, wrote, 'among the shells and bullets there had been no pride, no air of superiority from our European comrades-in-arms. We drank the same tea, used the same water and lavatories, and shared the same jokes. There were no racial insults, no references to "niggers", "baboons" and so on. The white heat of battle had blistered all that away and left only our common humanity and our common fate, either death or survival.' British officers felt the same bonding process under way. Captain

Charles Carfrae, leading Nigerian troops through the Burmese jungle, wrote, 'colour and other racial differences signified little. We lived together, ate the same food, carried the same back-bending loads, suffered privation equally and fought literally side by side.' John Hamilton, who was working his way down the Kaladan with the Gambian battalion, just a few miles ahead of Major Murphy and Isaac, said it was 'difficult to see how you could not like men who tolerated so much so patiently, and…with such good humour and so little grumbling'.

A sense of common purpose and shared sacrifice – these are surely prerequisites for the success of any army fighting against a formidable enemy. The British in Burma in 1944 were not the first to discover this, just as they were not the first to do away with many of the protocols of hierarchy during the heat of battle. But the British Army had to remain an effective fighting force, and there were limits to the process of fraternisation. No doubt General Slim was sincere when he wrote that 'the wants and needs of the Indian, African and Gurkha soldier had to be looked after as keenly as those of his British comrade', and that any soldier in his army 'was judged on his merits without any undue prejudice in favour of race, caste, or class'. But his was ultimately an army where the African was at the bottom of the pile. It was inconceivable to almost everyone in it, white or black, that things could be otherwise. Imminent danger may have brought men together, but it also reinforced the need for rigid discipline. Besides, even British officers who lived and fought in close proximity to Africans for many months felt there was a great gulf in thinking and morality between themselves and their men. Sergeant James Shaw, who trained Nigerian soldiers in Kaduna before accompanying them on a harrowing march in Burma, wrote that one of his men had been caught stealing extra rations in the jungle, and was tied to a tree and whipped as punishment. He wondered if the thief felt guilty but concluded that 'the percentage of Africans possessing consciences is something no white man can judge accurately; they're much too enigmatical'.

Some British officers asked themselves what on earth their African soldiers made of the sacrifices being asked of them, now that they were in the midst of war. The Nigerians, according to Captain Carfrae, 'found themselves in a forbidding country pitted against strangers altogether irrelevant to them, a people they hadn't known to exist and with whom they could have had no conceivable quarrel until we made our enmity theirs…The Nigerian soldiers, most of them peace-loving and none with the least urge for self-sacrifice, fought simply because they had promised their white leaders that they would. We imposed greatly upon their generosity.' Still, most officers were convinced that the British had done the right thing in taking Africans to Burma. Trevor Clark, slogging down the Kaladan Valley in early 1944 with the Gambian battalion, wrote, 'I never for one moment questioned whether we, *and our Africans* [his italics], were right to be fighting the war, both to defeat the totalitarians and to save the parts of the Empire that they had taken (or intended to take) from us; nor have I ever since.'

As the men of the 29th CCS carried on downriver, and the hill country gave way to the broad floodplain, they made quite a spectacle. They stayed on the river through the worst heat of the day, and, as they began to pass a few settlements, the local people, mostly Buddhists, came down to the water to stare at them. When afternoon arrived, they would steer the rafts over to the river's banks and tie up. Villagers crowded round the rafts. Many of them had hidden in fear from the combat units that had passed by in previous days. Now they ran their fingers up the Africans' arms and through their hair, touching and feeling a black person for the first time in their lives.

The soldiers, for their part, admired the herds of wallowing buffalo and the precision with which the villagers waded along rows of partially submerged bamboo fish-traps, checking for any catch. The soldiers had underestimated how much food they should have carried on the rafts, so, on the second and third evenings of their journey, some of them took to raiding the farms along the river. It was shameful, Isaac felt, a violation of the order not to deprive civilians of their property.

It was also a betrayal of the trust of those villagers who had greeted them with well-intentioned curiosity. But the soldiers were desperate to eat something fresh after the unexciting diet of recent weeks.

The officers chose to ignore the thefts, it seemed. As for the villagers, they silently directed the Africans to the best fruit, carefully avoiding eye contact. Their very meekness encouraged everyone to join in. Isaac grabbed melons, papaws and cucumbers – a feast. But his theft would nag at him.

Two other incidents troubled Isaac during those days on the river. The first was when Lance Corporal Felix Okoro slipped off a raft, and disappeared into the brown water. He was there, and then he was gone. When the men eventually managed to recover his body the next morning, all they could do was dig a shallow grave at the riverside, lay the corpse inside and shovel mud over it. The second occurred on the evening of the burial. Maybe it was the death of Lance Corporal Okoro that had affected Major Murphy's mood. He had hoped to get his unit through the war without a fatality, and he had failed. The men were boiling up tea after supper, laughing and joking, when the Major came storming over. 'Don't you know you're in the battlefield?' he hissed, and kicked the kettle off the fire. He ordered them to turn in immediately. 'I beg, master, we know we are in the battlefield, but before we go die make you no forget my *chop-o*,' someone muttered under his breath.

The Major, like Captain Brown, was considerably older than most of the men under his command. He'd left a wife, Margaret, and a son and a daughter behind in Scotland. In the last mail drop, he'd received a letter from Margaret, letting him know she was expecting their third child. Major Murphy didn't doubt that all of his men wanted to get through this war alive. But sometimes he looked at these young African soldiers, and couldn't help feeling that he had a more acute sense of what they stood to lose, of which risks were worth taking, and which were not.

At five o'clock on the evening of 1 March, at the end of their fourth day on the river, the 29th CCS put ashore on the west bank of the Kaladan. There was still enough daylight for some of the men to walk to the nearby village, and a sergeant went with them, to see if he might buy some bags of rice. Along with the rice, they brought back some encouraging news. The village, the place they called Mairong, was Muslim, not Buddhist, and the local people were friendly. Major Murphy was reassured. The death of Okoro had delayed them, but they had only another eight miles to go. They would be in Kyauktaw the following afternoon.

Just before dusk, the Major received an unexpected visitor, a British officer who was travelling in the opposite direction. Lieutenant Colonel John Hubert was heading upriver with two of his men in a dugout canoe with an outboard motor. They pulled over to spend the night with the 29th CCS. Hubert was in charge of a battalion of Punjabi troops who had recently taken up a position further north in the Kaladan Valley. He was returning to his unit, having spent the day south of Kyauktaw, in talks with General Woolner.

That night, the sky was clear, the stars a million glittering lanterns, and the Southern Cross shone brightly. As they sat overlooking the river, Hubert told Major Murphy that the bulk of West African soldiers were now some way south and west of Kyauktaw. As a consequence, the 81st Division was stretched over a considerable length of the Kaladan Valley. But there were many things that these two officers could not have known that night.

They could not have known that the Japanese, trying to regain the initiative after their defeat at the Battle of the Admin Box, were about to launch a counterattack of their own. Or that, at that very moment, a Colonel Hiroshi Koba was leading thousands of Japanese soldiers through the paddy fields on the east side of the Kaladan River, with an eye to storming Pagoda Hill. Or that Colonel Koba's advance patrols were already pushing northwards, all the way to the riverbank opposite of the 29th CCS's temporary camp. In short, they could not have known that they, and the few dozen British and African men who slept peacefully around them, were in great danger.

7

JUJU ON THE RIVER KALADAN

||||||||||||||||||||||||||||||||||||||||||||||||||||||||||||||||||||||||||||||||||||||||||||||||||||||||||||

*Some of the Africans think there is a juju on the River Kaladan and I am
beginning to believe it myself.*

> Captain Stephen De Glanville,
> the Arakan, 26 March 1944

||||||||||||||||||||||||||||||||||||||||||||||||||||||||||||||||||||||||||||||||||||||||||||||||||||||||||||

2 March 1944
Mairong, Burma

After the shooting, there had been screaming. And after Captain
Brown had come back to try to help the wounded, the Japanese
had taken him away. This much Isaac could remember. He knew also
that he had been shot twice. He could feel a searing pain in his right
leg, but there was also blood coming from the left side of his stomach,
just beneath his rib cage. Warm and sticky, it oozed down his side. He
must have drifted in and out of consciousness in the hours that had
followed. He craned his neck to try to identify the bodies around him.
There was Archibong Bassey Duke with his red tea mug. And there
was Private Essien. And was that Lance Corporal Daniel Adeniran,
also lying face down? None of them was moving. Isaac was alone,
and everything was quiet. He began to weep.

Why had the Japanese not killed him, as well? he wondered. He was
dimly aware that they had ransacked the medical equipment on the

rafts, then combed through the belongings of his dead colleagues. With that done, they'd gone back to the river and boarded motorboats. They seemed to have headed upstream. How strange that they had just left him lying there, on the riverbank. But then, Isaac was able to grasp the cold truth. The Japanese had decided not to waste a bullet on him. He was going to die anyway.

He heard voices. Some militiamen in uniform, local people, he thought, came upon the scene. They looked around and quickly departed, without saying a word. A little later, he had a faint impression of a crowd swarming around the rafts, looting whatever the Japanese had not taken. There was bickering – a flourish of hands, raised voices – and then they were gone. Then, just as it turned dark, he woke to see yet more visitors. Men, they looked like 'Indians' to Isaac; he supposed they must have come from the nearby village of Mairong. He was right. The Muslim men had come to collect the bodies of two boys who had been killed during the attack.

Slowly, it came back to him. The boys had come down to the riverbank in the morning to take a look at the British and African soldiers. They were still standing there when the Japanese opened fire, and they'd paid for their curiosity with their lives. Perhaps these men were relatives of those boys. They carried the boys' bodies away, and Isaac was left in the dark, alone again.

But then the men returned. Two of them walked over to where Isaac was lying on the ground. They seemed to be showing signs of sympathy, but they spoke no English. He knew that he needed their help; he had to get away from this place, as soon as possible. If the Japanese came back and found that he was still alive, they would surely kill him on the spot. He could feel the pain in his stomach as he stretched to open his breast pocket. That's where he kept his pay book, with a five-rupee note folded inside. It was all he had.

The men took Isaac's money and lifted him from the ground. They carried him some distance away from the river, he could not say how far, to an area of open vegetation, and laid him down in some tall grass where he would be concealed from passers-by. They spoke to him in their language, but he could not understand. They seemed to be saying they would be back, that they would come with food. And then they walked away into the evening gloom. Would he ever see them again? He passed a sleepless, feverish night, his leg and stomach throbbing, his throat desperate for water. He was horribly wounded, in a land he did not know, at the mercy of an enemy from whom he could expect no pity. What would become of him?

But Isaac was not, as it turned out, alone. Because the following morning, the Muslim men did come back, with rice wrapped in leaves and water in a bamboo container. He ate a handful of the rice and gulped down the water. The men seemed nervous, and spent only a few minutes with him before returning in the direction from which they had come.

Soon afterwards, Isaac spied a cloud of black smoke rising over the nearby jungle. Then he heard cracking noises, and caught sight of flames dancing above some of the trees. It was a fire, and it was being fanned by the midday wind directly towards him. He lay there, helpless. It would have been better, he thought, to have been shot by the riverbank like Bassey Duke or Essien than be slowly roasted to death, too weak to escape the blaze. He closed his eyes and prayed. Shortly afterwards, the skies clouded over and a gentle rain fell. The fire died down. He had been saved, he thought, by divine intervention. 'Incredible, unbelievable,' he mumbled to himself.

He tried to form the words of another prayer, but his head ached, and he passed out once more. Darkness fell, and the rain started again, much heavier this time. He was soaked, and feeling alternately feverish and cold. But he could not move his broken body, and so he lay there, waiting for his long night to end.

The two men returned the next day, with more rice as well as some herbs. Isaac ate but he could not sit up. He propped himself up on an elbow and tried to examine the mess above his right knee – the pulpy, red flesh and the gash of white that ran through it. He recalled what he'd been taught at the army hospital in Abeokuta: that was his femur, exposed and broken. The men rubbed herbs into the wound, and gave him some straw to lie on. They came back the next day, and the one after that, always with small parcels of rice, until the days blurred one into another.

Isaac started to think of the villagers as the 'good Samaritans'; they meant well, he could see, even if their gestures were pathetic. He felt his body getting weaker and weaker. He was losing weight. At night, his sleep was disturbed by his sweat and groans. Lying there, in the tall grass, he thought of home, of his aunts and uncles, of his father. Faces danced before his eyes, but he could not remember names.

Maybe a week had passed, or so Isaac thought, and it was the middle of the afternoon. He had spent the days in a dull daze, semi-conscious most of the time. So he was only half-aware of the group of villagers walking towards him. They were new faces, not the familiar men. And trailing behind them was, well, how could it be? It was a black man in British uniform. It looked like David Kargbo, the sergeant from Sierra Leone who had been his rafting partner in the days before the attack. They were coming closer now, and Isaac could see clearly: it *was* Sergeant Kargbo. He was limping, from what looked like a wound to his right ankle, but otherwise he seemed okay. In fact, he had an expression of relief on his face. He was smiling! For the first time since he'd been shot, Isaac felt a burst of hope. He was in pain, he was hungry, but he was sure that David Kargbo, leaning down to embrace him, had been sent by God. He had somebody to talk to, somebody to share this ordeal with. As the villagers went away, they indicated that they would come back with some food. By now, Isaac knew to trust them.

Still, as he and David tried to piece together what had happened during and after the attack, they spoke in whispers. David had been shot and, like Isaac, had been left to die of his injuries, somewhere in the grass near the rafts. David said that some men from Mairong had found him and had carried him to the village, where they hid him in a hut. The following morning, they'd indicated that it was too danger-ous for him to stay there, because the Japanese sometimes came by and searched the huts looking for enemy soldiers. They'd carried David back into the jungle, and he'd gleaned that the village headman had given instructions that he should be fed for a month. For some reason, it seemed the village had decided it was safer to unite the two Africans. Maybe different groups of benefactors had learnt what the other was up to, and decided to pool their meagre resources to assist them.

Isaac told David what he knew of Major Murphy, of Captain Brown's attempt to rescue them, and that he had seen Bassey Duke and Essien, both shot dead. But that left about seventy-five, maybe eighty, men unaccounted for. How many more had been killed? Were there others injured, perhaps scattered in the nearby jungle, who needed help but were too weak or frightened to call out? And there was still another possibility, one which they clung to. Surely, most of the men had managed to escape, in which case, wouldn't help be on its way? They weren't being unrealistic, they thought. But how little Isaac and David knew.

After weeks of steady progress, the fortunes of the British Army in the Kaladan Valley had suddenly turned. At 7.30am on 2 March, at about the same time that the 29th CCS was coming under fire on the west bank of the Kaladan River, the Gambian battalion of the 81st Division was busy crossing over to the east bank, eight miles or so to the south. The river at that point was some 750 yards wide, and the Gambians were ferried across in small boats. They had been sent to rescue the situation on Pagoda Hill.

The previous night, a unit of lightly armed East African scouts had been attacked by a much more powerful Japanese force. This was the beginning of Colonel Koba's surprise counterattack. At divisional headquarters, on the west bank of the Kaladan near Kyauktaw, an anxious General Woolner could hear the sound of mortar explosions and gun-fire coming from the hill. He ordered that it must on no account fall to the enemy. His instructions were in vain. As the bombardment intensified, some of the East African soldiers fled.

If Pagoda Hill was to stay in British hands, everything would depend on the Gambian soldiers who took up their positions the following morning. The British officers who led them, including John Hamilton and Trevor Clark, remembered a strange and confused battle, in which some platoons and companies fought valiantly, while others waited and waited for an enemy who never appeared, and were then mystified when ordered to withdraw without having fired a single shot. General Woolner's verdict was that the battalion commander had dispersed his forces too widely, and thus allowed the Japanese to infiltrate their ranks during the night of 2 March.

To add an element of farce to this dire situation, a Sierra Leonean battalion that had been sent under cover of darkness to help the Gambians landed on an island in the middle of the Kaladan River but believed it to be the river's east bank. They soon realised their mistake, but had to wait until dawn on 3 March before they could join their colleagues. By then, the Gambian defence had disintegrated. Pagoda Hill was lost, and the various African units were hurriedly ferried back to the west bank of the Kaladan.

All told, the Battle of Pagoda Hill was, in Woolner's words, 'a disaster'. Accurate artillery and mortar fire from the heights of the hill could reach across a long stretch of the Kaladan Valley. As a result, the 81st Division was forced to retreat, ceding control of the area to the Japanese. The recriminations were bitter. A number of British officers were removed from their positions in the coming weeks and months, including Woolner himself. Some officers blamed Lieutenant General Philip Christison, the overall commander of British troops in the Arakan. They said his instructions to Woolner were unrealistic, and even contradictory. While General Christison had ordered the 81st Division to hold Pagoda Hill and the town of Kyauktaw, he also told Woolner to carry on advancing, so as to cut Japanese supply lines and thereby assist British and Indian troops further to the west. This, Woolner said, had presented him with a 'grave dilemma': he had been asked to attack and defend at the same time in different places, without enough men or equipment to carry this off. The result was that, when the Japanese attacked Pagoda Hill, many of his soldiers were ten miles to the south. Woolner did not have sufficient men to try to retake the hill until 4 or 5 March, by which time he believed that the Japanese would have prepared strong defences. He also thought that crossing the wide Kaladan River, this time right under the noses of newly placed Japanese guns, was too dangerous, all the more so since the muddy banks afforded no cover for boats. It was simple. The Japanese, Woolner conceded, 'had been too quick for us'.

Woolner's official report on the events of Pagoda Hill was written in measured language, and he refrained from criticising even those colleagues whom he felt had let him down. In private, however, he was less diplomatic. In later years, he referred to one of the officers involved in the hill's shambolic defence as 'not only a dud but a coward too. He was flown out from the next Dakota strip' – unfit for further command in Burma, in Woolner's assessment. Another key officer 'chose that moment to crack up'. He too was flown out at the first opportunity.

The reverse at Pagoda Hill was also a very personal disaster for Isaac and David. It meant that they were now stranded in Japanese-controlled territory. In effect, they had been abandoned by the British. They did not know it yet, but there was no prospect of their being rescued. In fact, as his defence of Pagoda Hill was unravelling, General Woolner was aware of the fate of the 29th CCS. On the afternoon of 2 March, while Isaac lay wounded on the riverbank, a shaken officer from the unit had arrived at the divisional headquarters. He had managed to escape to the south on foot amid the confusion, and staggered ten miles in search of safety. He told the General what had happened.

Major Murphy's unexpected guest, Lieutenant Colonel Hubert, had also got away, but in the opposite direction. He and his two Punjabi soldiers fled into the jungle and took cover. After they had gone a little way, one of the soldiers, Lance Corporal Kesar Singh, bravely offered to turn back and retrieve their canoe. It was the quickest way to put some safe distance between them and the Japanese, he reasoned. He stripped out of his uniform, so as to pass himself off as a local farmer, and returned to the scene of the attack. But, when he got there, he decided that it was too dangerous to take the canoe.

The Japanese might be advancing north, and travelling on the river would leave them exposed. The three men then headed off on foot, and eventually arrived safely back at Paletwa, where they rejoined their regiment. Hubert estimated that there had been some fifteen Japanese soldiers involved in the attack, armed with two machine guns. It was a small number, but they had the element of surprise, and more firepower than the 29th CCS.

When General Slim took command of the British Army in Burma, he had stressed that there was no such thing as a non-combatant in jungle warfare. He wrote, 'Every unit and sub-unit, including medical ones, is responsible for its own all-round protection, including patrolling, at all times.' Major Murphy and his men clearly had been caught off-guard, and they paid a heavy price. Many of the soldiers in the 29th CCS had been ambling back from the village of Mairong when the Japanese opened fire. If the Japanese had waited only a little while longer, and allowed the men to board their exposed rafts, they would have inflicted even greater casualties.

On 5 March, the Punjabi regiment received information that the bulk of the survivors from the 29th CCS were walking north up the Kaladan Valley, following the route that Hubert and his men had taken. Seventy-seven of Isaac's colleagues would struggle back to Paletwa over the next few days, many of them wounded. They were joined by more than thirty Gambian soldiers, survivors of the Battle of Pagoda Hill who had lost touch with their commanders in the chaos of the defeat.

Unfortunately for Isaac and David, Woolner had far bigger problems to contend with than a handful of missing soldiers from the 29th CCS. With Pagoda Hill abandoned, the 81st Division was hemmed in by wide rivers, and, just as he had feared, it was coming under fire from Japanese gunners. Colonel Koba sought to divide and destroy the 81st Division on the plains around Kyauktaw. Woolner could see that his troops were shaken, 'unable to understand why their long and victorious advance had suddenly become what felt like a retreat'. He sensed that his men were not suited to a fight in the open country, and decided to make a move for the forested hills to the north-west. 'It had become necessary to go into close harbour, hidden in the friendly jungle, for a period of moral consolidation,' he said.

As the West Africans waited to cross yet another *chaung*, panic set in, especially among the unarmed porters, who felt the most exposed in the paddy fields. There were some stampedes. In a secret memo dispatched to his officers on 8 March, Woolner admitted that 'a dramatic change came over the situation' with the Japanese now on the offensive, and that this had 'produced a feeling of frustration and even of bewilderment' among his men. In truth, the 81st Division was exhausted. The West Africans had been marching and fighting for ten weeks without a pause, and their mobility was severely hampered by the large number of casualties they were carrying. Yet Woolner spurred his troops on, gathering them together in a safe position in the jungle hills. There, at a place called Kyingiri, they were able to build a landing strip for Dakotas. Casualties were flown out, and food and equipment flown in.

In the days that followed, the 81st Division regained its composure, and carried out a number of successful ambushes against the advancing Japanese. Despite these efforts, lasting damage had been done to the division's reputation. When Woolner flew by Moth plane to meet with General Christison on 23 March, he was appalled to discover what people at Corps HQ had been saying about him. He wrote, 'A completely erroneous impression prevailed about the morale of the Div. It seemed that it was believed to be in a state of demoralisation amounting almost to disintegration. Grossly exaggerated rumours had been spread by stragglers from Pagoda Hill and by sick personnel flown out, including some senior officers who should have known better.'

These 'calumnies' had their effect; Woolner would be relieved of his command in the coming months. He took the news with dignity, assuming full responsibility for the decisions he'd made. And what of his West African men? In a final report, he said it was 'impossible to express in words my gratitude to them for their irrepressible

cheerfulness under all circumstances, or for their unfailing and enthusiastic support whatever I asked of them'.

Shortly after Isaac and David's reunion, the villagers brought some
unexpected visitors to see them: a British captain, accompanied by
two Gambian soldiers. Maybe this was the rescue party they had
hoped for? Far from it. The captain explained that he and his men
had been cut off from their unit during the retreat from Pagoda
Hill. They had spent the past several days wandering through the
countryside, trying to discover in which direction the 81st Division
had moved. The captain had painted his face dark green, and he was
armed with a Sten gun. Despite the perilous circumstances, he exuded
a calm confidence. The two Gambians, who had lost their weapons,
appeared more anxious.

Isaac and David learnt about the defeat at Pagoda Hill. While they
were exchanging information with the new arrivals, there was a further surprise. Out of the jungle emerged Tommy Sherman, another
member of the 29th CCS, who had been hiding nearby and was not
injured. A Sierra Leonean, Tommy had always been a self-confident
character, and now Isaac was struck by his fresh and healthy appearance. Tommy told them that only the previous day he had buried
the body of one of their colleagues, another Sierra Leonean by the
name of Moigboi Jagha.

As Isaac and David absorbed all this news, the captain announced
that he wanted to escape from the area as quickly as possible. This
was Japanese-controlled territory, after all. He was prepared to try
to take Isaac, David and Tommy with him, but insisted they leave at
once. He made the villagers understand that he needed two men to
carry Isaac on an improvised stretcher, and this was agreed. The party
set off along the edge of a paddy field, making for the hills and – they
hoped – British positions.

They made slow progress. The stretcher-bearers did their best,
but stumbled over the ridges and troughs of the paddy field. Isaac
tried not to scream, but he had no support for his fractured femur,

and every jolt brought tears to his eyes. David hobbled along beside him. They had not gone far when a group of men from Mairong came running up with news that several Japanese soldiers had been seen on the route they were planning to take. The captain stopped and assessed the situation. He studied his map and worked out an alternative route. He also checked his ammunition, and saw that he had fewer bullets than he had thought. He would struggle to defend the group if they came under attack.

A decision had to be made. The captain could see that Isaac was a liability, and he was also sceptical of David's ability to complete a long strenuous march, or run if necessary. He ordered David to accompany Isaac back to the hiding place where he had found them. Perhaps the captain realised that Isaac would certainly die if he were left alone. Whatever David's thoughts at this time, he had to obey the orders of a senior officer. Isaac, however, felt sure that David, a devout Christian, would have volunteered to stay behind and look after him, even if the command had not come. The captain took down their names and numbers, and promised to pass on the information should he get through safely.

Then, just as Isaac, David and the stretcher-bearers were turning back, an argument broke out between Tommy Sherman and the captain. Tommy said the new direction that the captain proposed to take would lead them straight to the Japanese. The captain again consulted his map, and insisted he had the right route. He pressed on with his two Gambian soldiers, while Tommy set off alone in the opposite direction, carrying a small parcel under his arm. Isaac watched him disappear into the trees. Tommy was never seen by his colleagues again. The captain, meanwhile, managed to get through the Japanese lines, and would duly report to his superiors that he had seen two injured members of the 29th CCS, stranded near where their unit had been attacked, so many days before.

Isaac and David were in a deep gloom. The captain had explained to them that all signs indicated that the 81st Division had pulled out of the Kaladan Valley. They could not see where help would come from now. Soon the monsoon rains would begin, during which any change to the military situation was extremely unlikely. The British would not even think about a new offensive before the dry season began in November. That was eight months away. Isaac doubted whether he would survive that long.

He was in a wretched condition. He had not washed for weeks, and his hair was filthy and matted. He had already lost so much weight that he could see the outline of his rib cage jutting through his grey, clammy skin. The injury on the left side of his stomach, where the bullet had not penetrated as far as his intestines or vital organs, no longer hurt so much. But his right leg was sore and swollen, and pus seeped out of the messy wound. The stench was so bad, he noticed in helpless shame, that the villagers held their noses whenever they had to come close to him. An angry swarm of flies hovered above him during the day. He did not have the strength to wave them away, but tried to protect the wound with an old blanket he had been given by one of the villagers. He struggled to turn on his side when he needed to eat, scooping up rice with one hand, and straining to raise his head to sip water from a bamboo cane. He was not strong enough to sit up unassisted, let alone crawl, so he went to the toilet where he lay, and the foul smell of his shit and piss mixed with that of the pus and the exposed flesh of his leg.

David pleaded with the villagers to bring some sort of improvised shovel, so that he could clear away Isaac's mess from time to time. He chose to sit and sleep several yards away from Isaac. In part, this was to escape the stench, but there was another, unspoken reason. He was giving himself a chance of escape should a Japanese patrol hear Isaac's periodic groans of pain and despair.

Isaac knew that he had no chance of staying alive without David's help. David, for his part, could see that they would both die unless the villagers from Mairong were prepared to carry on feeding them and keeping them informed about Japanese troop movements for many months to come. For now, the villagers appeared to be friendly, and there was no doubting their pro-British sentiments. But how long would this last, now that the Japanese were once again firmly in control of the Kaladan Valley? At some point, the people of Mairong were going to conclude that co-operating with the Japanese was their best option. It would take only one person to betray David and Isaac, with fatal consequences. So they needed to do everything within their limited powers to ingratiate themselves to the villagers. They had no money or possessions to hand over, but they did have faith. Or at least, they could pretend to have it. The villagers had already asked them several times if they were Muslim. Now, David and Isaac set out to convince them this was indeed the case.

David found it easy to pass himself off as a Muslim, because he had been born one. His original name had been Umaro, and his father, Foday Marro Kargbo, was a teacher of Koranic verse known as a *karamokoh*. There was no mosque in their village of Rogbin in northern Sierra Leone, but the *selkendeh*, a pebble-littered clearing reserved for daily Islamic worship, was just next to the family home. This was where the children gathered round a fire every evening, to hear Rogbin's *karamokoh*, including Foday Kargbo, recite the Koran in Arabic. Young Umaro had learnt the verses by heart. He had only converted to Christianity, and become David, when he went on to the American Wesleyan Mission Primary School in the town of Gbendembu, some ten miles from his village. Throughout his life, he had benefitted from the discipline of rote learning. He could still recite large parts of the Koran, and had an enviable knack for remembering spelling, literary quotations, poetry and mathematical formulae. The villagers of Mairong were suitably impressed. Isaac, on the other hand, knew no Arabic, and little about Islam. It was only since joining the British Army that he'd spent any time with Muslims; there had been very few in Owo and the surrounding countryside during his childhood. He tried to explain that he had been taught Koranic verses, but only in English. Somehow, communicating mainly through hand gestures, he and David managed to persuade the villagers that they shared their religion.

The African men were also quick-witted enough to give themselves Islamic names. Isaac said that he went by the name of Suleman, and David introduced himself as Dauda Ali. Perhaps it was David's fluency with Islam that covered up for Isaac's hesitations. In any case, the ruse worked. The villagers fell for it.

For a while, they received food from a trickle of people, different each time, who sneaked over from Mairong to their hiding place. Isaac started to recognise some words in the villagers' language, which he assumed to be a dialect of Bengali. '*Pani kaigha? Bath kaigha?*' the villagers asked. 'Do you want water? Do you want rice?' Isaac learnt to reply, '*Pani ni, Bath ni,*' meaning they had no water and no rice. Sometimes he would say this even when it was not true, in the hope that he and David would be given extra portions to tide them over on the many days that none of their friends came visiting. But they had nowhere secure to keep the food; on some mornings, they would wake up and find that the little pile of rice that they had carefully set aside was covered in ants and other insects. At times, the villagers would come, pressing their hands to their hearts as they looked down on the injured Africans, and say, '*Bahut togolip, bahut acha.*' Isaac could only presume it was an expression of sympathy, or apology.

Gradually, the trickle of visitors bearing gifts dried up. He couldn't blame them, really. The villagers had little to give away and, with no prospect of the Africans being rescued, they couldn't be expected to bring them food indefinitely. David would limp out of their hiding place, to a nearby track, where he would beg passing villagers for food. This was a risky move. If a Japanese soldier, or even an unfriendly person from a nearby Buddhist village, were to walk past, David could have been caught. But he had no choice. The alternative was that he and Isaac would starve to death.

Isaac's mind was rambling. He often thought of Captain Brown, and the enormity of that officer's courage now struck him. The Captain must have waited for hours before deciding to return to the scene of the attack to try to help the wounded. When the Japanese appeared, Captain Brown had not reached for his weapon, but had allowed himself to be taken prisoner. Had the Japanese shown him some mercy? It seemed unlikely, but Isaac hoped so. He did not know then that one day in late March a small British patrol had ambushed five Japanese soldiers in the hills to the west of the Kaladan River. The Japanese ran, and so did their porters, numbering more than thirty men, all of whom dropped their loads as they fled. The British soldiers rummaged through the boxes and found that they included the medical supplies taken from the 29th CCS. Among the kit was a greatcoat with the tab of an Edinburgh tailor and a nametag that read 'Captain Brown, Royal Army Medical Corps'. It was to be the last, and only clue, as to his fate. Captain Brown, the draper's son from Aberdeen, left a grieving mother and sister behind, tormented for years by the loss of their beloved Richard. 'He just disappeared,' his sister would say to her neighbours many years later, and shake her head sadly. The little information the family received from the British authorities only added to their distress. At first, the Army reported that Captain Brown was missing, and believed to have been killed. In June 1944, for no apparent reason, his status was changed to 'prisoner of war'. It wasn't until 11 March 1946, more than two years after the Japanese soldiers led him into the jungle, that the War Office issued a death certificate for Captain Brown.

It became more and more difficult for Isaac and David to keep track of the passing time. They had no watch, no calendar, not even a pencil or scrap of paper. So they weren't sure whether it was late March, or even April, when a villager came to them, and said that another African was nearby, and that he needed help. David limped away with the man to see who it could be, and was astonished to find Sergeant Moses Lamina, a fellow Sierra Leonean with the 29th CCS, lying under a tree only fifteen yards away from where he and Isaac had been hiding. Sergeant Lamina was delirious, muttering only a few incomprehensible words. He looked weak and pale, and he had a leg wound that had become badly infected. In vain, David tried to ask him where he had been and how he had survived the previous weeks. In the following days, David hobbled over to where Sergeant Lamina lay, bringing him a portion of the food that the villagers had donated. Isaac, still unable to move, asked that David pass along messages of support. But Sergeant Lamina would not eat, and he died about one week later. David had no tools to bury him, and anyway he doubted that he had the strength to use a pickaxe or shovel. That night, David and Isaac heard jackals fighting over their colleague's body. The jackals came back the next night, and on the third night they were still howling, fighting and snarling over whatever remained of the Sergeant. David could not bear it anymore. The following morning, he did his best to sweep the torn limbs and bloodied and gnawed bones under a pile of leaves. Then he and Isaac prayed for Sergeant Lamina's soul.

Isaac had stayed awake those nights, listening to the jackals. He couldn't fight back the horrible thought that they would be feasting on his body next. He was clinging on to life against the odds. His leg pounded him with pain. He remembered what Major Murphy had told them in their training about diseases in the jungle, how germs and bacteria multiplied in the heat and humidity. Isaac knew that, if his wound turned gangrenous, he was finished. Two days passed, and nobody from the village came to them. He felt faint and weak with hunger. At times, he knew that David was talking to him, speculating about whether their friends had run out of food, or were too frightened to help because more Japanese soldiers had moved into the area. He could not summon the strength to reply.

Their next visitor was not from the village. He was a young Buddhist man, someone they had never seen before. 'English,' he said, pointing in the opposite direction to Mairong. He repeated the word again and again, pointing more emphatically now. He seemed to be saying that British soldiers were nearby, and that Isaac and David should follow him. He was tugging at David's shirt. Even in Isaac's condition, there was something about this stranger, his nervous eyes and breathless voice, which made him uneasy. Feebly, he tried to tell David not to go with him, but, when he looked up, he saw that David was on his feet. 'We are dying here, we have nothing to lose,' David said. 'If our soldiers are close, we must find them. They can rescue us.'

Isaac watched David follow the young man into the jungle. Some fifteen minutes later, the young man returned, alone and carrying a dagger. He looked down at Isaac, and pulled a knife from his *longyi*, which he held to Isaac's throat. Then he took Isaac's jacket, torn and covered in blood though it was, and his stinking, pus-stained blanket. Clutching his bounty, the man ran into the forest. Shortly afterwards, a crestfallen David reappeared, wearing only his trousers. In the nearby undergrowth, he too had been robbed of his jacket.

They were in a fix. The thief had been callous enough to rob them in their desperate condition. He would surely not hesitate to inform the Japanese of their presence, in the hope of further reward. He would use their British Army jackets as proof that there were injured enemy soldiers hiding in the jungle, and he would guide the Japanese back to where they lay. That same night, their fears were confirmed. They heard the crunch of footsteps on the dry leaves, and voices. Isaac strained to listen. One man was talking quickly, as if he was giving orders, but Isaac could not understand the language. The footsteps grew louder, then there was a long silence, broken by two gunshots in quick succession. The shots came from the place where David had tried to cover up the remains of Sergeant Lamina. Isaac grew still, his cheek pressed tight against the soil. He could hear himself panting, and felt the sweat running down his brow, and stinging his eye. It was a bright, moonlit night. The footsteps came even closer, and seemed to go round and round in circles. The Japanese knew they were there, and were looking for them. Then, the sounds started to grow fainter.

Isaac and David knew they had no time to waste. They had to move. They held a tense, whispered conversation, trying to concentrate on where they should go. They knew little of the geography of the area where they been hiding these past weeks. David suggested they cross the nearby paddy field, and look for shelter in the dense jungle on the far side. Isaac doubted he could make it that far, but resolved to give it a go. They set out around midnight, by which time they were reasonably confident the Japanese soldiers had gone away. Isaac sat up, but even this was enough to make him feel dizzy and nauseous. David staggered ahead, trying not to put too much weight on his damaged ankle. Isaac followed, pulling himself along the ground, with his back facing the direction he was going. His fractured leg dragged along behind him, a useless inconvenience. It was an awkward and slow way to move, and it wasn't long before he collapsed. By now, he had reached the paddy field. David came back and urged him to carry on. If Isaac stopped here, on open ground, he would be seen by the Japanese come daylight. They would kill him, David said, and pleaded with him not to give up. Isaac replied that anything, even death, was better than this. Then he passed out. David left a bamboo flask containing the little water they had, and limped on alone to the far side of the field, and the safety of the jungle.

Isaac woke at dawn, on a ridge in the middle of the field. The sun rose and blazed down on him all day. He was naked, save for a pair of shorts. He drank the water David had left him, but he was soon delirious with thirst. He urinated into the bamboo container, and tried to drink his own piss, but recoiled in disgust from the taste. At one point, he thought that two villagers had come to look at him. They were above him, shaking their heads slowly, but, when he opened his eyes again, they were not there. He could not hide from the fierce sun. For the first time since the day he'd been shot, he prayed to God to put an end to this agony, to end his life.

When Isaac next came to, the moon was out again, and he could feel a cool breeze on his face. He started to sing his favourite hymn, 'Abide With Me', in Yoruba, just as he knew his father Joshua did every evening, back in Emure-Ile. He didn't care if his voice was weak or croaking or that the Japanese might hear him. In fact, he still wanted to die. But let him first drink from the comfort of those familiar words, and the memories they evoked; of a village in a clearing in the Nigerian forest, of the laughter at dusk as people walked back together from the fields, of the smell of wood-smoke and of the rhythmic, homely thud of pestles on wooden mortars, and of the candlelit face of his father, mouthing the words of this hymn in their family home:

Wa ba mi gbe, alẹ fẹrẹ lẹ tan
Okunkun nṣu, Oluwa ba mi gbe
Bi oluranlọwọ miran ba yẹ
Iranwọ alaini, wa ba mi gbe
Ọjọ aye mi nsare lọ s'opin
Ayọ aye nku, ogo re nwọmi
Ayida at'ibajẹ ni mo n ri
'wọ ti ki yipada, wa ba mi gbe

In the silver moonlight, Isaac saw two people coming towards him, one carrying a large piece of wood, the other a bamboo container full of water. They were from Mairong, and they had come to save him, no matter what he wanted now. They gave him water, lifted him onto the plank and carried him into the jungle, where David was waiting for him. Dear Sergeant Kargbo. He had spent an anxious day, trying to attract the attention of any passing villager, then struggling to explain to them that his friend needed rescuing.

They slept on the bare ground in their new hiding place. They were safer, but they felt miserable nonetheless. They had lost their blankets, and most of their clothes, and by now Isaac, so restricted in his movements, had developed bedsores along his back. The sores had started as a line of purple welts, like bruises, on his spine and hip, but they soon burst open, livid red craters. The flies buzzed above him that afternoon with renewed fury. In the evening, it started to rain, and it did not stop for hours. They lay there, getting soaked. Even after the rain stopped, they could not stop their shivering. The following evening, it rained again, and once more they were soaked to the skin.

David suggested they pray three times a day, at morning, noon and in the evening, to keep their minds focused. What he meant was to try to keep the will to stay alive. Isaac mouthed the prayers, but he thought the end was near. They had gone without food for days, and the hunger had grown almost unbearable, when another Indian man came to see them. He was older than most of the other villagers, perhaps in his mid-forties. He wore a tattered shirt and a faded *longyi* wrapped around his waist, and he was barefoot. His thin face was filled with his large mournful eyes, so at odds with his small moustache. Much later, David would describe this moment, mixing biblical undertones and West African vernacular, as well as a canny sense of what a British censor might want to read:

> After twelve days hunger lying down hidden in this jungle, we saw an Indian Mohammedan coming towards us. On his arrival in this jungle he said unto us, 'Oh African brothers, have you had chop?'
>
> We said, 'Oh, our father, for twelve days we have had no chop.'
>
> Tears ran down his eyes, and he said to us, 'I will sacrifice my life to be feeding you from today till your troops come; no matter what will be the cost to Japanese wickedness.'

This man, the Indian Mohammedan with tears in his eyes, said he was called Shuyiman.

8

COVER ME, LORD

||||||||||||||||||||||||||||||||||||||||||||||||||||||||||||||||||||||||||||||||||||||||||||||||||||

Let this world cease
In a cool deluge drowning consciousness;
Cover me, Lord, with the lovely oblivion of rain.

Captain K.R. Gray,
Royal Signals, 'Monsoon'

||||||||||||||||||||||||||||||||||||||||||||||||||||||||||||||||||||||||||||||||||||||||||||||||||||

June 1944
Mairong, Burma

It was a gradual process, but, as the weeks passed, Shuyiman became more important to Isaac and David than all the other villagers who had helped to keep them alive. Their first big challenge together was the coming monsoon. Shuyiman built a shelter for the Africans, a simple structure fitted along the side of a slope in which they could lie side by side. The low roof, which gave them just enough height to crouch and look out, was made of raffia mat smeared with cow-dung – camouflage. Shuyiman laid down a floor of straw and brought them a blanket that they could share at night. He also gave them a pair of British Army jackets. Isaac and David wondered how this Muslim man had come across them. Maybe he had joined in the looting of their rafts after the Japanese surprise attack. Or perhaps someone in the village had found a load of airdropped British supplies that had gone astray. But, in the end, what did it matter? They had some clothing again.

That cramped shelter was to be Isaac and David's home for the monsoon season. It was neither snug nor dry – the cow-dung roof leaked, and rain poured in from the open sides – but they were more comfortable now than at any stage since the attack. It was just as well. The rainy seasons that they knew back home in Southern Nigeria and Sierra Leone could bring long and violent downpours, but this was even worse. Day after day, they lay huddled under their blanket, watching the sky turn grey, then slate, then near black. Eventually, the first drops would fall, then get faster and faster, heavier and heavier. Isaac thought it was as if somebody above them was deliberately emptying bucketload after bucketload. It went on for hours. The hills around them were covered in a gurgling sheet of running water. The trees shook as great gusts of wind from the Bay of Bengal tore up the Kaladan Valley. It was so noisy they could not even talk. Then, and often quite suddenly, the rain would stop, and the sun would come out. They would smell the damp earth, admire the glistening vegetation, count the seconds it took for the mist to rise from the trees and enjoy the concert of birds singing in dizzy celebration. But over time such interludes grew briefer and briefer, and the rain pounded down for longer and longer. At one point, Isaac thought, it must have rained for five days without pause.

Shuyiman brought them rice, water and, on occasion, fresh milk. He did not make it to the shelter every day, but, when he'd missed one, he would often reappear the following morning looking anxious and apologetic. With a regular supply of food, Isaac began to feel stronger. His stomach wound and bedsores had healed. The inflammation around his leg injury had come down, and the flesh had hardened and sealed over the previously exposed bone. But he noticed that his right knee had stiffened, with his leg stuck at an angle of about 160 degrees. He was able to crawl a few yards from the shelter to empty his bowels, but, when he tried to stand up, he still felt sick and wobbly. For the first time, it occurred to Isaac that, even were he to escape from this jungle alive, he might never be able to walk properly again. One day, Shuyiman brought an ointment, a mysterious grey paste, which he indicated should be rubbed onto Isaac's leg. David did this, dutifully, day after day, week after week, but they never knew if it made any difference.

Shuyiman's visits started to last a little longer. In the beginning, he would hurriedly drop off the food and rush back in the direction of the village. He seemed – understandably – to be worried that the Japanese might catch him with the wounded Africans. But now, he was eager to talk. This was difficult, as they struggled to follow the meaning of his words, but this did not seem to deter Shuyiman. He spoke at length, and with more and more passion, using his hands for emphasis. 'Allah' was invoked many times, of that Isaac and David – or Suleman and Dauda Ali, as they tried to think of themselves – were sure. David would reply by reciting a Koranic prayer in Arabic, and Shuyiman would beam with delight. But their conversations, if that's what they might be called, started to stray beyond religion.

One day, Shuyiman stayed a long time, perhaps more than an hour. With movements of his hands in the air, and then with the aid of diagrams that he drew in the dirt with his fingers, he tried to convey information to them about the state of the war. 'Japan', 'English', those words he knew. He seemed to be saying that the Japanese were surrounded by the British. But how could he know this? Surrounded where? After Shuyiman left, Isaac and David discussed the meaning of what he had told them. Could help be on its way? It seemed unlikely, in the middle of the monsoon season. They had not even heard any fighting since the days immediately after they'd been attacked. No distant artillery, no aeroplanes overhead. Isaac told David that he was worried Shuyiman was only trying to lift their spirits. Their friend, he said, was doing his best to keep a little hope burning in their hearts.

Despite Shuyiman's efforts, Isaac and David felt utterly isolated. For how long, they asked themselves, would they have to lie in this shelter, cowering from the rain and relying on the charity of impoverished strangers? For how long would they have to pray that the Japanese would not find them? Apart from their fleeting contact with the Captain and the two Gambian soldiers, they'd had no news of what had happened to the 81st Division, or how the war was going. To their frustration, they had completely lost track of time. Was it Monday, Tuesday or Friday? And which month were they in anyway? Try as they might, they were unable to make Shuyiman understand this question, or maybe they could not make sense of his answer.

At dusk, as the darkness deepened, Isaac and David would sing 'Abide With Me'. Their voices were tired and frightened, and rarely in harmony. But, as they sang the hymn evening after evening, they found that the familiar words brought solace: 'When other helpers fail and comfort flee, help of the helpless, o abide with me.' They had to cling to their faith. And, in Shuyiman and the others who'd kept them alive, they did have helpers.

They were encouraged when a new visitor came to see them from the village. He was relatively well dressed, and made them understand that his name was Lalu, and that he was a teacher. Yet even Lalu could not tell them the date. However, he did give them the piece of paper and pencil that they had been wanting. With these tools, Isaac and David set about calculating. They didn't have much to go on. They knew they'd been attacked at the beginning of March, that the rains had probably begun sometime in May, and that they could compare the amount of time they had spent in their shelter to the time where they had been before. They dutifully ticked off the passing days, and, when they had covered their single sheet of damp paper, Shuyiman brought them a piece of split bamboo that they could also mark. But they carried out their calculations with no real confidence. 'We are like cavemen,' Isaac said to David, flinging the bamboo aside in frustration, 'hopelessly cut off.'

There were whole days when they said very little to each other, and did very little, when Isaac slept, and David watched the rain come down. But there were other days when David, in particular, was full of schemes: patching up the roof; building a platform to keep food away from the ants; scooping out channels of dirt to drain water away from the shelter. On those days, when David was busy with his hands, he liked to talk. He talked about his beautiful fiancée, the woman who was waiting for him back home, and he talked about his life in Freetown before the war.

He'd worked at a newspaper, he said, as a sales clerk for the Sierra Leone *Daily Mail*, at the office on Rawdon Street. It wasn't much of a job, he had to admit. The pay was poor, and the hours were long. He had to be in the office long before dawn, ticking off the bundles of newspapers as the boys came to collect their loads for delivery. Sometimes David would help them, dropping off the papers at the *Krio* shops on Westmoreland and Trelawney Streets. Isaac would close his eyes, and try to picture David, walking up and down the steep streets of Freetown, newspapers under his arm. The best thing about the job, David said, was that he could read about what was happening in the world. He knew there was a war coming, and that young men would probably be wanted for the Army. Soon people on the streets were talking, all excited, about joining up to fight Hitler. One morning, David saw a khaki Bedford truck parked on Rawdon Street, just beside his office. He weighed up his options in a flash. The British Army offered adventure, certainly more than he was getting at the time, and he'd heard that the pay was good. Young men were leaping onto the back of the truck. He held out his hand, and somebody pulled him aboard. He didn't even have time to go back to his office to tell them what he was doing. The truck had already pulled away and was heading in the direction of Juba barracks. David was measured for his uniform that same day.

Just like Isaac, David had taken an impulsive decision, with little understanding of where it might take him. As they talked, the two men learnt that they had other things in common. They were both the first of their siblings to have gone to school. This had brought them opportunities, but also a sense of separation from their families. For David, this feeling grew stronger when he converted from Islam to Christianity at the Wesleyan Mission School. As a small boy, he had been inquisitive, often mischievous. At school, friends admired him for his sharp memory and wit. They gave him a nickname in their Temne language – *An sarr a kli*, meaning 'the stone that has life', taken from the first epistle of Peter, in which God chooses his 'living stones'. David proudly adapted this nickname to 'Livingstone', and thereafter came to be known as David Livingstone Kargbo. It was a name derived, he always liked to say, not from the famous explorer, but from his own mental prowess.

In turn, Isaac told David about Emure-Ile, and about his sisters and his mother and father. Both men wondered what sort of news, if any, had reached their families in West Africa about the disaster that had overcome them. Sometimes they tortured themselves with these thoughts. Perhaps it was just as well that there were things they could not know. Of how, for example, after David Kargbo was listed as 'Wounded and Missing' in the Sierra Leone *Government Gazette*, his parents had gone to the father of his fiancée and asked that they return the dowry payment they'd made the previous year. Or of how, one morning in Emure-Ile in June, a government messenger boy arrived by bicycle. He'd come from Owo as fast as he could, not even slowing down on the final hill, because he was carrying an important message for Joshua Fadoyebo, the church scribe. The letter was in a brown envelope stamped with the red crown of the English king. It was market day, so most people in the village were gathered outside. When Joshua turned and saw the sweating boy offering him the envelope, his body went cold. He tore it open, held the letter tight and let out a cry of despair. Everyone rushed home. 'The market just vanished that day' was how a cousin remembered it. The letter said that Isaac was 'Missing in Action', but wasn't that simply the way the white man, the *Oyinbo*, tried to soften bad news? Joshua's worst fears had been confirmed. He should never have let Isaac go. The news spread around Emure-Ile, and then around Owo, first among Isaac's relatives and then his school friends. Over time, 'Missing in Action' became 'Had Not Seen'. The British Army Had Not Seen Isaac.

★

Isaac and David's only hope was to stay alive and undetected. They did not know it, but time was on their side. Because, far from the Kaladan Valley, far from the Arakan itself, events were unfolding that would change the whole course of the war in Burma. On 6 March 1944, just four days after Isaac and David were shot, the Japanese had begun their long-anticipated offensive. This was when the British commanders realised that February's fighting in the Arakan had been a mere sideshow, intended to pull in their reserves and obscure the fact that the Japanese were deploying a much greater force some three hundred miles to the north. In the momentous weeks that followed, the Japanese swept down onto the Imphal plain, in Assam, in north-east India. The general leading the attack, Renya Mutaguchi, argued that, if his men were victorious in Assam, they should push on, and take Bengal. General Mutaguchi believed that the presence in his ranks of anti-British Indian soldiers, as well as memories of the recent famine, would ensure his force would be greeted as liberators in India. Calcutta would be theirs, and the famous 'March on Delhi' would begin. Other Japanese generals were more sanguine. They argued that the destruction of General Slim's army at Imphal was a valuable objective in its own right. Once and for all, the threat of a British return to Burma would be excised. They also hoped that the capture of Imphal's huge airfields, which the Americans were using to stage supply runs to Chiang Kai-shek's army, would transform the war in China.

Whatever the ultimate Japanese objective, General Slim was in no doubt that the Battle of Imphal could 'change the course of the World War'. He was caught off-guard by the scale of the attack, but he sensed an opportunity. This great Japanese offensive, he realised, could be turned to his advantage. If he could inflict a serious defeat on the enemy on ground of his own choosing, a counterattack into Burma, even through the daunting mountain country, would be that much less perilous.

It was a close thing. The British hurriedly flew in reinforcements from the Arakan, but General Slim had also underestimated the strength of a second Japanese force attacking the ridge at the mountain town of Kohima. If the Japanese could take Kohima, they would certainly cut the road to Imphal, where the bulk of British forces were concentrated, and establish a clear route to advance further into India. The fighting on Kohima Ridge was ferocious, but a small British garrison held out for days until reinforcements finally arrived. Slim later admitted, 'I was saved from the consequences of my mistakes by the resourcefulness of my subordinate commanders and the stubborn valour of my troops.'

The Japanese attack around Imphal itself was also repulsed, and by the beginning of May the British started to move forward. It now became apparent that General Mutaguchi had risked everything on the assumption that he would smash through the British lines and seize their supplies. His troops were exhausted, already running short of food and medicine. They trudged back over the mountains, abandoning their artillery and transport and, increasingly, their sick and wounded. When the monsoon started, cholera, dysentery and malaria spread through the weakened ranks. Tens of thousands of Japanese soldiers died, most of starvation and disease. Many soldiers simply collapsed on the mountain paths, or committed suicide in pacts with their colleagues. A British lieutenant leading East African troops would be haunted by the sight of piles of decaying bodies for the rest of his life: 'Glossy black scalps lay inside khaki field service caps, separated from the skull by decomposition. Clusters of writhing maggots feasted on the wounds of the dying and in the eye-sockets and mouths of the dead. Sated flies lay like a black cloth on the bodies that had fed them; swarms of hungry flies hummed ceaselessly over-head as they waited for their place at the table.'

The British pursued the Japanese with a confidence and ruthless-ness they had not shown before. As in the Arakan, the Allies had the advantage of complete supremacy in the air, meaning those Japanese still strong enough to march were forced to do so at night to escape the relentless strafing and bombing from above. The Japanese called their retreat into Burma the 'Road of Bones'. It was as crushing a defeat as the Germans had suffered at Stalingrad, and in the context of the war in Asia, as significant. If the Battle of the Admin Box had taught the British that they could beat the Japanese, the Battles of Imphal and Kohima convinced them that they would win the war in Burma.

In the Arakan, however, the monsoon rains made for wretched conditions, whether fighting or merely trying to stay alive. Following the defeat at Pagoda Hill, and the difficult marching in the weeks that followed, General Woolner had received orders to withdraw the 81st Division back to the Indian frontier until the rains were over. This news came as a relief to his weary men. The West Africans set off back to the hills, on tracks turned liquid. The water was a perpetual sheet, from the sky to the ground. The overwhelming sensation, according to Kofi Genfi from the Gold Coast, was one of never being dry: 'For three weeks you are not taking off your top dress, you are not taking off your shoe…oh! Woe betide you when you take off your shoe! The foot will be very white, as a pig's trotter. And – it – will – *stink*!…up to a mile away! Oh dear, dear, dear!' Many men suffered from stinking boils and sores, as blisters and cuts invariably turned septic in the filthy and damp conditions.

In the soaking vegetation and raging *chaungs*, they also discovered a new enemy: leeches that clung to their skin. These slimy creatures with concealed fangs could work their way between trouser leg and boot, or even through lace-holes. Arthur Moss remembered that his men's feet were 'a soggy, bloody mess when at night they removed their boots'. The leeches became bloated, up to eight inches in length, as they gorged themselves on the soldiers' blood. Initially, the men tried to pull them off, but this caused a wound that often became infected. The best way to get rid of the maddening bloodsuckers was to burn them, they learnt, using a flame or cigarette; rubbing salt into their slimy skin also worked. Even then, it was difficult to stem the bleeding or stop the wound from festering; with more experience and a bit of luck, some soldiers noticed that ash from a campfire did the trick.

The jungle's ubiquitous insects presented other dangers. There was scrub typhus, spread by mites that lived in the dense vegetation. Victims became debilitated as they lost their appetite, and often grew mentally confused and depressed. One British officer reported that Nigerian soldiers with the disease committed suicide. However, malaria was a far greater worry for General Slim. The disease had severely weakened British troops in the defeats of 1942–43. The General estimated that the annual rate of malaria was 84 percent in the British Army in India and Burma, and even higher among the troops actually fighting in the jungle. Many of the West Africans were distrustful of the mepacrine tablets that turned their white colleagues a jaundiced yellow. It was rumoured the drug could affect a man's potency. In any case, when the African forces joined the war in Burma in 1944, their malaria rates turned out to be far lower than in their British or Indian counterparts.

By the beginning of June 1944, the West Africans had pulled all the way back to Chiringa, where they had started out six months earlier. General Woolner estimated that the average infantryman in his division had marched an astonishing 1,500 miles during the campaign. In Chiringa, they recuperated, in preparation for a renewed offensive down the Kaladan Valley once the rains eased off. They would, however, be without General Woolner. He was replaced in August by Frederick Loftus-Tottenham, who'd spent most of his career in India and proven himself at the Battles of the Admin Box and Kohima – 'dashing and brilliant…a jungle go-getter', the newspapers called him.

As one of his last duties as commander of the 81st Division, General Woolner tallied the casualties from the first Kaladan campaign. He had lost more than a thousand men to death, illness and injury; a further 157 men were missing. Among these, of course, were Isaac and David, who were trapped inside Japanese-controlled territory, about seventy miles to the southeast of the Chiringa.

There were other Nigerian soldiers who carried on fighting and marching through much of Burma's monsoon season that year. At the end of 1943, shortly after the 81st Division had arrived in India, a whole Nigerian brigade, several thousand men, were told that they would not be joining the rest of their colleagues in the Arakan, but instead had been put under the command of Major General Orde Wingate, mastermind of the Chindit campaigns. General Wingate had developed a theory of 'long-range penetration', whereby a substantial British force should operate deep inside Japanese-held territory, disrupting communications and supply lines in guerrilla actions, while simultaneously bolstering Allied morale. The Chindit campaigns were certainly exploited by the British for propaganda purposes, though some generals remained unconvinced of their military effectiveness, given how they drained precious resources.

The Nigerian Chindits were flown by Dakotas into remote jungle 'strongholds' in northern Burma at the end of March 1944. There, behind coils of barbed wire, they withstood days and nights of ferocious Japanese assaults, all the while choked by the stench of bodies rotting around them. By the time the Nigerians were ordered to evacuate their stronghold and begin a march to the north, the rains had come. Unlike the 81st Division, the Chindits made their trek with the help of mules, but the animals flailed about on the treacly mud slopes and would frequently slip and fall, thrashing and kicking frantically, with no way to get back up on their feet. Then, the Nigerians would remove the wireless sets, batteries, mortars and machine guns from the mules' backs and stagger up the hills with the heavy loads on their own heads. Their courage, strength and generosity of spirit made an impression on many British officers. Captain the Reverend Miller, a senior Army chaplain with the Chindits, recalled, 'When the sick and wounded were so exhausted that they could only sink down by the track, it was the West African who bore them to safety on his wide strong shoulders. When men were dying from hunger a West African would be the first to share his own rations. As far as I know no one has sung their praise in this campaign. But their unwearied, unselfish and Christ-like service will not be forgotten by the men who came to rely on them.'

Captain Charles Carfrae led Nigerian soldiers on the second Chindit campaign. He wrote, 'Rain was absorbed by and penetrated packs, haversacks and pouches, adding so greatly to their weight that we staggered under them. Hoarded food was ruined, cherished letters from home became shreds of sodden paper.' The men marched on and on, and more and more of them collapsed. Jack Osborne, also commanding Nigerian Chindits, remembered hurried burials by the pathway, without any time for a service. 'We didn't even keep a record of where we left them,' he said. Carfrae estimated that in his column, for every man who had been killed or wounded, a dozen fell sick to malaria or typhus. And still it rained, 'the sun wholly deserting us, dry clothes a dream of wildest luxury, and worst of all the occasions when flames couldn't be conjured from soaking wood', making even a cup of tea an impossibility. Everyone and everything was covered in mud, and at night even the most ingenious shelter could not keep the water out. Food drops from the air became less and less reliable as the weather worsened. General Wingate himself was killed when his plane flew into mountains during a thunderstorm, and, by the time Carfrae's men were finally withdrawn, they were too weak to march further than two or three miles a day.

The rain also brought the farmers from Mairong out into the rice fields. Isaac and David could hear the men shouting '*Bor bor tit!*' at the water buffaloes, yoked in pairs, as they slowly ploughed up and down the paddies. David, grateful for any distraction, would creep from the shelter to a secluded position, and watch the farmers urge the animals through the mud and water for hours. At times, the rain fell so heavily that he could not even see across the field, but, when it relented, the gleaming buffaloes and the stoic farmers were still there, making their steady way up and down the mud ridges. Isaac tried to accompany David on these little expeditions, but still lacked the strength to move more than a few yards.

Mosquitoes, or *po*, as Isaac had heard the villagers call them, were now a major pest. They came out in swarms at dawn and dusk, but at the height of the monsoon they never really went away. Isaac and David were reduced to forlornly waving their hands in a half-hearted attempt to keep them at bay.

Time passed listlessly, and there were days when the boredom, the discomfort and the ever-present worry was too much, and the two men snapped at each other. One subject of contention was David's smoking. Of course, he had no cigarettes, but Shuyiman brought him a regular supply of locally grown tobacco, which he called *pata*. Shuyiman also supplied *bena*, a type of rope that would burn slowly over many hours, so that David could light his *pata*. Isaac argued that a passing Japanese patrol might see or smell the smoke, but David ignored him. In the end, Isaac also took up *pata* smoking. At least it was something to do.

One afternoon, Isaac was sleeping when David woke him with a shake. Two Japanese soldiers had just walked past the shelter. They had been carrying rifles and they looked alert, as if they were on patrol. David's eyes were wide with fear. He said that they must move immediately. They might not get another chance. Isaac resisted. He felt too weak. He wasn't convinced. How could they be sure they were going somewhere safer? Maybe right here was the best. He argued that, if the Japanese found their abandoned shelter, they would conclude there were British soldiers in the area anyway, and carry out a more comprehensive search until they found the new hiding place. So what was the point of moving?

Isaac drifted back to sleep, and into a familiar dream. He was walking into Emure-Ile. Villagers were lining the streets, waving at him, but he could not hear their voices. He entered a room, everyone greeted him, but once again he could not remember their names. His father was talking to him, but his words were drowned out by the howls of hungry jackals, and then a long *cough-cough* of machine-gun fire. The hacking bursts in his dream woke him up. There was no machine gun. It was only him coughing. And he saw that he was alone.

David, fed up with what he took to be his friend's fatalism, had determined to at least save himself. He had climbed out of the shelter, and hidden in the undergrowth a few hundred yards up the slope. There he waited, but the Japanese did not come back, and he returned to the shelter at dusk. The two men were too proud to greet each other. Isaac kept himself busy that evening waving away mosquitoes, while David studied their improvised calendar with great intensity. The next day, the chill between them had thawed, and they told Shuyiman about the Japanese soldiers. According to Isaac, Shuyiman did not seem overly worried, but calmly cut some branches so as to make their shelter harder to see.

But David remembered the events of this episode slightly differently. He said that, after they had seen the Japanese pass by several times, Shuyiman came to them in the middle of the night with some other 'Indians', and dug a deep hole which he then covered with grass. Henceforth, Isaac and David would retreat to this hole whenever they heard Japanese soldiers nearby.

After the shock of the Japanese patrol had worn off, they started to befriend other villagers. Two young boys in particular seemed to enjoy visiting them. Mohammed Ali was about eight years old and Ismael Suleman roughly fourteen. Ismael, a 'rascal' according to Isaac, was eager to teach the local language, patiently using his hands to convey his meaning. He liked to boast of his father's wealth: '*Am bap gur rupee pisi, colombasa ase, hamoni ase,*' he would say – 'In my father's house there is a lot of money, there is a gramophone and a harmonium.' Mohammed explained that he was an orphan. Could he accompany them, he wondered, back to Africa one day?

Isaac found that it was getting much easier for him to communicate with the villagers. They had a name for him: *Sutha Bacha*, 'The Young One'. His vocabulary grew larger and larger. Chicken, he learnt, was *murghi* or *koora*, because the villagers liked to say that the noise a fowl made sounded like *koora ki, kiri-ki, kiri-ki, kiri-ki*. Rice was *kana*. Milk was *doof.* Beef was *grugusa*. He was enjoying learning, and was secretly pleased that he'd picked up more of the language than David. If David had done a better job of convincing everyone that they were Muslims, now Isaac was able to make himself useful in a different way.

Isaac and David's hair had grown over the months into filthy, tangled mats. Their heads itched, and crawled with lice. They looked like lunatics, they would say to each other. So they were grateful when Shuyiman offered to cut their hair off, and to shave David's beard, with a razor and a bowl of water. Afterwards, Isaac crawled to a stream some twenty yards from their shelter, and lowered his body into the cold water. He had not washed since the day he had been shot. He had no soap, but just to feel the cake of mud and sweat fall off his skin was exhilarating.

Something was changing, and it wasn't only that the rain had all but stopped, and the nights were a little cooler. They had more and more visitors, including some villagers whom they had not seen for months. Shuyiman, who had never faltered, seemed more upbeat. He brought happy news one day; his wife, Khatoun, had given birth to a baby boy. He had already spoken many times of his young daughter, Gulasha. In fact, many of the other villagers referred to him as *Gulasha bap*, or 'Gulasha's father'. Now Isaac and David shook his hand, and Shuyiman beamed. His attempts to convey news of what the 'Japan' and 'English' were up to carried a greater air of certainty, a more convincing sense of optimism.

One night, David shook Isaac awake. He'd heard noises coming from the direction of the other side of the river. It sounded like artillery, he thought. Isaac did hear something, but it was far, far off, and could have been thunder, so he went back to sleep. The following night, it was David who was asleep and Isaac who lay awake, listening to faint thuds. Maybe David was right; they did sound like explosions.

The next morning, Shuyiman came to them. He was not carrying food. He said they should prepare for a short journey after dusk that day. He would be taking them to his house in the village, where they would be staying from now on.

9

LOYALTY AND PATIENCE

||||||||||||||||||||||||||||||||||||||||||||||||||||||||||||||||||||||||||||||||||||||||||||||||||||||||||||||||||||||||||

I have come to love and respect these Mussulmen. They are liars 'par excellence' and are out for what they can get. But who is to blame them; they've done us well enough. They have had to put up with two British withdrawals, and yet they have come back with us and fought, and died with and for us. I sometimes wonder if any other people in like circumstances can tell the same story of loyalty and patience as can these Mussulman Arakanese.

British officer,
writing about the Muslims of the Arakan, 1944

||||||||||||||||||||||||||||||||||||||||||||||||||||||||||||||||||||||||||||||||||||||||||||||||||||||||||||||||||||||||||

August 1944
Mairong, Burma

Isaac was anxious during that final afternoon in the shelter. He was not convinced that he and David would be safer in Shuyiman's house than they had been in the jungle. But he also knew that they were beholden to Shuyiman after so many months of assistance. They had no right to doubt his good faith, and they were in no position to spurn his invitation. They would simply have to trust him. David saw things differently. He worried there were more Japanese troops moving through the area, and it was only a matter of time before they were discovered. Better, he argued, to be in the village, where they would be more likely to have some warning that the Japanese were coming.

Just after dusk, Shuyiman returned with two other men from
Mairong. The village, which Isaac had never actually seen during
his months in hiding, turned out to be only five hundred yards or
so away. Still, it took him about an hour and a half to cover the
distance. Shuyiman had brought him a roughly hewn walking stick,
but this snapped under his weight almost immediately after he'd
left the shelter. Isaac was left to crawl and pull himself round the
edge of a paddy field, trying with all his might not to slip into the
water. At one point, he fell and lay in the mud, wishing he could
be carried on a stretcher. He thought he could make out David and
Shuyiman, about twenty yards ahead of him, anxiously beckoning
him to follow. Isaac knew that they were keeping their distance
from him in case a Japanese patrol came past. Then, he would be
on his own. He looked up and rallied himself. He could feel mud
plastered on his cheek and the damp of his tattered jacket clinging
to his skin. He clenched his teeth and dragged himself forward.
When he finally reached Shuyiman's house, he was at the point
of collapse.

It was the greatest physical exertion he had made in months, but
there was one final obstacle. Shuyiman's bungalow was raised several
feet above the ground. David and Shuyiman had already climbed the
bamboo ladder into the house and he could see them peering down
at him. Isaac nestled his back against the ladder, and pulled himself
up close to it with his arms. He reached behind him, feeling in the
dark, until his fingers found the notches carved on the first rung.
He tightened his grasp as much as he could. He was pouring with
sweat. His heart was pounding. He lifted himself up one rung, then
another. Then he felt someone's arms around his waist, pulling him
over the threshold into the house. He lay there panting, and as his
eyes adjusted to the candlelight he realised that his thin body was
covered in leeches. Shuyiman held a small stick of burning bamboo
to the bloated creatures and, as they released their grip on Isaac's skin,
pulled them off one by one. Then he removed Isaac's dirty jacket and
brought him a bowl of water to wash in.

Shuyiman introduced his wife, Khatoun, and their daughter Gulasha, a little girl who must have been six or seven years old and who stared at the two African men with astonished wide eyes through a tangle of dark hair that draped across her face. Then Shuyiman handed Isaac and David the sleeping baby boy, Kalu, and they held and embraced him in turns. Shuyiman had moved his family out of the only bedroom so that Isaac and David could sleep there. They were honoured guests. That first night, Isaac lay awake. It felt strange, lying on a reed mat in a dark enclosed space after months in the jungle. He heard Kalu crying softly in the room next door.

In the morning, he and David got a better sense of their surroundings. They were in a *basha*, a typical house of the Kaladan Valley. Its frame and floor were built of bamboo, and the whole structure was raised on stilts. The African men were confined to a single room, shielded from view by a blind hanging over the entrance to their door, but they could still manage to see something of the village from their new hiding spot. The weave and latticework of the walls had many gaps, and they would peek out through these, confident that nobody passing by – villager or Japanese – would realise they were there. They glimpsed water through the vegetation, and worked out that they were just yards from the banks of the Kaladan. A path ran past the house, parallel with the river, and they could see everyone who walked along it. There were a couple more *bashas* within their limited range of sight, identical structures to the one they were in. A few dozen houses built from bamboo, strung alone a muddy lane. This was all there was to Mairong.

Shuyiman brought rice and stew to them twice a day. Isaac was sure that his hosts were making sacrifices to accommodate them, but to his embarrassment he found that after months of deprivation he now struggled to eat more than a small amount, so he often returned most of the food that Khatoun prepared for them. Khatoun was soft-spoken and modest. He and David rarely saw her, but her voice grew reassuringly familiar, as did Gulasha's. When Khatoun finished cooking, Isaac could hear mother and daughter calling out to Shuyiman: '*Eh! Gulasha Bap, Eh! Gulasha Bap, bath kai, bath kai, bath kai!*' Shortly afterwards, Shuyiman would push aside the blind and appear smiling, carrying the food on banana leaves. They ate with their fingers. Once in a while, when he had some milk, Shuyiman would bring *cha*, tea, in a bamboo cane, jokingly referring to himself as the *cha-wallah*. Discreetly, each evening, he would remove the bedpan from the corner of their room.

At night, the village was quiet. There was no sound of radios, no distant engines or generators. Occasionally, a dog would bark or a jackal would scream in the distance, or Kalu would start to cry next door. Then Isaac would hear Khatoun's murmurs of comfort, and he pictured her holding her baby in her arms, rocking back and forth. He liked to think he was at home in Emure-Ile, where the nights were also dark and still, just as David imagined that he was in his own village of Rogbin. But sometimes here in Mairong there was a splash from the river, perhaps a fish leaping out of the water, or a trader drawing up in his *khisti*. They would wake with a jolt, and hold their breath until they felt sure that it wasn't the sound of a Japanese patrol. And then, as dawn broke, was that an Imam, a *Moulovi*, calling for prayers to Allah from the far side of the village? Isaac would strain to listen, feeling a sudden puff of wind as a bat fluttered across their room. Otherwise, there was silence. At night, he could make out one or two flickering lanterns swinging from the roofs of surrounding *bashas*.

Just as in the jungle, days passed into weeks, and Isaac and David faithfully marked them off on their bamboo calendar. From their *basha* spy-hole, they had a new clue about the passing of time. They noticed that on particular days the men who walked along the path wore their cleanest *longyis* and little white lace caps, while the women were in their smartest saris. Shuyiman, too, seemed to dress up for this day. And they were all walking in the direction from where they heard the *Moulovi* calling. It was *Jumaat* – the Muslim Holy Day, or Friday. Once they had worked this out, Isaac and David knew the day of the week, but they were none the wiser as to the actual date.

The morning after one such *Jumaat* Shuyiman rushed into their room. 'Japan, Japan, Japan!' he said, with a panic-stricken face. David was on his feet and Isaac was already crawling towards the door. Japanese soldiers had returned to Mairong. They were carrying out a house-by-house search. It was only a matter of minutes before they'd be at Shuyiman's door. Shuyiman and David carried Isaac down the ladder at the front of the *basha* and shoved him into the undergrowth. He crawled deeper into the vegetation, trying to keep up with David, scratching around for a safe place, thorns slicing into his face. David had rushed ahead. Where had he gone? Isaac realised he was only wearing his shorts; there had been no time to grab his jacket. But he had to press on.

He found himself lying face down in the reeds by the Kaladan River, just as he had on the day he'd been shot all those months ago. He sensed that David was somewhere nearby, but he could not see him. His mind raced with the possibilities. The Japanese must have received some information that had prompted their search. Had somebody betrayed them? In recent days, some of the villagers who had brought them food in the jungle had turned up at Shuyiman's house. Isaac thought he had heard the villagers asking Shuyiman about them. Two black African soldiers in a *basha* in the middle of a village – it was too fantastic a story to keep under wraps for long. If only, thought Isaac, he had insisted that they stay in the jungle.

It was dusk by the time they saw Shuyiman on the riverside path, making signals with his arms that all was well, and that they could emerge from their hiding place. That night, Isaac and David talked in hushed voices about the risk Shuyiman was taking. Isaac was in no doubt: if the Japanese were to find them in the hut, they would be killed, but so too would Shuyiman. The Japanese would make an example of him, argued Isaac. Shuyiman was looking after the enemy, and, from the Japanese point of view, that made him an enemy as well. Isaac's worries were not unfounded. Anthony Irwin, the British officer who survived the battle of the Admin Box, was a major with V-Force, the reconnaissance and intelligence operation on the Burma–India border. He described what happened to a Muslim village chief when the Japanese learnt he was supplying information to the British. 'They stripped him. They laid him down in the sun and then pinioned him to the ground with bayonets through his hands and feet, and then carefully, and with skill, they stripped the skin from his back and rubbed rock salt into the tortured flesh. His village was forced to watch this execution, and stay watching until he was dead, which, though he was over sixty, did not come to him until six hours later.' Shuyiman's fate would presumably be just as gruesome if the Japanese ever found his African guests.

In the nights that followed their narrow escape, Isaac listened carefully not just for any sound of the returning Japanese, but also for arguments between Shuyiman and Khatoun. By giving shelter to Isaac and David, Shuyiman was putting his entire family in grave danger, and yet Isaac never heard any serious disagreements coming from the other part of the *basha*. Khatoun remained a kind, but near-invisible presence. If she was anxious or angry about the effect all this would have on her family's safety, she did not seem to show it to Shuyiman in their home.

As the weeks progressed, Isaac came to think of Shuyiman as much more than a friend. Shuyiman had done everything in his power to keep him and David alive. He was their saviour.

The Second World War, through its scope and scale, spread violence and cruelty across much of the globe. Strangers killed or maimed strangers, sometimes at close quarters, sometimes, with the aid of mechanisation, in large numbers from a great distance. Invariably, soldiers didn't know the names of the people they were fighting, nor did they often care much for the others' race or culture. But amid this savagery, the war also created the occasional, wonderful tie between very different kinds of people. The bond formed by two Africans and a Burmese Muslim in the Arakan jungle was an unlikely but beautiful thing. They came from opposite sides of the world, they struggled to communicate with each other, and they faced seemingly insurmountable odds. Yet an attachment grew up between them, one that would inspire each of them for the rest of their lives. The war brought the basest of human instincts to the fore, but also the finest. Shuyiman found strangers in deep trouble on the doorstep of his own village, and he responded with compassion.

All of which does not mean that Shuyiman's actions were entirely selfless, or that he was not looking to the future. Isaac and David had the constant impression that the various villagers who had brought food to them in the jungle were hoping for a reward one day. Many eventually stopped coming, apparently disillusioned at the prospect of the British Army ever returning to the Kaladan Valley. Shuyiman was the exception, and he was at pains to remind Isaac that he had brought food after the others had given up. Later, when Shuyiman invited Isaac and David into his house, there were those in the village who thought he was being foolish, that he was taking an enormous risk that he would later regret. Shuyiman listened to these warnings, but shrugged them off. At home, he liked to tell Khatoun of the generous present the British would surely give him if they were to discover their wounded soldiers safely under his roof.

Shuyiman knew that he was taking a dangerous gamble, but he had calculated the odds, and, as the months passed, he grew increasingly confident that he had made the right decision. By October, the monsoon rains had begun to clear and traders working up and down the Kaladan Valley from Akyab and Kyauktaw brought news of the British advance following the battles of Kohima and Imphal. Time was running out for the Japanese. As he worked alone in the rice fields, Shuyiman thought carefully about what he was doing. He had a strong idea that it would somehow be *honourable* if the British were to discover the African soldiers in his house. It would show that he had been a good host, in a deeply hospitable culture.

If Isaac and David suspected some of Shuyiman's motives for helping them, there were others of which they were unaware. For Shuyiman was being swept along by events, which, he believed, compelled him to help the British cause in any way he could. When he and the other villagers had rescued Isaac and David in March 1944, they would have had every reason to doubt that the British were capable of winning the war in Burma. After all, the British had only just recorded their first-ever victory over the Japanese, at the Battle of the Admin Box. This had brought an end to the long list of defeats and retreats that dated back to the Japanese invasion of Malaya in December 1941, but it was far from a guarantee that the British would emerge triumphant. And yet the villagers of Mairong desperately wanted the British to win. This was because they were caught up in another conflict that tore through the Arakan in the early 1940s, one that pitted Muslims against Buddhists. The larger war between the British and Japanese had both influenced and encroached on this local struggle, and Isaac and David became unwitting beneficiaries of this overlap. Shuyiman had come to believe that the future of his family, his village and indeed all his fellow Arakanese Muslims, depended on a British victory over the Japanese.

Many Burmese had welcomed the Japanese invasion. 'Asia for the Asiatics', said Tokyo Radio, promising independence for the Burmese if they would co-operate in getting rid of the British colonisers. The British, after all, had toppled the Burmese monarchy in the 1880s, looted the Mandalay palace and ruthlessly suppressed revolts ever since, right up to the Saya San rebellion of 1930–32.

In 1941, the Japanese had transported a group of thirty Burmese nationalists to Tokyo, where they were given weapons and training. One of these 'Thirty Comrades' was a young man called Aung San. At Rangoon University, he had been an austere and socially awkward figure, but his passionate devotion to the overthrow of British rule and establishment of an independent Burma impressed both his contemporaries and the Japanese. Soon enough, Aung San was the leader of the newly formed Burma Independence Army.

When Japanese soldiers marched into Burma in January 1942, the soldiers of the Burma Independence Army were by their side. The two armies were greeted as heroes and liberators in the towns and villages where they arrived just as the British fled. '*Dobama!*

Dobama!' – 'We Burmans! We Burmans!' shouted Aung San's men and the welcoming crowds in unison. The Japanese, for their part, celebrated a victory for Buddhist solidarity 'over exploiters and blood suckers and devils who intended to hold East Asiatics in perpetual bondage'. A British general trying to stem the Japanese advance complained that the Burmese were providing the invaders with 'information of our every movement', as well as practical support in the form of guides, rafts, ponies and elephants. To the general's dejection, these were things the British 'could not get for love, and only with great difficulty, for money'.

The British watched the Japanese progress with a rising sense of panic, but there were many other groups in Burma who shared their fears. Burma was a diverse and fractured country, and the apparent sudden end of British rule evoked varied reactions among different peoples. When the British drew up Burma's borders in the nineteenth century, their primary concern was to keep out the French and Chinese, not to define the boundaries of a viable nation-state. The majority ethnic Bamar, also known as the Burmans, were concentrated in the central plain of the Irrawaddy River. But around this fertile and flat land was a horseshoe of mountains inhabited by the Karens in the east, the Shans in the north-east, the Kachins in the north, the Chins in the west and a myriad of smaller groups, many speaking mutually unintelligible languages. Under the British, these minorities enjoyed autonomy. They had willingly provided many of the recruits for a colonial army and police force. Christian missionaries, who struggled to make inroads with the devoutly Buddhist Bamar, had more success in the hills and mountains, finding converts among the Karens, Kachins and Chins. The minorities came to feel they had a vested interest in British rule, and some were prepared to fight to defend it. The Bamar, in contrast, felt the humiliation of colonial subjugation far more acutely. It was their kingdom that had been overthrown by the British, and it was primarily they who in 1942 rallied to Aung San's cause. As the Burma Independence Army advanced with the Japanese, there were attacks and massacres of

Karen villages, reinforcing the impression that this was as much an ethnic Bamar militia as a nationalist army.

There was another important group that feared a victory for Japan and Aung San's army. One of the defining characteristics of the decades of British rule in Burma had been a huge influx of immigrants from India; by 1942, they numbered more than one million. The Indians, with their understanding of both the English language and British administration, were better placed than most Burmese to take advantage of the opportunities offered by colonial rule. Alongside the minorities from the hills, they formed the bulk of Burma's pre-war army. Many of the Indian and Gurkha troops were, in fact, descendants of soldiers who had originally conquered Burma under British command during the nineteenth century. Indians also dominated other parts of the public services: the railways, post office, prisons, police and so on. In Rangoon, where Indians outnumbered Burmese by a ratio of almost two to one, Indian landlords owned much of the property and Indian shopkeepers and traders controlled commerce. Burmese living in Rangoon were advised to learn not only English, but also Hindi, if they wanted to advance their careers. There were also many Indian labourers, or 'coolies', doing manual work for pitiful wages, and, if successful Indians were resented for their wealth and influence, the coolies were despised for their poverty. Just like in East and South Africa, the Indians in Burma were the unassimilated middlemen of Empire, with their own distinctive languages, castes and religion.

During the economic downturn of the 1930s, the already strained relations between the Indian migrants and the Bamar took a marked turn for the worse. The farmers who had borrowed heavily from Indian moneylenders, the so-called *chettiars*, sank into debt when the price of rice plummeted during the Depression. When these farmers defaulted, as eventually many did, their land passed into Indian hands. Most of the soldiers who put down the Saya San rebellion were Indians. There were anti-Indian and anti-Muslim riots in 1930 and 1938, and, as the British retreated ahead of the Japanese in 1942, there were more attacks on the Indian community.

Some Indians were nationalists themselves, eager to see the end of the British Raj, but, as the Japanese and the Burma Independence Army closed in on Rangoon, fear spread through the entire community. The wealthiest were able to pay for passage out by sea, but the majority set off for the Indian border on foot, abandoning almost everything they owned. The Indians looked to the British Army for protection, only to find that the British were more intent on ensuring the success of their own retreat and would limit the numbers of refugees allowed on the roads. Tens of thousands of Indians died of starvation and disease on that journey; an estimated two hundred thousand eventually staggered over the mountains to Bengal and Assam.

In the pre-war years, the Arakan, behind the barrier of the Yomas Mountains, was something of an irrelevance to Burma's British rulers. Burma's most valuable products – rice, teak and oil – came from the centre of the country or the Irrawaddy Delta, and were exported through Rangoon.

An indigenous Muslim minority, Indian in appearance, had lived in the Arakan for centuries. But, during the more than one hundred years of British rule, Indians had also emigrated from the Chittagong region of neighbouring Bengal. The Arakan appeared to enjoy stronger ties with India than it did with the rest of Burma, according to one British soldier who visited in the 1920s. 'Akyab reads Indian and not Burmese newspapers,' he observed. 'It has four mails a week from Calcutta and only one from Burma.' In Akyab, prosperous Indian traders had built elegant houses. As a result of all this activity, the Arakanese Buddhists were growing 'apprehensive about the steady invasion of their country by hordes of Chittagonians', he wrote. The impending collapse of British rule offered the majority Arakanese Buddhists a chance to reassert their supremacy. Sectarian rivalry swiftly descended into bloody conflict.

Even before Japanese soldiers entered Akyab on 24 May 1942, Arakanese Buddhist gangs, some loosely affiliated with the Burma Independence Army, were plundering and murdering their way through Muslim villages, before setting them on fire. The Muslims retaliated in the northern part of the Arakan, destroying Buddhist pagodas and monasteries and carrying out massacres of their own. Anthony Irwin described the conflict in chilling terms: 'Whilst it lasted it was a pretty bloody affair. Where the Maugh [as the British called the Arakanese Buddhists] predominated whole villages of Muslims were put to the sword, and vice versa. My present gun-boy, a Mussulman who lived near to Buthjedaung, claims to have killed two hundred Maughs. For weapons they used a great two-handed Dahs, with a blade in some cases four feet long.' There was panic in both the Buddhist and the Muslim communities, and refugees fled in opposite directions. Muslims consolidated in the north of the Arakan, and Buddhists in the south. Irwin's V-Force, operating close to the Indian border, relied on Muslim support. 'If they see a British soldier lying wounded and lost in the jungle they will get him in somehow. If they see a Jap body, they will cut off the head and proudly bring it to me, demanding Backsheesh,' he wrote.

The Muslims around Kyauktaw fared particularly badly during the turmoil of 1942. 'A considerable number were massacred…and by the end of the year only a few thousand were left out of an estimated 40,000,' according to a British official. In January 1943, the British briefly recaptured Kyauktaw, during their first and ultimately unsuccessful attempt to retake the Arakan. Their advance set off a renewed wave of ethnic and religious violence around the town, which was now on a lethal fault-line between predominantly Muslim and Buddhist areas. A British official wrote that 'large numbers of Mohamedans bent on loot and revenge followed in the wake of our troops as they re-entered Buddhist territory'. One informer for the British wrote a vivid report of the triumphant mood among the Muslim militias at this time. They took *khistis* and *sampans* by force from the Buddhists, and 'related lively stories of their adventures to the admiring crowds of Muslims who received them wherever they went'. By February, the British military commanders in Kyauktaw were strongly advising their superiors that a battalion should be stationed there, specifically to keep the peace between Buddhists and Muslims. In the event, the British would soon be withdrawing. But nobody in the Arakan, and nobody around Kyauktaw specifically, could forget what had happened, and the tensions were still very much alive by the time the West Africans arrived the following year.

This explains why the Muslims were so pro-British. It also explains why many Arakanese Buddhists supported the Japanese – at least until the tide of the war turned. Isaac and David's great piece of luck, if that's what it can be called, was to have been shot and nearly killed next to Mairong, a village of Muslims who identified with the British cause – and were more than ready and willing to help them. For instance, on 2 March 1944, the same day as the attack on the 29th CCS, the civilian affairs officer with the 81st Division, a Major P. Burnside, wrote to his superiors: 'the Indians in the Kaladan have had a bad time and another lot of them around the mouth of the Pi Chaung were slaughtered after we evacuated in 1943!...Their cattle have been stolen and they have had to pay ransom. They are very glad to see us back but are still not sure that we are here for keeps.' If David and Isaac had been lying injured by a Buddhist village a few miles up- or downstream, they would probably have been turned over to the Japanese, or perhaps abandoned to a slow death in the jungle.

Isaac and David had the nous to further strengthen their bond with Shuyiman and his friends and family by pretending to be Muslim. It's difficult to know how important this white lie was in motivating the villagers to help the injured soldiers. British and New Zealand pilots who were shot down or crash-landed behind enemy lines elsewhere in the Arakan left accounts of how Muslim families went to great lengths to conceal and protect them, despite the risks of reprisals from the Japanese. But the communal violence in the Arakan would have created a heightened sense of religious solidarity, which Isaac and David used to their advantage.

The Japanese did fulfil their promise and granted independence to Burma in August 1943. The ceremony in Rangoon was grand, and the leader of the government, Ba Maw, dressed up in elaborate silks and gave himself the title of *Adipadi*, 'He Who Stands First'. Aung San was named his deputy, and the Burma Independence Army became the Burma National Army. But it was all something of a sham, a puppet independence recognised only by Japan and its Axis allies. Real power in Burma remained with the Japanese military, and their priority was the increasingly difficult task of winning the war.

The independence ceremony had produced a flush of patriotic pride, but Burmese dissatisfaction with their new Japanese rulers soon turned into a burning hatred. Khin Myo Chit, a young Burmese intellectual who had been a fierce opponent of British rule, wrote an extraordinary account of life under the Japanese. In it, she recounted innumerable instances of cruelty and torture, saying, 'I am glad for the people who died somewhere before 1942, for they never knew what Japanese rule was like.' Most feared of all were the *Kempeitai*, the Japanese military police. People who lived next to the *Kempeitai* headquarters in Rangoon would 'shudder as they relate the shrieks and howls which it was their misfortune to hear every night – shrieks of mortal fright and howls of deadly pain and agony'. And, although the Japanese spoke of pan-Asian solidarity, they showed little respect for native Burmese culture. In particular, the Burmese resented the Japanese practice of face-slapping anyone suspected of disobedience. 'This was regarded by the Burmese people as the greatest humiliation of their lives,' wrote Khin Myo Chit, who blamed the Japanese for 'a crass ignorance...for which they were soon to pay dearly'.

The economic situation, which had already grown precarious in 1943, worsened in 1944. Japanese soldiers seized whatever food they needed, and forced young Burmese men to build their roads, bridges and railways. Burmese women, desperate for food and clothes, sold themselves to Japanese soldiers. People began to say that 'the British sucked Burman blood but the Japanese went to the marrow of the bone'.

In the Arakan, the Japanese commandeered canoes and boats, depriving local people of their means of transport – indeed, in many cases, their means of making a living. An agent working for the British in the Arakan in early 1944 painted a bleak picture of life in the villages around Kyauktaw.

> The people here are very poor. They are in rags as they have had no clothing to purchase since 1942. There is no salt, matches, cooking oil and *ngapi* [fish paste]. Cattle have died in numbers due to Rinderpest and the shortage of bullock power has made rice cultivation impossible. They have just enough rice to live on as the Japs have taken away all their rice, poultry, pigs, cattle etc. They live on the land and the villagers are forced to give them all their requirements. The people are suffering from small-pox, skin diseases and malaria as there are no medical aid since the Japs came in. There is poverty and distress all over and the people are praying that the English may take over the place soon.

The agent was no doubt writing what his British masters wanted to read, but his account was consistent with many others at that time. It was into this situation that the West Africans made their advance down the Kaladan Valley.

The relationship between the Japanese army and Aung San's Burma National Army was also deteriorating. Burmese soldiers in training camps complained that their Japanese instructors were sadistic. When Japanese soldiers inevitably slapped Burmese recruits during their training, clashes broke out around the barracks.

The British disparagingly referred to the Burma National Army as the 'Burma Traitor Army'. In fact, Aung San was secretly developing plans to turn against the Japanese. By late 1944, when Isaac and David were still in hiding, British intelligence officers were in contact with Aung San, but urged him to bide his time. He did, and it wasn't until

March 1945 that his soldiers suddenly attacked Japanese positions in
the countryside near Rangoon. Overnight, in British military com-
muniqués the Burma Traitor Army became the Patriotic Burmese
Forces! Aung San's Burmese soldiers would fight against the Japanese
for the remaining months of the war, stressing their independence
from British forces through every battle they waged.

In the Arakan, the local militia that was affiliated with Aung San,
known as the Arakanese Defence Army, ultimately swung round to
the British side, as well. In May 1945, in the days after British soldiers
had recaptured Rangoon, General Slim met Aung San for the first
time. The two men got on rather well.

'"Go on Aung San"', wrote Slim in his memoir, with a famous
account of their conversation, '"You only come to us because you
see we are winning!" "It wouldn't be much good coming to you if
you weren't, would it?" [Aung San] replied simply. I could not question the truth of this...I liked his honesty. In fact, I was beginning to
like Aung San.'

However, these changes in fortune were still many months away.
For now, all that Isaac and David knew was that the war was getting
closer – uncomfortably so. They could hear planes above the *basha*
during the day, dropping their bombs and strafing targets in the hills
around them. One explosion was so loud that the house shook. The
planes had to be British, surely, as no one had seen or heard any sign
of the Japanese air force for many months. Sometimes at nights they
could hear the rapid fire of Bren machine guns, very different from
the slow Japanese 'woodpeckers'. It was impossible for them not to
be a bit hopeful, even as the fighting seemed to be edging up to their
doorstep. They noticed Shuyiman beaming with joy on some days;
that had to be a good sign. His friends had started to bring presents
of food to the house – plates of *gurugusa* and *murgi* curry – which
were shared with Isaac and David.

One night when the moon was full, Isaac and David looked
through the bamboo latticework and across the silver waters of

the Kaladan. A large boat was drifting downstream, packed full of Japanese soldiers. The men seemed to be standing still, lifeless almost. The following night, they saw more boats, with more Japanese soldiers, heading in the same direction. The signs were unmistakable. The Japanese were pulling back from the Indian border, and towards Akyab. It was a silent retreat, carried out under cover of darkness because it had become too dangerous for the Japanese to use the river during daylight. Three or four days later, Isaac peered through a small gap in the bamboo wall, and saw more Japanese soldiers, this time walking down the path at the front of the house. He stood there, transfixed, as they passed by, just yards away. They were so close he could smell their sweat. There were perhaps a dozen, their rifles on their shoulders, and ammunition slung round their waists. Their steps were heavy, their eyes dull and their faces unshaven. They marched right through the village of Mairong, and they never looked up.

Another week passed. The rice crop Shuyiman had planted when they were in the shelter was now ready for harvest, and he was working long days in the fields. He would bring Isaac and David cups of tea just before dawn, placing them silently by their mats, before heading out for the day. On this particular morning, the village was very quiet for some hours after Shuyiman had gone. It must have been about ten o'clock when Isaac and David heard the noise outside. It was a noise unlike any they knew. It sounded like people shouting, far off in the distance. They looked at each other in fear and moved back to the shadows at the far side of their room. But was that also cheering they could hear? Whatever the noise was, it was getting louder and louder, and it was coming in their direction. And then it was right outside the *basha*. Suddenly, someone threw open the blind.

Khatoun and Gulasha were standing in the doorway. Khatoun was laughing and praying and telling them to go outside, all at once. 'Get out, get out!' she said. Isaac was pinned to the far corner of the room, shielding his eyes from the bright sunshine. 'Come out, why?' he asked, even as she implored them to follow her. It made no sense, but they went anyway. David was first and Isaac crawled behind.

Outside, Isaac blinked and struggled to focus – he had not been in bright light like this for nine months. Nor had he seen so many people for a long time. For they were surrounded by a crowd, and now it wasn't only Khatoun, but everybody in the village of Mairong who was laughing and praying. Gulasha was jumping up and down beside them. All these smiling faces, all these arms reaching out to touch and feel them. It seemed as though everyone had known in which house they'd been hiding all this time. After the months of darkness and whispers, of secrets and fear, David and Isaac were finally being welcomed into the village. And only then did they understand why.

The crowd that had been pressing against them had parted. A soldier was walking towards them, with a smile of disbelief on his face. He was holding his hands out, in what looked like a gesture of peace. He was wearing a British uniform.

10

HOME AGAIN

||||||||||||||||||||||||||||||||||||||||||||||||||||||||||||||||||||||||||||||||||||||||||||||||||||||||||||||||||||||||||||

The most famous ballad of all is 'Home Again'. The intensely home-loving African sang it as he embarked for India; he sang it during the voyage, and he will greet his native land with it when his ship steams into Lagos Pool or Freetown Harbour, and there will be many a British soldier, too, who will sing it as he sights the shores of home.

Victory Magazine, 23 July 1945

||||||||||||||||||||||||||||||||||||||||||||||||||||||||||||||||||||||||||||||||||||||||||||||||||||||||||||||||||||||||||||

December 1944
Burma

The next few hours, days even, took on a dreamlike quality for Isaac. He could vaguely recall he and David hugging each other, and whooping with joy. They shouted 'Hallelujah! Hallelujah!' and 'Praise the Lord!', instantly forgetting that as far as the villagers were concerned, they were fellow Muslims.

There was so much to do. Khatoun immediately arranged for a party to fetch Shuyiman from the fields, while Isaac and David were desperate for information from the British soldiers. There were about a dozen of them, a small patrol from an Indian regiment that had been probing forwards ahead of the advancing 81st Division. Isaac's first question to them was what date it was. Their answer was 6 December, almost Christmas. He and David laughed. According to their calendar, they were sometime in late August. Out by four months. Then Shuyiman showed up from the fields, full of joy. He clasped their hands, smiled from ear to ear and dashed into the *basha* to wash and hurriedly change his clothes.

That at least was how Isaac remembered the day. David had a slightly different but no less colourful account of their rescue. It placed Shuyiman at the centre of the event, and went like this:

> In the month of December the 6 this man
> [Shuyiman] saw our patrols (Indian troops) in
> this village he ran to them and said 'Are you
> English soldiers?' The patrol NCO said 'We are
> English Troops.' This old man then said to these
> people, 'Oh my Indian friends, for nine months
> I had kept two wounded Africans under enemy
> condition. Please come and take them away'.
> The troops ran into the house with gladness.
> They shouted 'Praise be to God'. They brought
> us to our African friends once more.

Rescued. In those final few weeks, as Isaac and David heard the British planes and as they watched the Japanese retreat, they had struggled to suppress their rising optimism. Deep in their own thoughts, they had each reached the same irresistible, incredible conclusion. But an unspoken rule had formed between them that they would not discuss it, not speculate on how it might happen. It seemed safer, somehow, to stick to the same morbid topics they had dwelled on for these long, long months. What would the Japanese do to them if they were captured? Would they be shot straight away, or tortured first for information? Isaac had expected no mercy. The Japanese would see that they had made a mistake by not finishing him off the first time. They would not waste a second opportunity. Finally, he could banish these dark fears. Because Khatoun was still laughing, and Gulasha was still skipping round them. This was really happening.

The villagers were raising the hands of the soldiers in the air and ruffling their hair, and the soldiers were smiling bashfully in return. Everyone was speaking so fast that Isaac was struggling to understand what was being said. It was the corporal leading the patrol who called an end to the celebrations. He wanted to pull back from Mairong. He didn't have many soldiers, and nobody from the village could tell him with any certainty whether the Japanese were nearby. It was too risky to stay, and, in any case, the patrol was already a notable success. He organised two of the villagers to carry Isaac on a stretcher, and they were off. Just like that.

Isaac didn't recall saying goodbye to Khatoun or Gulasha. But one image stayed with him. When he lifted himself on his elbows to look back from his stretcher, he saw mother and daughter standing in the midst of the happy crowd, outside a *basha* on the banks of the Kaladan, celebrating a small miracle in the middle of this incomprehensible war.

The soldiers were already on their way back to their camp. David followed, and behind him were the stretcher-bearers carrying Isaac. Next came Shuyiman, and a ragtag group of men and women and many small children, who were forced to run to keep up with the soldiers' pace. At the edge of the village, the corporal told the crowd to disperse; only Shuyiman and the stretcher-bearers were allowed to accompany them any further.

They had a long walk ahead of them and it was evening by the time they arrived at the British camp. They had stopped at one point when they suspected a Japanese patrol was passing nearby. Isaac watched the Indian soldiers fan out into the bush, clutching rifles, machine guns and grenades. It was a false alarm. Their good fortune had not left them.

The camp was like a beehive. Everywhere, there were men digging trenches, unloading mortars from boxes, rushing from one company to the next with orders. There must have been thousands of soldiers, although the camp was skilfully designed to blend into the jungle. Isaac and David were taken to the field hospital, and an officer soon came to see them and offer congratulations. Word spread, and another and then another officer came to talk to them, each armed with a great smile and a thousand questions. Company commanders, battalion commanders, brigade commanders; all of them wanted to see and hear what Isaac and David had to say. One of them – was it a brigadier? – hugged Isaac and gave him a packet of Sea-to-Sea cigarettes and a bunch of bananas. Isaac was suddenly conscious of how filthy he was. He was still wearing the jacket that Shuyiman had given him months ago, just after they'd been robbed in the jungle. His hair was once again wild and unkempt. He stank. Yet here were these British officers, queuing up to embrace him.

But what of Shuyiman? He had been called away in all the confusion, soon after they entered the camp. General Loftus-Tottenham, the divisional commander, had heard the news, and had sent for the Muslim villager who had sheltered the two West Africans. Isaac and David expected that Shuyiman would return to the field hospital, but it was now dark, and they started to wonder whether he would be able to find them, in the warren of paths and camouflaged positions that made up the jungle camp. Time passed, and Isaac's fears grew. He wanted to tell Shuyiman that they owed him everything. He wanted to say farewell. But they never saw him again. Even amid the excitement of their rescue, this failure saddened him.

They slept that night on stretchers, underneath warm blankets, but the following morning Isaac and David were on the move again. This time, Isaac was carried by four stretcher-bearers, with a second team standing ready to take over as soon as they tired. They travelled all day, and slept again in the jungle. After dark, they heard shooting coming from across the valley. The soldiers dived for cover in the narrow trenches, which they'd dug when they'd stopped to make camp for the night. In the confusion they left Isaac out in the open, on his stretcher. He lay there, watching the tracer fire pass over his head, feeling strangely unperturbed. He had been through so much, what could possibly hurt him now?

The shooting stopped, and the shelling began. The Japanese gunners had got their range, and they were giving it everything they'd got.
Again the soldiers jumped into the trenches, and, once more, Isaac
lay there, listening to the shells, starting with a distant, soft bump,
like the sound of someone kicking a football far away, then a second
or two of silence, followed by a shrieking sound that got louder and
louder, and finally a crashing, grinding explosion in the jungle nearby.
Sometimes the shells landed in a *chaung* beneath their camp, and the
shriek would be capped by an almighty splash and spray. There'd be
a short pause, and then the whole thing would start up again, with
the distant, soft bump of the football being kicked. It was too much.
Isaac hauled himself off the stretcher and looked for a place to hide.
There, he saw it: a hollow at the base of a big tree, as far away from
where the shells were coming as he could manage on his own. He
huddled down in it. And that was how he spent his last night in the
Arakan, his last night in Burma itself.

At midday the following day, they arrived at an open paddy field.
There were hundreds of West African soldiers there, working hard
to level out the ridges of the field and fashion a rudimentary airstrip.
At one side of the field, from the cover of some trees, artillery and
mortar teams were firing in the direction from which the Japanese
had been shelling during the night. Isaac and David may have been
rescued, but the war was carrying on at full tilt. Out of the clear
blue sky a little Moth plane suddenly appeared, intent on making its
bumpy landing on the hastily cleared land. Isaac and David were to
be evacuated by air, but the Moth could only take one passenger at a
time. Another soldier had been severely wounded during the shelling,
his head bandaged, and he was the first to go. It was an hour before
the plane was back.

Isaac was loaded on board, lying on his back with his feet jammed
into the tail of the tiny compartment. As the plane took off, Isaac
craned his neck to see the jungle beneath him. It was the first time
he'd flown in an aeroplane. The pilot stayed low, so as to make it
harder for the Japanese to shoot them down. He lit a cigarette, and

then passed one back to Isaac. Soon, though, the dark-green jungle gave way to lighter-green paddy fields, and then a golden band of sand. Tears were streaming down Isaac's face. 'Am I free? Am I free?' he said, again and again. He had to pinch himself to believe it was real. Before he knew it, they were on the ground and he was being pulled from the plane and onto another stretcher. He raised his neck and could see palm trees, and beyond them the sea. As he was carried away, he turned to look back at the plane. The pilot, still smoking, was grinning and giving him the thumbs up through the cockpit's open window. The propeller never stopped. The pilot was already turning the Moth around so that he could take off and fly straight back to the jungle strip to pick up David and bring him here too.

They were in India, where they would spend the next three months, moving from one hospital to another, always heading in a westerly direction. On that first evening, near Cox's Bazaar, a Sikh nurse disdainfully removed Isaac's jacket and threw it in a dustbin. He bathed Isaac with warm water, soap and a sponge. Later that night, lying on a clean bed, under clean sheets, with a mug of tea and plate of warm food, Isaac found that he was crying again. 'Am I free? Am I free?' he was still asking the nurses who passed by his bed. They must have taken him for a fool, he realised. Their smiles were weary but sympathetic.

A few days later, Isaac and David were on a Royal Navy ship headed up the Bengali coast with other wounded soldiers. On board, Isaac shared his story with one of the sailors. 'Eh! One of our African boys speaks good English and has a hell of a tale,' said the sailor. In no time, officers and men were crowding round Isaac's bedside and begging him to relate his adventure once more. He didn't need too much persuasion. He was the centre of attention, and he loved it.

They spent Christmas near Calcutta, at what was known as a convalescent depot, with hundreds of other injured African soldiers. The Army laid on entertainment, with singers, dancers, conjurors and magicians, even a concert party all the way from Ceylon, attending to the soldiers' spirits, if not their wounds. During the screenings in the cinema, a British officer noted that, whenever the Africans saw a scene in which a man and woman were alone in the same room, they cried in amazement, shouted ribald comments and sometimes shrieked with laughter. The war in the jungle seemed far away.

The Emir of Katsina, one of the traditional leaders of Northern Nigeria, was sent by the British to bolster the morale of African troops in India and Burma. He arrived at the convalescent depot with an entourage of handsome dark men in long white robes and turbans, and presented magnificent leopard skins to the drummers in the depot's marching band. The British and Indian nurses admired them, and the Nigerians felt proud of their distinguished visitors. When the emir returned home to Nigeria, he faithfully conveyed the wishes of the soldiers whom he'd met, telling the newspapers that the men wanted 'more letters from their friends and relations and particularly from their wives they left behind'.

Isaac and David wrote long letters home, letting friends and family know that they were alive. In fact, the good news had already reached Nigeria. An eager and attentive reader of the official news-letter for the colony, the *Nigeria Gazette*, might have noticed the following announcement in small print on 1 February 1945: 'The undermentioned, who was previously reported missing has been located with our Forces. NA/46573 Pte. Isaac Fadoyebo.' Unlike some of his counterparts in other parts of Nigeria, the district officer in Owo did not have many military recruits coming from his area, so, as soon as he was alerted by Lagos as to this unexpected develop-ment in the case of Private Fadoyebo, NA/46573, he dispatched the messenger boy back to Emure-Ile. Again, the boy cycled as fast as he could up the hill from Owo, with another brown envelope stamped with the red crown. This time, the telegram said, or so the villagers would remember, that the British 'had seen' Isaac Fadoyebo once more. He was very sick, but recuperating, in a hospital in India. The traditional ruler, the *Olowo* of Owo, Oba Olateru-Olagbogi, also sent a message to Emure-Ile after he had spoken to the district officer and felt assured of this happy news. But Joshua and Ogunmuyonwa could not shake off their doubts. Joshua had long ago decided that official announcements were one thing; seeing was quite another. The Nigerian soldiers had set out for Burma such a long time ago, and he had not yet heard of a single one that had returned home. Why should he hold out any hope for *his* son?

Maybe somebody also tried to alert David Kargbo's parents in Rogbin. In the *Sierra Leone Gazette* of 8 February 1945, one Sgt Kargbo SL / 109486 had mysteriously slipped across from the 'Wounded and Missing' column to the merely 'Wounded' column, but had anyone noticed this? David's family had hardened their hearts. They too had come to believe their son was dead, and, anyway, newspapers rarely found their way as far as Rogbin.

Isaac and David were pleased to receive a visit from a group of their friends from the 29th CCS. This delegation brought a gift of money, raised from within the unit, to give thanks for the two heroes' survival. Everyone wanted to congratulate Isaac and David and hear their story first-hand. The 29th CCS had been evacuated from the jungle shortly after the attack, and had spent a quiet war, treating sick and injured soldiers in hospitals in India, far from the battlefront. In fact, the disaster that befell the 29th CCS had taught the British a lesson: jungle warfare called for more mobile and better-defended medical units than a casualty clearing station could provide. For the remainder of the war, troops in Burma were supported by smaller field ambulance units, which performed necessary surgery and provided other emergency care in the jungle until an injured patient could be carried to an airstrip for evacuation.

The excitement of the reunion was tinged with sadness. Isaac and David confirmed what their colleagues had long feared: that Archibong Bassey Duke had died, and so had others, including David Essien, Moses Lamina and Major Murphy. As for Captain Brown, nobody had any news at all, and there was every reason to fear the worst. The same too of the hot-headed Tommy Sherman, who had disagreed with the captain from the Gambian regiment and taken his fate into his own hands when he walked off alone into the jungle.

The Sierra Leonean men also brought bad news for David: they had heard his parents had claimed back the dowry from the family of his fiancée; he did not have a young bride waiting for him at home after all. Isaac tried to comfort David, pointing out that they were lucky to be alive, and that he would surely marry another woman when he got back to Sierra Leone. But David was inconsolable, and bitter. 'They should have waited,' he insisted, 'they were not told I had died, they were told I was missing!'

David and Isaac had other visitors, who came with official demands. A British intelligence officer ordered them to compile a report on their experiences. 'History of Our Nine Months Hiding Under Japanese Quarters' was written by David, with Isaac's approval. Just over two pages in length, it was broadly consistent with Isaac's own memories, which he would write down many years later, although, as an official document, it does not focus on their private hopes and fears. David spent a good portion of the report in describing the Japanese attack on the 29th CCS and the capture of Captain Brown and in listing the names of the dead.

David wrote that, after he and Isaac were shot, they were interrogated on the banks of the Kaladan by the Japanese, but they resolutely refused to give away any information. 'They all came to us asking, "Where are our English officers?" We answered "We have no English officers and we do not want you to ask us any questions for we prefer to die than to speak with you".'

But, if the tone is sometimes suspiciously self-serving, there is also generous praise for the man who rescued them. David emphasised the debt that he and Isaac owed to Shuyiman. 'This Indian Mohammedan sacrificed his life to feed us until the time comes when we shall be able to see our own people.' He even included a crude version of their friend's address – *Shuyiman, Gulasha Bap, M Village, Burma* – in the optimistic hope that this would be enough information for any British official who might want to find Shuyiman and give him some sort of reward. The report ended with a flourish, and a tribute to their Muslim saviours in the Arakan:

Oh my African brother, do not forget the Indian
Mohammedans for they are not enemies, but
friends. We are afraid of the Japs for we have
seen them and studied them. The land of
Burma shall be Britain's and not Japanese possessions. We have experienced Japs tricks but
they are all in vain.

Writer SLA/109486 Sgt David Kargbo

Approved by NA/46573 Pte Isaac Fadoyebo

The doctors and nurses at the convalescent depot were instructed to
get the African soldiers back on their feet as quickly as possible, so that
they could return to their units. But many of the soldiers were thinking of home, and it turned out they had an important ally on their
side. Major Savage, a doctor with the Royal Army Medical Corps, was
remembered as an immensely caring man. He was of mixed Scottish
and Gold Coast ancestry, and was married to a woman from one of
the Gold Coast's leading families; he would live in Accra after the
war. He did his best to ensure that his African patients at the depot
were repatriated and not sent back to the Arakan. Not that Isaac and
David were ever in any danger of such a fate. The severity of Isaac's
injuries, the length of their ordeal and the disbandment of the 29th
CCS all made them high-priority cases for repatriation.

In early 1945, Isaac and David travelled back across India, to
the military hospital at Poona. David, as an 'up patient', was free to
leave the ward and explore the town whenever he wished. Isaac, who
needed crutches to move around, was put under the care of a British
doctor, one Lieutenant Colonel Neil, a dedicated and compassionate
man. After examining Isaac's leg, Neil told him the news that he had
long feared: he would never be able to walk properly again. However,
Neil hoped that, by removing Isaac's broken right kneecap, he would
be able to straighten the crooked leg. With luck, said the doctor, this

would enable Isaac to walk without crutches, or even a stick, albeit with a permanent stiffness. He urged Isaac to study the gait of one of the elderly colonels in charge of the hospital. This colonel also had a stiff right leg. He would often walk up and down the wards, looking over the patients and giving Isaac many opportunities to scrutinise his bearing.

In the event, Isaac's operation was only partially successful. He had his kneecap taken out. That had gone to plan. But his leg, now in plaster, assumed an awkward bow shape, and a fortnight later the doctors decided to carry out a second operation. Isaac was in such pain that he needed to be put under anaesthetic simply to have the plaster removed. He woke up after the second operation to find his leg in plaster once again, and with livid red blood stains already seeping through. But the curve had been corrected. On his many subsequent visits to Isaac's bedside, Neil encouraged him to believe he would make a good recovery.

Slowly, with comfortable sleep and regular meals, Isaac began to feel like his old self. His shattered body was recovering, and so too was his mind, after the months of tension and strain. He played board games, and enjoyed long, drowsy afternoons. One day, he was touched to receive a Yoruba Bible through the post – a gift from Major Moynagh, the commanding officer of the 29th CCS back in Sierra Leone. Isaac was now, for the first time since he'd signed up for the Army at the end of 1941, beginning to see beyond the end of the war. He would soon be returning to civilian life. He was not sure what career to pursue, nor whether his disability would get in the way of his plans, but, lying in that hospital in India, he felt some of his old resolve coming back. His first ambition once he got home, he decided, was to build on his few years of education and resume his studies. He would persevere, and he was ready for a struggle.

In the middle of March, Isaac and David were on the dockside at Bombay, surrounded by other wounded West Africans, all waiting to board a hospital ship for home. Some of the men were blind. Some had lost limbs. Others seemed to be mentally incapacitated. More than a year and a half had passed since the West African contingents had disembarked on these same docks with the task of protecting the British Empire from the Japanese invaders. Each of these men had survived the Burma campaign, but some had been broken in the process.

Isaac was carried aboard on a stretcher by four friendly Italian prisoners of war who, despite their lack of English, managed to express sympathy in their own language, and showered him with cigarettes. They took him to his cabin, shook his hand, and left, talking loudly among themselves.

It was also in March 1945 that the 81st Division finally pulled out of Burma, to recuperate in India. During the division's second offensive, the West Africans had advanced, once again, down the Kaladan Valley, driving the Japanese back in a series of small battles and skirmishes. And, once more, they had marched long distances for months on end, supported by the Allies' air forces. Otherwise, they had been cut off from the rest of the British Army. In that sense, the West Africans had fought something of a private war.

One of the strangest moments came on 9 December, a few days after Isaac and David's rescue. On an airstrip deep in the Kaladan Valley, British officers organised a cricket match. They called it the 'Kaladan Lords', and arranged for bats, balls, stumps and pads to be flown in by Moth planes. The players wore jungle green and the game was played to a background of mortar and small-arms fire. There were frequent interruptions as planes flew in and out, throwing up clouds of dust that made play impossible. Some African soldiers watched the game, bemused. But Lieutenant Colonel Philip van Straubenzee, a great cricket enthusiast from a distinguished Yorkshire military family who had been assigned to the Sierra Leonean regiment, wrote, 'despite the Jap mortar fire great enjoyment was had by all'.

The long-awaited prize of Akyab, the port at the mouth of the Kaladan with the important airfield, finally fell into British hands on 3 January 1945. The Japanese, surprised by the speed of the West

African advance, feared they would be trapped, and had pulled out a few days earlier, which allowed British and Indian soldiers to land on the beaches unopposed. They found deserted Japanese bunkers as well as Japanese graves. The jetty at the port was damaged beyond use, the harbour silted up and full of wrecks. The soldiers looked round what was left of the town, and saw that British bombing raids had destroyed much of Akyab. One British official wrote: 'I estimate that about 98 percent of the buildings are damaged to some extent ie considerably more than had been estimated from appreciations of air photographs....The whole town was overgrown with jungle, only a few streets being comparatively free from it, and this enhanced the impression of utter desolation.' A small number of frightened Muslims were living in the ruins. They pleaded with the British to send more soldiers quickly, to avoid a repeat of the communal massacres of 1942. Akyab's pre-war grace was gone for ever, but the British were relieved to have it in their hands. And the town's capture was a victory for the West Africans, even if they had not been there to take it themselves. According to one senior British general, 'the battle that might have been fought on Akyab's beaches had already been won in the jungles to the north'.

Instead, the 81st Division was preparing for its final battle in and around the jungle- and mist-shrouded hills of the historic city of Mrauk U on the Kaladan floodplain. Established in the fifteenth century, Mrauk U had been the capital of the old Kingdom of Arakan, where Portuguese and Dutch envoys paid tribute to a monarch who had grown wealthy through trade across the Bay of Bengal. Mrauk U's political and economic influence had long since waned, leaving the ruins of dark stone pagodas and temples. Their steps were covered in grass and weeds, their walls thick with emerald-green moss. Inside, rows of stone Buddhas stared stoically at whoever arrived with offerings. The Japanese had used Mrauk U as an administrative centre, and turned some of the temples into brothels for weary soldiers.

By this stage of the war, the Japanese were in no position to mount a counterattack. Their forces were depleted and many of their troops had already been transferred away from the Arakan to the central Irrawaddy Valley, where their generals were trying to stem the advance of General Slim's army towards Rangoon. By now, a whole new contingent of West African soldiers, the 82nd Division, had also entered the Arakan, and they shared in the capture of Mrauk U. The 82nd Division would carry on fighting until the Japanese surrendered in August, and most of its men would stay in Burma until well into 1946. Hundreds of Africans would be killed in these last months of the war; the Japanese may have been retreating, but they fought tenaciously until the very end.

The West Africans' campaigns were barely covered by the Allied war correspondents and photographers, for whom they held no glamour. British soldiers in Burma famously dubbed themselves the 'Forgotten Army', but what did that make the West Africans? John Hamilton wrote with frustration that they were the 'forgotten flank of the forgotten corps of the "Forgotten Army"'.

General Slim, blessed with the common touch that endeared him to his men, had made an effort to get to know the 81st Division before it advanced into Burma. But thereafter he was rather distant from the African troops, and never visited the soldiers fighting in the Kaladan Valley.

At the end of 1945, a Nigerian soldier, Lance Corporal John Ejirika, wrote to his officer to say that he had just seen the film *Burma Victory*, the official documentary account of the defeat of the Japanese, commissioned by the Supreme Commander of Allied Forces in South East Asia, Admiral Lord Louis Mountbatten. Lance Corporal Ejirika was dismayed by the film; not one African made an appearance in it. 'Only Indian, American and English troops were seen there. No record of African hard fighting in Burma even in Kaladan Valley where we lost so many African troops,' he wrote. The omission was all the more surprising given that British army cameramen had gone to great lengths to shoot some fascinating footage of West African soldiers in Burma in 1944–45. Yet, not a single frame was included in *Burma Victory*. No wonder a British officer wrote, with some bitterness, that the 81st Division 'went in anonymously, marched out anonymously, and it seems they have left anonymous dead behind them'.

Where the West Africans did attract media coverage – in Indian newspapers and official Army newsletters – they were invariably portrayed in a hackneyed and paternalistic manner, much as many of their British officers treated them. They were the 'Happy Warriors', singing and carefree. 'To the African, singing is almost as vital as his food or the rifle with which he fights,' reported *Victory* magazine. The *Madras War Review* said they were 'High spirited, gay, fond of joking and singing...at heart a simple, kindly and immensely strong people...They enter into everything with zest – that is the secret of the Africans and why they are loved...The humour, loyalty and optimism of the African soldier is irrepressible and infectious.'

The truth, of course, was more complex than such hoary racial stereotypes, and there were occasions when African soldiers did not make friends on the ground. On 26 February 1944, when Isaac was in the ruined riverside town of Paletwa and about to set out on his ill-fated raft trip down the Kaladan, a British civilian affairs officer, Captain De Glanville, was also there, busy compiling a report on the behaviour of the African troops. He wrote: 'in a day or two the last of the West Africans will have moved out of this area and there will be a sigh of relief from the coolies, villagers and myself'. The Africans had impressed the locals with their fighting qualities, and those in the infantry battalions were well disciplined, but many others, thought Captain De Glanville, seemed 'to have a touch of klepto-mania', brazenly stealing anything they wanted, including livestock and rice. The villagers were apparently terrified of the Africans, and with good reason. De Glanville observed that 'there have been three cases of rape true and undetected and one attempted rape of two women aged between 60 and 80', then noted 'this was the last straw and scandalised the locals'.

Similarly, Robert Mole was in the Burmese colonial service, and working in the Northern Arakan in late 1944 as a civilian liaison officer in an area recaptured from the Japanese and placed under the control of West African soldiers from the 82nd Division. He saw how the Nigerians, with their habit of bathing naked in the river, sometimes frightened the local population. (This had also been the practice of Japanese soldiers, who had likewise offended Burmese sensibilities.) More seriously, Mole said, Arakanese villagers came to him with numerous complaints about how they were treated by the West Africans. In one incident, soldiers went on a rampage through a village that had refused to supply them with women. They killed three people, he wrote, and set fire to many houses.

By the time Isaac and David set sail from Bombay, the outcome of the war in Asia was no longer in doubt, even if a Japanese surrender seemed some way off. In Europe, meanwhile, the Nazis were all but finished. The Mediterranean was safe for Allied shipping, and so the hospital ship took the injured men back to West Africa through the Suez Canal, instead of going round the Cape. It sailed unescorted; the convoys, the Navy protection and the zigzags through the sea that the troopships had used on the outward route were no longer necessary.

Isaac's journey home was blissful. He could move round the ship on crutches, and the British nurses and doctors, he recalled, were wonderfully kind. Some of the soldiers liked to play the guitar, or gather round tables for long games of cards, but Isaac was happiest sitting on the open deck. There he would enjoy the sunshine, whiling away the hours mesmerised by the white surf of the breaking waves and the dolphins that occasionally leapt out of the water around the ship's bow.

They travelled up the Red Sea – 'not red at all', one confused African soldier noted – and then through the Suez Canal, where they sailed past brightly dressed crowds of Egyptians waving from the shade of the palm trees. At Port Said, the ship was surrounded by traders in canoes, who frantically shouted up to the deck hoping to catch a soldier's eye and sell him some fruit, a basket or a dress for a wife or girlfriend at home. Much later, they stopped at Casablanca. They were heading south now, and the air grew warmer once more.

Isaac was resting in bed when David Kargbo came to his cabin. Overnight, the ship had arrived in Freetown harbour. There was something evocative in the breeze that morning, but it was only when Isaac looked out of the cabin window and saw the green mountains that he recognised it: the pungent scent of the West African coast, of smoked fish, rotting vegetation, human sweat and tar. Fragments of voices and laughter drifted up from the water, 'Oh how are you, my dear friend?' 'Are you in good condition of life?' 'How de body?' The questions were coming from dark figures in dugout canoes and launch boats bobbing on the waves beneath the ship. Many years later, Isaac would remember this moment. His writing style was always rather stiff and formal, but his account of David's departure hints at a sudden sadness that overcame both men:

> He came to me, shook my hand, and said: 'Isaac we have to part here. Goodbye. May God Bless You.' He spoke in a voice touched with emotion. I was speechless for a while and later I got up, gave him a big hug, and in a depressed and reflective mood I said: 'Cheerio Sergeant Kargbo. May God help you.' Minus his assistance I would have died of sheer starvation. He was the one doing the begging for bread and water to keep our bodies and souls together when we were in hiding in the jungle.

Then David was off, boarding one of the launch boats. As it pushed away from the hospital ship towards the harbour, it turned in a gentle arc and cut through a little fleet of wooden canoes still waiting to take on passengers. Isaac watched its progress from his cabin window. Everyone on board was waving, David standing prominently in the prow. Behind it were the mountains, white clouds draped over the lion peaks. At their foot, a muddle of sun-bleached clapboard and gables reached up the slope – Freetown, just as Isaac had first seen it in 1942. A song carried from the launch boat across the water, back to the hospital ship, its sad beauty initially clear, then becoming fainter and fainter:

Home again, home again
When shall I see ma home?
When shall I see ma native land?
I shall never forget ma home,
My farder be dere
My mudder be dere
When shall I see ma home?
When shall I see ma native land?
And never more to roam, oh, oh

11

GREAT AWAKENING

|||||||||||||||||||||||||||||||||||||||||||||||||||||||||||||||||||||||||||||||||||||||||||||||||||||||||||||||||||||||||||

This war has brought about a great awakening...The African...has been in the Middle East, Sicily, Arabia, Syria, Iran, Abyssinia, Madagascar, Ceylon, India and Burma. He has met not only the British, but also the South Africans, Americans, French, Greeks, Italians, Australians, Germans, Arabs, Egyptians, Mauritians, Sinhalese, Indians, Burmese, Chinese, Poles, Russians in Teheran, and other races like the Dutch, and he is learning from every one of them...

Robert Kakembo,
An African Soldier Speaks (1946)

|||||||||||||||||||||||||||||||||||||||||||||||||||||||||||||||||||||||||||||||||||||||||||||||||||||||||||||||||||||||||||

24 April 1945
Lagos

It was on a Tuesday afternoon, at two o'clock in the afternoon, that Isaac's ship docked at Lagos. The soldiers on board had left the city anonymously almost two years before, but they were given a warm welcome on their return. The Band of the Nigerian Police, lined up on Apapa wharf, played 'For They Are Jolly Good Fellows' and 'God Save The King', and a large and eager crowd – not deterred by what one newspaper called a 'broiling sun' – surged forward as the ship drew close. The great and the good of Lagosian society had turned up – colonial administrators, generals, budding local politicians, bishops, prominent businessmen and lawyers – white and black rubbing shoulders together. The most senior British official in Lagos at the time, His Excellency Sir Gerald Whiteley, had the honour of boarding the ship first and inspecting the soldiers. He was followed up the gangway by a posse of journalists, who swarmed all over the ship looking for injured men to interview.

The journalists knew that this homecoming was front-page news. The war might have seemed like a somewhat abstract affair to many Nigerians, but here was a chance for these determined reporters to show how their fellow countrymen had paid in sweat and blood. The soldiers on that ship were some of the first to return from Burma. They were living proof that Nigerians had played their part in the great fight against the dictators of Nazi Germany and Imperial Japan. 'The men were in high spirits and their faces beaming with joy as His Excellency and party went round the wards,' wrote the *Nigerian Daily Times*. Its editorial, 'Heroes from Burma', said Nigerians should be proud of their wounded soldiers, and 'appreciate the grimness of the ordeals they have had to pass through in their campaign against the Japs – the little yellow savages'. The *West African Pilot*, less inclined to toe the official line, noted that the men were in 'various stages of deformity but, nevertheless, genuinely and spontaneously cheerful'. The nursing orderlies, the *Pilot*'s correspondent added, were 'men from the counties of England and charming English maidens who seemed to have stood up well to an experience which perhaps men will never know till the war ends'.

The first journalist to talk to Isaac was, by coincidence, an Owo contemporary from the 1930s. Anthony Enahoro, the son of the headmaster at the government school, came from a more privileged background than Isaac, and, at the time when many young men were joining the Army, Anthony was a pupil at the elite King's College in Lagos, where 'he read as much as he ate' according to a friend, devouring every single book in the school library. In the past few years, Anthony had become interested in politics, often missing classes to attend meetings organised by the fiery lawyers and journalists in the capital who were beginning to demand an end to British rule. Now six feet tall with a round handsome face marked by an intense stare and scholarly glasses, Enahoro was a rising star of the newspapers with a growing reputation as 'the angriest young man in Nigeria'. Dressed in a white short-sleeved shirt and matching white trousers, he briskly strode onto the hospital ship, saw that Isaac's leg was in plaster, and asked him directly whether he would ever regain its full use. When Isaac replied that he would not, a cloud passed over Enahoro's face. It was as though, thought Isaac, Enahoro was asking himself why a young man should be permanently maimed in support of a cause that meant so little to Nigeria and its future.

At Enahoro's instruction, Isaac's war experience featured prominently in the *West African Pilot*'s report the following day. The paper's account was more or less accurate:

> One man had a stirring story of pathos and drama to relate. He was Private Isaac Fadoyebo of the Nigerian Medical Corps, who left Lagos in July 1943, bound for the Burma inferno. When his party fell into the hands of the Japanese Fascists on March 2, 1944, they did not find sanctuary until December 6, when they were aided by some Burmese peasants. Had it not been for the fact that the party of West Africans feigned unconsciousness, the Japanese guard who came daily to inspect them might have done something tragic.

For Isaac, it was a moment of fleeting fame in a lifetime spent largely in respectable obscurity. None of the other injured soldiers on board – who, according to the *Pilot*, included a shell-shock victim from Benin and a man from Calabar who'd had his toes amputated by the Japanese – were named in the newspaper reports. Even in their own country, Nigeria's soldiers were largely anonymous.

At three o'clock, Sir Gerald finished his inspection. The police band was ordered to continue running through its repertoire of marching songs while the big moment, the disembarkation of the wounded, finally started. Most climbed down the gangway without any assistance. The blind – 'never to see the land they love again', wrote the *Pilot* – were guided down to the wharf. Last came the stretcher cases, carried by the teams of stretcher-bearers who had been left waiting and wiping sweat from their brows this whole time. The soldiers were loaded onto ambulances and driven to the nearby military hospital at Yaba. The public, held back by the police, strained for a glimpse of the war heroes. They looked at us, Isaac thought, with respect and amazement.

None of those waiting on Apapa wharf that afternoon could have imagined that the British Empire was so close to collapse, and few would have had any intuition of the political changes that were about to sweep across their continent. Britain may even have appeared stronger than ever to many in Nigeria and the other African colonies – victory in the war was all but assured, and the King's mighty ships were starting to carry His Majesty's soldiers home. When Japan surrendered, Lagos society came out to celebrate. There was a 'Great Victory Dance' at Glover Hall (admission: four shillings, with promises that the bar was 'fully stocked for a grand celebration') and special events at the Island and Polo Clubs. The Victory Service was held on 19 August in the neo-Gothic splendour of the Cathedral Church of Christ on the Marina. The church was packed, maybe two thousand British and Nigerians crammed in together, rows of fluttering hand-fans barely stirring the hot and still air. The Bishop of Lagos, A.B. Akinyele, gave a rousing address, comparing the Empire to the great rock at Akure, the granite inselberg that rises over the Yoruba bush not far from Isaac's village of Emure-Ile. 'So long as the British Empire remain steadfast on the Rock of Age,' said the bishop, 'that Empire shall never perish.'

There were many soldiers in the congregation that day, and the generals who had led Nigerians in Burma assumed the sun would not be setting on their Empire any time soon. The service included a special message from Lieutenant General Montagu Burrows, the Commander in Chief for West Africa, who described the triumph of the Allies as the greatest victory in the history of mankind, in which 'the achievements of the West African soldiers are now famous throughout the Empire'. Major General Hugh Stockwell, who had led the 82nd Division in Burma, was blithely confident about the future. He looked forward to seeing a new generation of African soldiers 'uphold the traditions of their fathers when taking their place alongside other soldiers of the British Commonwealth of Nations in the furtherance of Imperial strategy'.

Not everyone was prepared to accept that things should just carry on as before. Maybe it was Anthony Enahoro, upset about Isaac's injuries, who wrote the leader in the *West African Pilot* entitled 'Welcome Heroes!' It said that the Nigerian journalists who saw the injured soldiers 'felt an intrinsic pride that, after all, backward though some of us had been labelled in certain quarters, we had done our humble bit and fulfilled our fair share in the effort not only that democracy might live but also in order that the stature of man might be revived'. In other words, some Nigerians sensed that a new world order was coming, and they felt they deserved to be part of it.

Just eight years after his brief encounter with Isaac on the Apapa wharf, the same Anthony Enahoro, by now a politician, would stand up in the Nigerian parliament and move a motion for independence from Britain. A decade further on, Britain would have left most of its African territories, including Nigeria, and was making final preparations to quit the remainder. To many of the African soldiers who'd fought for King and Empire, this must have been an astonishing, and deeply confusing, turnaround. And yet it was the war itself that was the catalyst for change.

Britain had won a pyrrhic victory that had reduced its place in the world. At the end of the fighting, it was economically exhausted, like all the other old European powers. In the general election of July 1945, the British people voted Winston Churchill out of office. The

Isaac Fadoyebo. 'I saw people joining the army, and I followed suit. Not knowing that I was heading for trouble.' (courtesy of Fadoyebo family)

Left: David Kargbo. He and Isaac clung to life – and cheated death – together. (courtesy of Ramatu Kargbo)

Right: Major Robert Murphy, Isaac's commanding officer, pictured on his wedding day before the war. (courtesy of Veronica Brennan)

West African recruits take an oath of loyalty to King and Empire, Zaria, northern Nigeria. Most West African recruits signed up for money and adventure. (courtesy of Jill Hopwood)

Sizing up whether a recruit is soldier material. British officers said Hausa soldiers 'had very good physique'. (courtesy of Jill Hopwood)

Training in Nigeria before the journey to India, 1943. General Woolner said his soldiers were 'absolute beginners'. Regardless, they would be taking on the Japanese. (courtesy of Jill Hopwood)

The West African
81st Division
marched long dis-
tances through the
dense, hilly Arakan
jungle, carrying
loads on their heads.
(Imperial War
Museum)

Above: Mrauk U, capital of the
ancient Arakan kingdom, and
site of a key victory of the West
African troops in Burma.
(PHOTOBYTE / Alamy)

Left: Traditional *basha* near the
Kaladan River, the Arakan.
Shuyiman's house was built in
this style. (© John Warburton-
Lee Photography / Alamy)

Left: Soldiers welcomed home from Burma at Lagos, Apapa docks, 1946. When Isaac arrived the previous year journalists swarmed over his ship, hoping to collect their war stories. (courtesy of Jill Hopwood)

Right: Proud soldiers parade through the streets of Lagos. In the words of Robert Kakembo, 'the war has shown the world that we are men, and given the opportunity, we are a match of anybody else in the world'. (courtesy of Jill Hopwood)

Prime Minister Tafawa Balewa (at right) addresses the nation at Nigeria's Independence Ceremony, 1 October 1960. Princess Alexandra looks on. (Time & Life Pictures/ Getty Images)

Tokunboh Street, Lagos, As Isaac would have known it in 1954...
(courtesy of Jill Hopwood)

...and in 2013 (Barnaby Phillips)

Post-colonial hospitality: Isaac (middle row, far left) and other Common-wealth civil servants at a training course in England, 1969 (courtesy of Fadoyebo family)

Family man: Isaac, Florence, and all their daughters, c.1970 (courtesy of Fadoyebo family)

A memorial to the African
soldiers who died in
Burma to save the Brit-
ish Empire, in Taukkyan
Cemetery near Rangoon
(Barnaby Phillips)

Shuyiman's grandson,
Roshi, and son, Adu,
Pagoda Hill, June 2011
(Barnaby Phillips)

Sittwe, June 2011. A few months later, the town would be convulsed by fighting between Rakhine Buddhists and Muslim Rohingyas. (Barnaby Phillips)

Isaac tells his story, Emure-Ile, Nigeria, 2011. (Barnaby Phillips)

new Labour government would concentrate its scarce resources on building a welfare state at home, rather than on defending an Empire abroad. The United States and the Soviet Union, the new undisputed superpowers, vied to spread their influence, but both were vocally opposed to old-fashioned European imperialism.

Nigeria's educated elite, keen readers of the *Pilot*, had drawn their own conclusions from both the conduct of the war and its consequences. They read of how the civilised white man had bombed cities and committed unspeakable atrocities; in many parts of Europe, the people had been reduced to starvation and begging. They read about the Atlantic Charter, which, at America's insistence, proclaimed 'the right of all peoples to choose the form of government under which they live'. And they read that Britain had decided to give India complete independence once the war was over. This last piece of news, according to a British intelligence officer in Nigeria, created 'an electric shock throughout Lagos'. If India could have it, then why not Nigeria? That was the inevitable question, and the British did not have a satisfactory answer.

During the war, Nigeria, like several other British African colonies, had suddenly become a much more important place. There was global demand for its rubber, palm products, tin and cocoa, its ports were busy handling massive convoys on their way to Asia, and, of course, some 120,000 of Nigeria's young men had enlisted in the armed forces, of whom about one-third ended up in Burma like Isaac. These men had left their hitherto isolated villages and towns and been exposed to a whole new world – many had set off merely looking for adventure, but all of them would be changed by their experiences.

The African soldiers had crossed two oceans, encountered an ancient civilisation and emerged victorious in a struggle with a mighty enemy. They had risked their lives alongside British and Indian soldiers. They had seen that, when put to the ultimate test, all peoples, regardless of colour, share the same mix of qualities and frailties that make us human: courage and cowardice, wisdom and foolishness, altruism and selfishness.

Britain had depended on Africa and African soldiers to save its Empire, but had not necessarily understood all the consequences that would follow. The soldiers came back as travelled, more confident men. Some were prepared to criticise aspects of colonial society, and a few to even question its existence. Robert Kakembo, the Ugandan author of the censored booklet 'An African Soldier Speaks', put it eloquently:

> Having fought for liberty, equality and for all the four freedoms expressed in the Atlantic Charter, we are determined not to remain behind in the world race. We have every right to claim a share in the future advantages and opportunities of development. We have a very long way to catch up with the senior races, but the war has shown the world that we are men, and given the opportunity, we are a match of anybody else in the world. I speak with the Rt. Hon. Winston Churchill:
> Give us the tools and we will finish the job.

So had the British actually sown the seeds of their African Empire's dissolution? By defending their imperial interests in the short run, did they ultimately undermine them?

Waruhiu Itote was not yet twenty years old when he joined the King's African Rifles in 1941. He signed up out of boredom and poverty, but also because of the British propaganda that warned that his homeland, Kenya, was in danger of being overrun by Germans and Italians, whom, he would write in his memoir, 'we could only imagine as the worst monsters on earth'. And yet Waruhiu had already felt the injustice of British rule in Kenya, from the seizures of land by white settlers in the Highlands, to the separate public toilets for different races. There was much about the Army that he would also learn to dislike. He was frustrated at the discrepancies in pay between African and British junior officers and humiliated by the separate messes and lavatories. But it was his experiences in Burma that would turn him into a nationalist and committed anti-colonialist. A young British soldier, lying by his side in the jungle, asked him why Africans were fighting to protect the Empire, rather than fighting to free themselves. '"At least if I die in this war," the British man said softly, "I know it will be for my country. But if you're killed here, what will your country have gained?"'

In Calcutta, a black American soldier gave him further reason to doubt his choice, warning him that the British who fought in the war would always be heroes in their own country, whereas the Africans would quickly be forgotten. Waruhiu also met an Indian nationalist in Calcutta, who told him that Africans should have demanded independence in return for fighting on the British side, just as the Indians had done. Each of these encounters, Waruhiu would later write, made him think of himself as Kenyan for the first time. Travelling to India and Burma had helped him understand where he came from, and what needed to change in his homeland.

By the time Waruhiu returned to Africa, he was determined to help bring independence to his people. He would go on to become a leader of the Mau Mau movement, adopting the nom de guerre 'General China' in a guerrilla campaign to force the white settlers from his native Kikuyu land.

By December 2009, John Nunneley must have been one of the last men alive in Britain who could say that his father had fought in both the Boer War and the Great War, and he was surely the only one who had led a future Mau Mau general through the jungles of Burma in 1944. He still had clear memories of Corporal Waruhiu Itote crouched in a foxhole beside him, clutching his rifle and peering through the jungle in anticipation of a Japanese attack. Waruhiu was 'a good looking young man, diligent...an almost silent presence in the officer's mess, responding to orders, "Whisky and soda, please"'. It was only natural, said Nunneley, that Waruhiu went on to try to remove the British from Kenya: 'why shouldn't he harbour those thoughts?'

During the Mau Mau rebellion, Waruhiu would use the same tactics in jungle fighting that the British had taught him in Burma. Many of the soldiers, white and black, who pursued him through Kenya's mountain forests were former colleagues from the Second World War. He was eventually caught and sentenced to death. But the British decided not to execute him. His life term in prison became more comfortable when a district officer recognised him from their time together in Burma and insisted that Waruhiu be released from solitary confinement.

Waruhiu Itote was not the only African soldier who said that his travels to India and Burma had converted him to nationalism. The political atmosphere in India was extremely volatile in the early 1940s, as the British struggled to control the 'Quit India' movement. Marshall Kebby from Nigeria recounted how he went to see Mahatma Gandhi give a speech at the Madras racecourse. Kebby travelled there by bus, the only black soldier among a million Indians, and managed to make his way to Gandhi's side, he said. He asked him what he was going to do for Africa now that India was on the verge of being free. Gandhi replied that India would give Africa moral support, provided the struggle against the British was not violent. The day made a profound impression on the Nigerian. He said, 'Gandhi taught us that the worst home rule is better than the most benevolent foreign rule. We wanted freedom first, before anything else.'

Whatever the fears of British officers, the vast majority of African soldiers were unlikely to pick up subversive ideas from Indian nationalists. They had few opportunities to meet ordinary Indians, and it was rare that they shared a language in common. African soldiers were overwhelmingly illiterate and from rural backgrounds. Most came from conservative regions, such as Northern Nigeria with its strong tradition of loyalty to local emirs, and it was to these conservative regions that they returned when the war was over. Back in his remote village, without decent road or rail connections, much less a telephone, such a soldier was not in a strong position to challenge the colonial order, even if it had occurred to him that he should. Instead, the agitation for independence came from small and educated groups in the cities – lawyers, doctors and newspaper publishers who had gone to secondary school and even university, and most of whom, if anything, looked down on military service during the war. This was the elite that Isaac had aspired to join in 1941 when he asked his father to pay for him to go to a prestigious secondary school. It was his father's initial refusal that had impelled him to volunteer for the Army. Military service was the option Isaac had grasped only when other doors had closed on him.

Isaac had expected to die in Burma. On his journey home, he was relieved simply to be alive. But the mood of many other African soldiers at the end of the war was not so benign. After they withdrew from Burma in March 1945, Isaac's colleagues in the 81st Division were transported to a camp near the town of Karvetnagar, some one hundred miles from Madras. It was a bleak and isolated place. 'The whole area appeared under-populated and decaying,' John Hamilton wrote, and 'few Indians were to be seen and those almost all looked half-starved.' Initially, the British generals had planned to give the West Africans a period of rest after their time in Burma before sending them on to Malaya, the next colony they were aiming to recapture from the Japanese. Thankfully, the Japanese surrender on 15 August 1945 made this plan irrelevant. Soldiers from the Gold Coast stationed near Karvetnagar celebrated with the slaughter of a bony bullock, much beer and dancing. It was time to go home.

But the Africans would discover that they were not a priority. Britain's shipping resources were stretched, and officials in London decided to concentrate on first bringing home British soldiers, as well as the tens of thousands of British prisoners-of-war who had suffered in camps in Singapore and Malaya. The Africans waited in India, with little information as to when they would be travelling, and their resentment grew. It wasn't until the end of 1945 that the British made any ships available for the 81st Division. 'One cannot help but wonder what would have happened if British troops, after more than a year in the jungle, had been stuck for nine months or more in bamboo huts on a featureless, hot and dusty plain remote from anything more closely resembling civilisation than the railwayman's club at the nearest junction,' wrote John Hamilton.

The soldiers watched films while they waited. They saw newsreels showing the aftermath of the atomic bomb in Hiroshima, which horrified them. The Nigerian soldier J.O. Ariyo attempted to put the devastation into context for those back home. 'Man will kill himself by his own hands,' he wrote, 'if one of these bombs lands in Lagos, within one minute, all the people up to Ota, all the trees and all the animals, will just disappear. Even those in Abeokuta would not escape the aftereffects. The following day, another bomb would make Ibadan disappear. It wouldn't be long before all of Nigeria disappeared.'

Aside from mulling over such grim thoughts, the West Africans had precious little by way of distraction. To make matters worse, many of the division's British officers had managed to secure passage home, leaving behind their bewildered and resentful troops.

Most of the 81st Division showed remarkable patience during this long hiatus, but, in October 1945, a mutiny broke out involving several hundred soldiers in the Sierra Leonean regiment. The Sierra Leoneans chased and beat up their commanding officer, and were threatening to kill another. When they tried to raid the armoury, they were beaten back by a group of Gambian soldiers. The dispute that sparked off the trouble, a disagreement over a special haircut allowance, was relatively trivial. Some officers were convinced that their men, who suddenly began to refer to their commanders as 'Britishers', had been 'got at' by Indians hostile to the Raj, though many of the mutineers simply complained about the long delay in their repatriation. Some ninety were arrested; a portion of these men were sentenced to prison in a court martial. A British officer, writing almost forty years later, was still deeply saddened by the memory. The mutiny was, he said, very unexpected, 'a devastating blow to our pride in what we regarded as a cheerful, hard-working and disciplined unit'.

That was not the end of the unrest. Headley Vinall, a soldier attached to the 82nd Division who had repaired wireless radios behind the frontlines in Burma, wrote in his diary that West African soldiers went on strike in October 1945 as they waited to sail from Bombay to the Gold Coast. Then, in the days before the soldiers embarked on a Dutch troopship, the SS *Ruys*, on 6 November, Vinall feared there was 'plenty trouble brewing'. By 11 November, he was writing that his prediction had come true, and that the main instigators of the disturbances would have to be taken off the ship by armed guards. The SS *Ruys* put in at Port Said on 14 November, where eighty British soldiers armed with machine guns and 'stacks' of military police were called in to quell the trouble. One policeman was stabbed, and fifty African soldiers were arrested.

Hugh Lawrence, also in the 82nd Division, was in Burma until April 1946, when he returned to West Africa with his Nigerian soldiers. On the journey home, he had the definite impression that the men had run out of patience; 'they started being less punctilious with their manners'. When they eventually arrived in Lagos, Lawrence found the streets full of soldiers who had just disembarked from India. 'I was very struck,' he said, 'by the fact that, as I walked past these chaps on the streets, nobody saluted me, they didn't see me. They'd had enough of the Army and wanted out. I don't think it was an anti-British sentiment, but they'd had enough of Army discipline.'

Life after the Army often proved to be disappointing to these West African men. Whatever hardships the soldiers had endured in India and Burma, they had at least had the security of an income, decent food and housing. Now the British sought to dissolve their African army with, if anything, even greater haste than they had recruited it. Britain was bankrupt, and so the pre-war principle – that each of the African colonies should be physically and financially responsible for its own defence – was quickly re-adopted. This meant a rapid scaling down of the enormous force that had been built up during the war. By the end of 1946, more than 160,000 West African soldiers had been demobilised, almost two-thirds of them from Nigeria.

The vast majority of war veterans returned to farms in rural areas, but there were others who had been hoping for paid employment, and the chance to use newly acquired skills. Robert Kakembo wrote that these soldiers 'have learnt the value of money and they have been taught to love necessary luxuries – things like cinemas, wireless broadcasts, newspapers…Toilet, soap, hair cream, razor blades, cigarettes are becoming indispensable in a soldier's life… The African must get a reasonable salary to enable him to get some of these things at least.' The British imposed some quotas, forcing companies to employ a proportion of ex-servicemen, but the supply of jobs could not meet the demand. In 1947, just under half of the demobilised soldiers in Nigeria were listed as unemployed. Many felt that they had been badly let down.

Letters from African soldiers to their British officers in the years after the war testify to their frustrations. Gyam, from Ashanti, in the Gold Coast, wrote to John Hamilton in January 1947. He had been on a waiting list for a post office job since the previous May, but had 'given up all hope of being employed there'. He had gone on a training course but felt he was being given menial tasks: 'the ex-servicemen who attend the course do all the nasty works there. We learn practically nothing…There is not much happening in this country at present,' he reported to Hamilton. A former soldier from the Gambia also wrote to Hamilton, expressing his alarm at shortages of soap and rice, 'just like we did not finish the war in Burma'.

Across Africa, soldiers were complaining of woefully inadequate gratuities and disability allowances, and that promised pensions had not materialised. In Nigeria, the *West African Pilot*, not a newspaper to understate the situation, described the ex-servicemen's plight: 'Our World War II veterans must be made to enjoy the fruits of victory just as they were made to pass through the furnace of horror, by baptism in the crucible of savagery and by communion in the vortex of the whirlpool of human and mechanical barbarism'.

In 1948, in the Gold Coast, the anger of the former soldiers boiled over. On Saturday, 28 February, the Ex-servicemen's Union marched to Christiansborg Castle in Accra to present a petition to the governor that complained of the high level of unemployment among their members and demanded larger pensions for the disabled as well as the payment of war-service gratuities. Policemen blocked their way and opened fire, killing three former soldiers, including one Sergeant Cornelius Adjetey who had fought in both World Wars and had recently returned from Burma. Dozens of other protestors were injured. The very men who'd risked their lives for Britain lay on the ground, dead and dying. Riots broke out in Accra and several other towns, and British-owned shops and businesses were burnt and looted. Victor Nunoo, a Burma veteran remembered, 'every white man we saw, we had to stop him, beat him and burn his car...any white man's store, we had to break it, loot it. I took part in this myself. We became furious. It turned us back into reliving our experiences in Burma – that war type of madness.'

The historian Basil Davidson wrote, 'looking back it may not seem much in comparison with the tumults of the world today. But the effect then was shattering. There went up in the smoke of those burning stores the whole myth of the model colony, law-abiding and content, always prepared to be patient and respectful in its every-day behaviour.'

The British responded by arresting leading local politicians, but their bluff had been called; they had neither the means nor the desire to rule the Gold Coast by force. British officials in Nigeria agreed to an immediate request to send soldiers to the Gold Coast, but soon began to worry about the consequences for the whole region. When they were asked to send reinforcements a few days later, a senior civil servant in Lagos wrote in his diary, 'I am opposed as there is always a danger of the trouble spreading and we are getting too thin on the ground.'

A new, emboldened nationalist movement emerged in the Gold Coast in the aftermath of the riots, in the form of Kwame Nkrumah's Convention People's Party (CPP). The CPP toured the countryside with loudspeaker vans, used clever posters and slogans and made bold appeals in the newspapers. In fact, it used the same tactics, and often

186 Another Man's War

the very same personnel, that the British had relied on to mobilise support for the war only a decade earlier. In 1957, the Gold Coast became the first British colony in Africa to achieve independence, with Nkrumah as its president.

This was probably not what the former soldiers who marched on Christiansborg Castle that February day had envisaged. They were certainly frustrated and disillusioned, but their grievances were more economic and social than overtly political. They were thinking about their own welfare, not freedom for the Gold Coast. But, by the time of independence a few years later, the ex-servicemen had already become part of Ghana's national story – they were the 'Burma Boys', and remembered as freedom fighters. The three who died were now seen as having paid the highest price in the noble cause of liberation. They had become martyrs.

It wasn't only in the Gold Coast that former soldiers were hailed as heroes of the nationalist struggle, and, as the years passed, it might have become difficult for them to claim otherwise. In his old age, Marshall Kebby from Nigeria insisted that 'every soldier who went to India got new ideas and learnt new things. He came back with an improved idea about life. We the ex-servicemen gave this country the freedom it's enjoying today, we brought this freedom, and handed it over to our people.'

Isaac's experiences were less romantic. Even after his return to Lagos, he rarely thought about politics, or questioned Nigeria's place in the Empire. Neither did a majority of his friends or family. In the 1940s, he recalled, people from Lagos still liked to boast they lived in a Crown Colony – 'we're in the Colony!' – whereas the rest of Nigeria was a mere protectorate.

A new breed of Nigerian nationalist was emerging – the likes of Nnamdi Azikiwe, Obafemi Awolowo and, of course, Anthony Enahoro – and they would soon inspire others to join them. It was these men, who didn't go to Burma, who campaigned for independence, not the likes of Isaac Fadoyebo, who did.

★

On a fine morning in Emure-Ile in August 1945, Isaac's mother Ogunmuyonwa woke up early, with a feeling of happiness that she could not explain. The news of the Japanese surrender had not reached the village, and, anyway, what would it mean to her? And yet she had a strong premonition that something was about to turn out well. In the market, she bought a large bag of bush-meat, to prepare a stew with onions and peppers. She returned to her house to cook.

Isaac stood on the back of the Armels Transport lorry as it bumped down the dusty road from Osogbo. Through the forest they went, jolting to a halt when they reached a village in a clearing. People got on and off, possessions were handed down and lifted up, but he barely noticed all the comings and goings. He held on tight to his new bicycle and was wrapped deep in his own thoughts. The weeks since he had returned to Nigeria had been difficult. At the military hospital in Yaba, the British doctor had removed Isaac's plaster, and taken X-rays of his leg. He showed Isaac the damaged femur. The doctor said that, if Isaac had been able to arrange an improvised splint straight after the attack, he might have stood a chance of making a complete recovery. Still, Isaac had been lucky. The bullet had passed within a whisker of his femoral artery. If the artery had been hit, or later severed by the sharp pieces of broken bone, Isaac would have bled to death. The challenge for him now was to try to walk on his stiff leg without the assistance of a stick or crutches.

His first steps in the hospital had been slow and tentative, and he leaned clumsily on the doctor to stop himself from falling over. He was, he thought, like a little child learning to walk for the first time. Day after day he had practised, until he reached the point where he could hobble up and down the ward by himself and without a stick. The doctor congratulated him. For the first time in fourteen months, Isaac was walking unassisted.

He left the military hospital, and at the beginning of June he was formally discharged from the Army on medical grounds. But much to his frustration his leg swelled up once more, and so the Army arranged for him to be sent to a civilian hospital in Ibadan. His wound had again turned septic, and the doctors removed a small fragment of dead bone. Despite the objections of a nurse, a British doctor insisted that Isaac should be treated in the 'clerks' ward' instead of the general ward. It was, Isaac noted with satisfaction, an honour to be in what he called a 'VIP apartment'.

Despite his limited mobility, Isaac had been relieved to discover that he could ride a bicycle well enough. Granted, he was still perfecting his technique, but he was pleased with his purchase. It was something to show for his earnings as a soldier. Now, at last, he was going back to his village, to see his people.

He banged on the side of the lorry, and the driver came to a halt, surprised. 'How can I stop for you here? No house, only bush!'

But Isaac knew exactly where they were. 'Never mind,' he said, 'I beg, pass my bicycle.'

The lorry drove off in a cloud of dust, leaving Isaac alone under the mango trees, with the bicycle and a large suitcase. Emure-Ile was about a mile away, down a track that descended into the gentle valley to the north. He saw a labourer walk by, a road-mender on his way back to his camp, and offered him four pence to help carry the load. 'Why not?' replied the road-mender. And so Isaac went ahead, limping but pushing his bicycle, and the road-mender came behind, the suitcase on his head. He had not walked such a long distance since he had left hospital, but he was determined to return to his village on his own feet. The sun was low in the sky. He smelled the dust and wood smoke, he heard the wail of the plantain eaters, he saw the hornbills gliding high overhead. It had been more than two years.

It was his sister, Adedeji, who first heard the commotion. People seemed to be shouting, up by the track that ran past the Anglican church. She wondered why, and went outside. A young man with a bicycle was coming down the hill, walking in a strange way. He looked like Isaac, only taller and thinner. But it was unmistakable now. The crowd was saying his name, again and again: 'Isaac, Isaac, Isaac.' Part of her wanted to run towards him, part of her wanted to run back to the house, to fetch her mother. But Ogunmuyonwa must have also heard something, because she had already come out of the house, and was running up the hill. Mother and daughter ran as fast as they could towards the young man with the bicycle.

Ogunmuyonwa could not believe it. It was her son, the son she had loved and then mourned. She embraced Isaac, then fainted and fell to the ground. Someone poured water over her, Isaac wasn't sure who. Now it was his father, Joshua, who was hugging him so tight that it almost hurt. There were drummers, and people were dancing, and a procession was forming round him, as they approached his family's house. He tried to push his way through the crowd, but it was no use. 'So many people,' he would love to say for the rest of his life, 'you would have thought I had stolen a goat!' Some people were shouting that he had come back from heaven, but there were others who were frightened, who said that he was a ghost. 'It was as if a dead man was back to life – resurrection of a sort,' Isaac later wrote. He stood in the middle of the tumult, happy but also confused. He had sent them letters. They should have been expecting him. They must have known he was alive.

Only later did he find out that his letters had been greeted with disbelief. In the village they had simply said, 'If he is alive, where is he?' Isaac understood their scepticism, when he played it over in his mind. After all, what did Emure-Ile know of the World War? How could he explain to them everything he'd seen? Of ships and oceans and far-off cities, of the jungle and the fateful Kaladan River? How could he ever describe the anguish and despair, the courage and the friendship, of the days, weeks, months, after the attack? All they knew in Emure-Ile was that Isaac was the only one who had gone from their place to fight, and that the *Oyinbo* had brought them a letter saying that he was missing. Then, some months later, they sent another letter saying he had been seen. But no one had seen him in Emure-Ile, despite the passing of so much time – until today.

The crowd stopped Isaac from going into the house. They chanted, '*Ma wọ'le, ma wọ'le!*' – 'Do not enter, Do not enter!' Emure-Ile had mourned the loss of Isaac. Now the villagers needed to perform a ritual, to confirm that he was not a spirit, before he would be allowed to cross the doorway of the family home. He could not resist them. In fact, he longed for their acceptance, to belong in his own village once more. They threw dust at him. If he were a ghost, he would disappear, but, if it were really Isaac, the dust would stick to him. And so they all bent down to fill their hands. He saw his grandmother, Aleke, bending down with them. Then the red dust of Emure-Ile was in Isaac's eyes, in his throat, on his sweating black skin. He was choking. But the dust stuck to him, and he did not disappear. He was not a ghost, just a young man who had cheated death and come home.

12

THE CRIES TURN TO LAUGHTER

||||||||||||||||||||||||||||||||||||||||||||||||||||||||||||||||||||||||||||||||||||||||||||||||||||||||||||||||||||||||

Your son went to the army
You were crying
The soldier returns now
The cries turn to laughter.

Popular Yoruba verse at end of the war

||||||||||||||||||||||||||||||||||||||||||||||||||||||||||||||||||||||||||||||||||||||||||||||||||||||||||||||||||||||||

August 1945
Lagos

There are some very old people in Emure-Ile who still remember the day when Isaac came back from the war, though they disagree on what had happened to him while he was in Burma. There are those, the majority in fact, who say that he returned with a limp because he had fallen out of an aeroplane while flying over the jungle and landed awkwardly in a tree before being rescued by passing hunters. His sister, Adedeji, would confidently dismiss that story, and share her own version of events. 'He was shot with another soldier,' she said, 'and a farmer found them in the forest. He hid them behind a big tree, and brought them bread. They lay there, beaten by the rain, exposed to the sun, their hair like Bob Marley people. Then one day a British helicopter was flying over. The farmer blew his whistle so the helicopter pilot would hear him. It landed, and flew them away to

Bombay.' Whatever had happened, everyone agreed that Isaac's return was one of the most memorable days in the history of Emure-Ile. 'There was joy on everyone's face,' said Olajide, a cousin of Isaac's, who was twelve years old at the time. 'Absolute joy.'

Joshua arranged the slaughter of his fattest goat. Family and friends feasted long into the night, and those who could not squeeze into Joshua and Ogunmuyonwa's house danced on the street outside. Isaac would remember the tears that filled his grandmother Aleke's eyes. She had visibly aged in the time he'd been away, and she looked tired. When he held her, he too began to cry. She told him, 'I knew I will see you alive before leaving the world, and now that you are back home it is time for me to bid you all farewell.' She said she had never given up, because the traditional oracles and fortune-tellers that she'd consulted had always insisted Isaac was alive. One had even told her that Isaac had been threatened with a knife, and was left in just a pair of shorts. Now that the oracles had shown themselves to be true, she was at peace. Aleke would die six months later in her sleep.

The only person for whom Isaac's return seemed to be bittersweet was Joshua. He was overwhelmed to have his son back, but could not hide his dismay when he learnt that Isaac would be disabled for life. 'Nineteen years old, this is not the start in life you need,' he said. He wished he could have handed over one of his good legs in exchange for Isaac's damaged one. Isaac remonstrated, 'Baba, what can we do? Let us just thank God that I'm alive.'

Early the following day, the two men walked to the Anglican church and prayed. Afterwards, Joshua said it was only on this second day that he really believed Isaac had returned; the previous evening had been too much like a dream. Still, he worried about Isaac's leg, and pleaded with him to visit a village healer. Isaac refused, saying, 'I was not prepared to have my leg further mutilated by traditional healers.' He tried to reassure Joshua. The Yorubas believe in destiny, Isaac said, whatever God has decided is going to happen to you will so happen. He had put himself in trouble, joining the Army of his own volition. Now, Isaac vowed, he would give life a good fight. 'Even if I fail,' he said to his father, 'people will see my efforts and will say, "This guy has tried."'

Joshua smiled but remained unconvinced. He found it hard to believe that a young man with a limp could ever do well in life.

Within a year, Joshua started to fall ill with what his daughter Adedeji would call 'severe arthritis'. Isaac scraped together what money he could find to pay for medicine. Then, on 20 May 1947, there was a total eclipse of the sun over Emure-Ile. Many people were convinced that the world was coming to an end. Shortly afterwards, Joshua died. It was, wrote Isaac, an 'unexpected and premature departure from the world…it was sad that he did not live long enough to enable me to reciprocate his kindness and affection.'

Isaac was true to the promise he'd made to his father in the village church. He did not dwell on the past, but got on with trying to build a new life for himself. In February 1946, he paid a courtesy call to the district officer at Owo, who told him that he was entitled to a gratuity of eighteen pounds for his war service (about six hundred pounds in today's money). More importantly, he was also eligible for a disability pension, backdated to the day he had been discharged from the British Army. The Army did not pay pensions for war service (in Africa, other colonies or Britain itself), but it did recognise its obligation to those who had come home wounded. Isaac was judged to have a '60 per cent disability', and, as the pension for a '100 per cent disability' had been fixed at thirty shillings a month, he would receive eighteen shillings a month for as long as he lived. Returning to Lagos, he took advantage of the quota system for ex-servicemen to secure a position as a temporary clerical assistant at the Department of Labour. He was, technically, the very lowest grade of civil servant. Isaac was a boy of, as he put it, 'obscure origins', but he now had a much-prized civil service job, with security and prospects.

The Department of Labour was on Catholic Mission Street, almost next door to the handsome Edwardian buildings of King's College. The famous school had experienced its own upheavals during the war. In 1944, the authorities had moved the boys out of their boarding houses and into lodgings on a nearby street, so as to provide temporary accommodation for soldiers. The boys protested. Dozens were arrested, and, to the enduring bitterness of many associated with the school, eight were forcibly conscripted into the Army. Two years had passed since those events, and things seemed to be getting back to normal. Isaac would see 'KC' boys every day, in their smart blue blazers and cricket caps, strolling along the colonnaded verandas that overlooked the racecourse, with an air of confidence in their future that he could only envy. He knew that his chance to enjoy the kind of education they were receiving was long gone. But Lagos offered many opportunities to distract Isaac from such emotions, and he grabbed them. He was a young man in the big city with a regular wage in his pocket. In his own quaint words, he was 'careless and fond of going out in company of friends to make merry'.

His colleagues at the Department of Labour warned him that, if he ever wanted to be more than a temporary clerk, he would need better academic qualifications. In other words, he needed to pursue more work, and less merrymaking. Isaac heeded their advice, and so, after he left the Department of Labour at the end of each day, he hurried to a backstreet night school, which arranged correspondence courses through Wolsey Hall, a college in Oxford. He took O Levels, and then A Levels, the night school sending the papers off to England for marking. He did well in English, Yoruba and economics, even history of economics, and battled manfully with the British Constitution. But he struggled with mathematics, especially algebra. Simple equations and simultaneous equations he could master, but, when the teacher got to quadratic equations, Isaac was flummoxed. He persevered, though, and, each time he passed an exam, his seniors at the Department of Labour encouraged him to take another. They admired this young clerk with the stiff leg and the remarkable war story.

In the middle of Lagos Island is an area that is sometimes called Oke Popo, but is better known as the Brazilian Quarter. It got its name from the thousands of slaves who settled there in the nineteenth century after they were freed from sugar plantations in north-east Brazil. Some had been born in Africa, often in the Yoruba interior, but had been sold off as children to Portuguese slavers; others had been born in the Americas, but never forgot their African origins. In Lagos, they and their descendants were known as 'Agudas', a relaxed mix of Roman Catholics and Muslims with names like da Silva, Dos Reis and da Costa. Many were fine stonemasons, bricklayers and carpenters, and in their work they developed a unique and cheerful style of architecture, the 'Brazilian Style', characterised by colourful, stucco-plaster facades, decorated doorways, sash windows and fine wrought-iron balconies. Isaac lived in the middle of the Brazilian Quarter, on Tokunboh Street, for some fifteen years, renting two rooms in a blue, single-storey house typical of the neighbourhood. Tokunboh Street was already paved, but in those days only the occasional car passed by. The noisy but much-loved steam-tram that had trundled down the middle of the street had stopped working back in the 1930s, leaving an empty median where children played table tennis on planks of wood.

Lagos had charm in the late 1940s and '50s, in a way that those who only know it from more recent years would find hard to imagine. It was greener and quieter, a more gentle place. The shops closed at noon to allow for a siesta and reopened in the late afternoon. In the evening, Lagosians liked to promenade along the Marina, for a mile or more, watching the boats come into the harbour. They'd stop to pay a few pennies to a photographer with an old wooden camera to capture a romantic pose under the palms. At the southeast end of the Marina was Lovers' Garden. 'The town was very quiet,' remembered Esther Salawu, 'the Marina was peaceful, you could stroll there in the evenings, sit on the benches, nobody would harass you. I would sit there with my husband and take the fresh air.'

Perhaps it's too easy to romanticise the city of that time. Lagos was built on a swampy island, with a humid, sticky climate, and space was always at a premium. There were slums, certainly, and pot-holed back streets, crammed with what one 1950s visitor called 'the tumble of houses of all shapes and sizes set at all angles, the stained steps, the rickety balconies and shuttered windows, the milling, variegated, talkative crowds'. There were pickpockets, small-time gangsters known as *jagudas* and teenage prostitutes in knee-length *bonfo* frocks, looking for business day and night. Many parts of the city did not have running water, and the open drains stank of offal and sewage. Indeed, 'night-soil men' walked down Tokunboh Street each night after dark, collecting pails of human waste, which they dropped in the lagoon. But Lagos was safe, the kind of town where women walked home alone at night at any hour, and families often left their doors unlocked.

On warm nights during the dry season, Isaac would pull a mat out onto the veranda at Tokunboh Street, and sleep outside. When he was much older, he would look back on those early years in Lagos with incredulity, comparing what the city was with what it had become. 'Crime then was much, much less. But nobody can sleep outside in Lagos now,' he would say, laughing at the very notion. 'They can come and kill you.' Nor did people have to worry about mosquitoes then, because the city authorities ensured that the gutters were swept clean and sprayed with insecticide. In those days, people in Lagos took electricity, or 'light', for granted. 'If they wanted to take out light, they'd warn you, but it soon came back,' remembered Isaac. 'It was reliable, very reliable. But now…light may go for weeks!' Like many older Lagosians, he would shake his head at the absurdity of it all, then let it go with a wave of the hand. The alternative, he said, was to get upset and angry, and what good would that do?

The fact was that Lagos had given Isaac a better life than he would have had if he'd stayed on the farm in Emure-Ile. Immediately after the war, the worst racial prejudices of British rule were finally breaking down. Today, Aduke Alakija is a vivacious nonagenarian, fond of sparkling conversation and an after-lunch brandy. Born in Lagos in 1921, she was the daughter of a prominent lawyer and publisher, Sir Adeyemo Alakija, who sent her as a young girl to Britain to receive a 'proper' education. She went to a boarding school in north Wales, and from there to the London School of Economics. In March 1945, she returned to Nigeria, a self-assured young lady. A few weeks later, Aduke was taken by Sir Adeyemo to see the arrival of Isaac's hospital ship. 'My father was showing me off at the time,' she said. The event left little impression on her; maybe she found it hard to relate to the experiences of the soldiers, mainly illiterate men from Northern Nigeria. In the circles she moved in, people were more interested in politics, education and getting a job in the government. But what she did recall, very clearly, was an occasion, a few weeks later, when a shop attendant ignored her in order to serve a white lady. Under Aduke's interrogation, the unfortunate boy confessed that it was the manager, Mr Jones, who had instructed him that white customers be given preference. 'What, in Nigeria?!' exclaimed Aduke. 'Never!' Mr Jones was called down to the shop floor where he stammered a denial that such an instruction had ever been given. On future visits to the shop, Aduke had to insist on not being given preferential treatment herself.

It was what became known as the 'Bristol Hotel Incident' of 1947 that signalled the true turning point in race relations in Lagos. The white manager of the famous hotel refused to admit a man of mixed Anglo-Sierra Leonean descent, not knowing that he was in fact leading a commission sent by the Colonial Office in London. The news spread across the city. Demonstrators stormed their way into the Bristol, smashing windows and furniture, and furious articles appeared in the *West African Pilot* and other newspapers. The governor quickly moved to outlaw racial segregation in all Lagos establishments, including at the best hospital and the most prestigious private club, the Ikoyi Club. A few years later, Aduke was admitted as the Ikoyi Club's first Nigerian woman member. 'By then they were begging us to join,' she said, 'so a group of us would go and drink there on Sundays.' Initially, some of the white members, 'most of them second rate' in her withering assessment, resisted the new state of affairs, but they soon moved on.

By the early 1950s, the social scene included Nigerians of different ethnic backgrounds mixing freely with Europeans, Aduke recalled. Now, divisions owed more to class and education than to colour. 'There were certain classes that you could never tolerate, the people who worked for railways and so on,' she said, 'but if you had the same type of education, and so on, you all got on.'

At Christmas and New Year, Europeans and Africans put on their finery and gathered together to watch the horses at the racecourse. Black and white jockeys raced side by side. In 1956, a young Queen Elizabeth came to visit. Aduke, who was presented to the Queen as one of Nigeria's first female lawyers, remembered that the monarch seemed rather nervous as she was introduced to Lagos society. Evidently, when it came to self-confidence, Nigeria's elite had nothing to learn from their British counterparts. It may have been this quality that helped ensure the 'colour bar' was never set so high, nor enforced so rigidly, as it had been in Southern or Eastern Africa.

Nigeria, just like the other West Coast colonies, had been saved partly by its climate. The 'White Man's Grave' deserved its malign reputation for disease. It had never been an attractive proposition for settlers, and this meant there was no significant European society to jealously guard its privileges, no white farmers prepared to shed blood to keep land they had taken. Elspeth Huxley, who had lived much of her life in colonial Kenya, visited Lagos in 1953 and perceived the 'inter-racial *bonhomie*' while having a wonderful time during a dance at the Island Club. The academic Margery Perham found the atmosphere in colonial Lagos in the 1930s to be 'utterly different' from what she had known in other African colonies. Here 'a proud assertive people...walked the streets in their bright flowing robes as if Lagos and its suburbs, its markets and its official buildings was entirely their city and subject to no suzerain power'.

It was as if the Nigerians *knew* what belonged to them, and the British were tolerated on sufferance. And by the 1950s the British were not only climbing down from their privileged social position, but they were also relinquishing political power. They had decided to go.

British officials worried in private that there were not enough trained Nigerian civil servants to run the country. But they also admitted that they were starting to feel out of place, that Nigeria was like a bored hostess, waiting for her self-invited guests to leave. Independence was coming.

There was no great struggle for freedom in Nigeria, no popular uprising that forced Britain to fight or leave. If there had been, the withdrawal would have happened even quicker. Instead, a group of able Nigerian politicians, with wildly competing agendas and different regional powerbases, found themselves pushing against an open door. The disagreements between these politicians and the British hinged on the exact timing of the departure and, crucially, over how power would be distributed between the regions. The champions of Southern Nigeria, Obafemi Awolowo of the Yorubas and Nnamdi Azikiwe of the Igbos, wanted the British out as soon as possible, while the leaders of the less developed North asked them to stay longer. These differences came to a head in the Nigerian parliament in 1953, after which Northern leaders were booed and heckled on the streets of Lagos, and there were anti-Southern riots in the North. It was a fevered atmosphere and there was much apprehension about the future. Many Nigerians, especially in the South, accused the British of 'divide and rule', of favouring the North. British officials maintained that the differences between the regions were real enough and insisted they were now doing their best to build bridges between them.

The original sin was Britain's. There was no unity in Nigeria because Nigeria was not, at least at that time and before, a country in any meaningful sense. Its borders had been shaped purely by imperial ambition, some two hundred different ethnic groups lumped together. Even Nigeria's name was a British invention, thought up by Flora Shaw, the wife of Lord Frederick Lugard, the colony's first governor-general. Awolowo put it with cruel succinctness in 1947: 'Nigeria', he said, 'is a mere geographical expression.' It's a moot point, though, whether any politicians did enough in those pre-independence years to reach beyond their own ethnic constituencies.

A few months before the British left, Nelson Ottah penned a damning, but ultimately prescient analysis for *Drum* magazine. Nigeria, he said, was in grave danger of falling apart because of tribalism, 'created and fostered by our own politicians. In their desperate quest for power the first word in their mind was never Nigeria. It was Ibo, Yoruba or Hausa. And they only began to pay lip-service to Nigeria after they had made sure that their greatest weapon, tribalism, was well set up behind them.'

The preparations in Lagos were frantic. Workmen tore down old buildings, put up new ones, widened roads and rushed to finish an expensive new hotel and stadium, all to make sure the city would celebrate Independence Day in a state of suitable grandeur. 'Never has there been such a delirium of activity,' wrote *Drum* magazine, which, with exuberant optimism, predicted the event would be attended by some 250,000 visitors from ninety countries. After all, as people in Lagos said, this was not just any old colonial territory about to step onto the world stage. Nigeria was by far the most populous colony in the British Empire; with a population of more than forty-five million, one-third of all imperial subjects were Nigerian.

Queen Elizabeth sent her cousin, Princess Alexandra, to the ceremony on her behalf, and thousands of Nigerians braved heavy rain to cheer her along the fourteen-mile route from the airport at Ikeja. The next day, 30 September 1960, the skies cleared. The excitement, observed the reporter for *Drum*, 'was almost unbearable'. At dusk, the crowds walked along the Marina, now decorated with festive lights depicting camels, parrots and other animals, towards the racecourse. The churches rang their bells, the ships in the lagoon joyously sounded their sirens and the Navy, stationed across the water in Apapa, fired a twenty-one-gun salute. The Princess drove round the thrilled crowds in an open-top car, waving her white-gloved hand. '*Abẹkẹ!*' shouted the Lagosians – 'We beg to cherish her!' – in appreciation of her beauty.

At precisely midnight, the Union Jack was lowered and, in a sudden flash of floodlights, the new green and white flag of an independent Nigeria was hoisted high above the capital. Nigerians sang their national anthem for the first time, their many voices straining with emotion: 'Nigeria, we hail thee, our dear native land; though tribe and tongue may differ; in brotherhood we stand'. The first prime minister, Tafawa Balewa, could not have been more gracious about the soon-to-be-departed British, of whom, he said, 'we have known, first as masters, and then as leaders, and finally as partners, but always as friends'.

When black Africa's other giant, the Congo, had won its independence from Belgium just three months earlier, the mood had not been nearly so conciliatory. The ceremony in Leopoldville was a disaster. The Congolese had listened in fury as the Belgian King Baudouin hailed the 'genius' of his rapacious and cruel great-uncle, King Leopold, in establishing Belgian rule in the Congo. The new prime minister, Patrice Lumumba, responded with a bitter speech, in which he denounced the 'humiliating slavery [and] atrocious sufferings' imposed by the Belgians, who, he said, had run a regime of 'oppression and exploitation'. In Nigeria, in contrast, people spoke of forgiveness towards the departing colonial masters. 'Nigerians, in their hour of triumph, deliberately forgot the errors that the British had made yesterday,' wrote *Drum*. 'They did not seek revenge. To millions of Nigerians the goodness of the British in Nigeria outweighed their badness.'

The Congo would unravel almost instantly, and Belgian settlers fled amid recriminations and racial killings. By the time Nigeria celebrated its independence, Patrice Lumumba had already been deposed in a military coup, three regions in eastern Congo were in armed revolt, and the Americans and Soviets were vying for influence from the shadows. Lumumba, whose legend endures today as a symbol of the strangled hopes and ambitions of an independent Africa, was murdered a few weeks later. Nigeria would not experience such a precipitous collapse, but many had a nagging feeling that all was not well, despite the exhilaration on the streets during the independence ceremony. As Aduke Alakija observed more than half a century later, 'I think we rushed independence. I mean, it was happy, we all had a wonderful time, but I think the handing over was too sudden. We should have taken another two or three years.'

Isaac did not live in the world of high society or political intrigue. He had no distinguished ancestors, and few friends close to the levers of power. He rarely ventured over to Ikoyi, where the British, and now a few Nigerians, lived comfortably in fine bungalows set in spacious gardens. He didn't get invited to the smart parties that Aduke Alakija frequented, where white-clad stewards served whiskey and gin and *small chop*, little plates of olives and canapés. But he had secured his own precarious foothold in the Lagos middle class, and he was trying his hardest to make sure he stayed there.

He married Florence, a Yoruba woman who worked as a clerk in a bank and whose family came from Abeokuta, the town in Southern Nigeria where he'd signed up for the British Army and spent his first months of military training. She had been married before, and had a daughter, Nike, whom Isaac raised as his own, while also encouraging the girl to stay close to her real father. By the end of the 1950s, Isaac and Florence had two more daughters, and the rooms at Tokunboh Street were beginning to feel too small. He could see the changes on the surrounding streets: the steel and cement high-rises going up all over Lagos Island, shining white, their plate glass glinting in the sunlight. And he could see the political changes coming at the Department of Labour.

When he joined the department, almost all the senior officials had been white. They had drafted Nigeria's Labour Code, negotiated with the trade unions, carried out the factory inspections and drawn up the rules to ensure the health and safety of Nigeria's workers. But in the late 1950s Isaac's British colleagues began to leave, one by one, and Nigerians took their places. 'Africanisation' was sweeping through the government. Chinua Achebe, the celebrated writer, was working at the Nigerian Broadcasting Corporation at the time, and saw a similar process under way there. 'Officers began to retire and return home to England...They left in droves, quietly, amiably, often at night, mainly on ships, but also, particularly the wealthier ones, on planes.' There had never been a large number of British officials in Nigeria – just a few thousand civil servants, policemen and soldiers spread across this enormous country. Now they were going home.

However, there was one institution to which the British would cling until the very end. In 1948, three years after the end of the Burma campaign, Lieutenant Louis Victor Ugboma became the first Nigerian to receive an officer's commission in the Army, but, at the time of independence in 1960, the vast majority of officers were still British.

The 1960s were Isaac's 'golden age'. His studying paid off, and he began to rise up the ranks of the new Ministry of Labour. Promotion brought with it opportunities to travel. He went on a training course to Oxford with a group of similarly earnest young men from Ghana, East Africa, Malaysia, India, Fiji and other parts of the Commonwealth. The 38th Labour Administration Course for Overseas Officials was an exercise in post-colonial hospitality, held by the British Department of Employment and Productivity. He also went to Washington in a group of fifteen young African civil servants. He was always smartly dressed on these trips abroad, in a suit and tie, and, when he posed on a cold sunny day for a photo outside the US Capitol, a proud smile beamed across his face. Africa's place in the world was changing, and Isaac was enjoying opportunities his parents could never have imagined. He had become, in Nigerian parlance, a 'Been-To'. He had been to the United Kingdom and the United States. In a modest way, perhaps, and not with the sense of entitlement of the sons and daughters of politicians who returned to Lagos from their British schools flaunting new accents and the clothes they had bought on Oxford Street, but he had achieved something nonetheless.

There were occasions on those trips abroad, in airport terminals or in the hotel bar, when the conversation would drift to the war, and then Isaac's travel companions would ask him about his limp, and his time in Burma. He told his story in a courteous and self-deprecating way. David Kargbo had been his 'comrade in adversity'. The Muslim villagers who had saved them were 'gentlemen and generous hosts'.

The Japanese had been cruel but they were also 'dogged fighters...a tiny set of men with big hearts'. But, if Isaac felt that he could recall events with equanimity after the passing of so many years, he did have one strange encounter that jolted him right back into the past.

It was at the end of the Oxford trip, on a grey December day, and he was passing through London on his way home. He sat in a restaurant near Victoria Station and noticed that an older white man was staring at him. The man walked over to him and spoke in Hausa. '*Sano*,' he said – 'Greetings'. He had seen Isaac entering the restaurant, and wanted to know why he was limping. As Isaac started to explain, the man's face lit up in recognition. He was a retired major who had led Nigerian soldiers from the 81st Division in Burma, and he knew all about the story of the 29th CCS, and the improbable survival of two of its men. 'By the way,' said the Major, 'that chap who hid you and looked after you, we made sure he did well. We gave him piles of rupees, and some cows as well. He became a rich man.'

Isaac listened, astonished. The Major put his hat on and walked out of the restaurant, and into the London gloom, swallowed up by the crowds heading towards the station. For years afterwards, Isaac would wonder why he didn't run after him, grab him and ask him what more he knew of Shuyiman's fate.

In 1962, Isaac and his growing family left Tokunboh Street and Lagos Island, and did what so many aspiring middle-class families were doing in Lagos at that time: they moved to a new neighbourhood, Surelere, which was being methodically laid out on the adjacent mainland. It was within easy reach of the city, and offered more space and more comfort. The meaning of *surelere* in Yoruba – 'patience is rewarded' – seemed to fit with Isaac's efforts to better himself. He'd secured a mortgage, and would be one of the development's very first homeowners. He had picked a bungalow on a cul-de-sac cleared from the bush, with newly laid electricity cables and water pipes.

His daughters remembered the sense of excitement of arriving in what was called 'new Lagos'. 'We would picnic under the trees, and a milkman delivered fresh milk every day from a nearby dairy,'

Nike recalled. There were parks, and a clean stream to play along-side. These may seem to be unremarkable memories, but for what Lagos became in the following decades. The houses were neatly laid out, for the civil servants, but also headmasters, writers, teachers and musicians who moved into the neighbourhood alongside them. Nigeria was a new country, and everything seemed possible. Almost fifty years later, Isaac would joke that he was the *oba*, or king, of the street – the first to arrive in Surelere and now the only remaining survivor from the early days. The neighbours had come and gone.

His leg continued to trouble him. He had a further operation in 1946, and two more in 1953, but the limp remained. He'd been excited to discover in the 1960s that he could drive a car provided it had automatic gears. His first car was a light-blue Hillman. It was that now distant time when Britain sold cars to the rest of the world and an ordinary Nigerian civil servant's salary went far enough to pay for one.

Isaac's only failure in this period, he said later, was that he never managed to secure a university degree. He had passed the preliminary exams to take a BSc in economics through his correspondence course with Wolsey Hall in Oxford, but somewhere along the way he lost impetus, and dropped out. He put this down to his 'laziness', but that seems an overly harsh self-assessment. Children – he and Florence had six daughters by 1965 – consumed much of his time after work each day. And, degree or not, he had risen to the eminently respect-able rank of chief labour officer.

Back in Emure-Ile, he was hailed as a local boy made good. When parents from the village were sending a teenage son or daughter to Lagos to try to make their fortune, they'd tell them to go and see Isaac Fadoyebo first. 'Go see that man, im go help you find work,' they'd say.

Isaac was prospering but Nigeria was beginning to lose its way. The precarious structure the British had left behind did not take long to crack apart. The competition between the regions for power and resources grew more pronounced, and none of the politicians proved capable of attracting any real support from beyond their own ethnic group. Oil, which was discovered in the 1950s, began generating more and more revenue but this encouraged corruption as much as economic growth. Nigeria's first republic collapsed in the military coups of 1966, amid a flurry of assassinations and then ethnic massacres. Worse was to follow.

One day at the end of May 1967, Isaac was washing himself at home when the news on the radio brought him to a sudden stop. The Eastern Region, dominated by the Igbo people, had unilaterally seceded, and declared itself the independent Republic of Biafra. The radio announcer said Nigeria's military government was not recognising this illegal act and would recover its territory. There was going to be a civil war. There were some in Lagos who were excited at the prospect, but not Isaac. 'I wasn't happy,' he said, 'because I knew what war was. People would be killed, people would be maimed, people would be impoverished, over what?'

The Nigerian government announced a general mobilisation of all ex-servicemen under the age of fifty. It didn't affect Isaac, who was not fit to fight, but thousands of the men who'd been with him in Burma more than twenty years previously were called up. The younger soldiers jokingly referred to these veterans of the Second World War as "*Yam-Maza*' or '*Mazan Jiya*' – 'Yesterday's Men'.

The civil war lasted for two-and-a-half years and resulted in more than a million deaths. And yet, at a superficial level, life for the people of Lagos stayed the same. Even after the panicked exodus of Igbos from the capital to the East in 1966, a Nigerian journalist wrote that Lagos was 'alive with girls, cars, parties and dances'. In the clubs, people kept on swaying to the Highlife music and the bandleaders kept on singing, '*Lagos, na so so enjoyment, you get money, you no get money, Lagos na so so enjoyment*' – 'Whether you have money or not, Lagos is a place to enjoy life'.

Isaac visited England on work during the siege of Biafra, and remembered being amused when his hosts asked how he had managed to travel at a time of war. They had seen disturbing pictures on television of starving people in Biafra. Isaac tried to explain to them that the impact of the war was not felt in the capital, as it was being fought out in the east, where he and many Lagosians knew practically nobody. It didn't affect him directly, he said.

However, Isaac was wrong. Biafra would surrender in 1970, but the impact of the war would last much longer, and would be felt by all Nigerians. It entrenched the military's hold over politics. Cliques of soldiers would rule the country for much of the next thirty years, presiding over ever-worsening corruption and the collapse in morale and integrity of a once-respected civil service. The various juntas became more and more reliant on oil revenues, and agriculture and industry fell into disrepair. Nigeria was in a downward spiral, and nobody, in any part of the country, would escape.

Isaac and Florence separated in 1976. His daughters remembered that their parents had been having disagreements for a while. The second youngest, Adetoun, was thirteen years old when her parents split up. She had been told her birth had been like a funeral, so desperate were Isaac and Florence for a son after four daughters. During the pregnancy, Isaac had passed on a message from his own mother, who said that Florence should take a potion from a traditional healer that would ensure she gave birth to a boy. Florence refused to do this. In fact, in an earlier pregnancy, she had delivered a little boy, who was tragically stillborn. After Isaac and Florence broke up, he took up with a younger woman. The relationship lasted only two years, and afterwards Isaac said he wanted nothing more to do with women. Except that, with six daughters, he was surrounded by them.

Tayo, Isaac's third-born, said that, as she and her sisters grew up and pursued successful careers in medicine, teaching and business, Isaac got over his yearning for a son. 'He's a human being and this is Africa so it was only natural he wanted a boy,' she said, 'but he could also see how many young boys got into trouble, and we never gave him headaches.' His parenting style could be quirky; he forced all of his daughters to take a daily concoction of a raw egg and milk when they were young to ensure they grew up strong. In later years, he said he was blessed to have had so many girls, and his pride at their achievements was obvious. And he grew closer to Florence again. In their old age, Isaac and Florence went to family celebrations together, even as they continued living apart. After Florence died in 2011, her coffin, in accordance with Yoruba tradition, 'lay in state' at Isaac's house, as friends and family came to pay their respects before the funeral.

In 1980, Isaac took voluntary retirement from the Ministry of Labour. It was an amicable parting; he was in his mid-fifties and had been there long enough – thirty-four years – to qualify for a civil service pension, to go with the small disability pension he'd been collecting since 1946. He was relieved to discover that his years at the ministry gave him some 'second-hand value', and he moved into the private sector. But the Nigerian economy was in severe difficulties, and neither of the two factories where Isaac worked in the early 1980s would survive the downturn. Thus, he found himself definitively retired in 1986, at the age of sixty.

In theory, Isaac's pensions should have put him in a comfortable position. In reality, inflation had eroded their value and he could never rely on them to be paid on time. The Nigerian Ministry of Defence had taken over responsibility from the British Army for his disability pension at independence, and in the 1990s the payment was increasingly erratic. Sometimes Isaac waited for a whole year before it was disbursed. He magnanimously put this down to 'administrative problems', but his daughters more caustically said the delays were the result of 'the Nigerian factor'. It was they who made sure that, pension or no pension, Isaac always had enough money to keep him going each and every month. Not that his needs were great. He took pleasure in looking after his children, and a growing brood of grandchildren, and from walking across Surelere to the nearby football stadium, where he could take in a match from the cheap seats. 'I live a simple and contented life,' he wrote in the late 1980s. 'My habits can almost be termed monastic.'

Like almost every Nigerian, Isaac liked to spend time diagnosing where his country had gone wrong. And, as he got older, he had more and more time to think about this. He had lived through not only a civil war, but also half a dozen successful military coups and any number of failed ones. Soldiers had ruled Nigeria from 1966 to 1999, save for one brief interlude when the politicians unsuccessfully tried to re-establish a democratic government. In the 1980s and '90s, Isaac watched in frustration as living standards fell, and universities, schools and hospitals decayed to become pale imitations of what they had once been.

In part, Isaac repeated the mantras voiced by many others. 'If you build on a faulty foundation, the super-structure can't last,' he would say, in a rebuke to the British legacy. But the dire quality of Nigerian leadership in the fifty years since the British had gone had made an unpromising situation much worse. 'Corruption and bad governance have delayed our progress,' Isaac said. 'They say Nigeria is the giant of Africa, and maybe they're right. But a giant should be able to perform like a giant.' A lack of cohesion seemed to be holding the country back, according to Isaac. 'We're too worried about ethnicity. If we see a Yoruba man up there, we support him whether he's doing well or not doing well, because he's our blood. That's not good, that's our main problem in this country.'

Yet, though Isaac's diagnosis was unremarkable, some of his proposed solutions were bold. The country, he said, needed a revolution. This would no doubt be accompanied by 'weeping and gnashing of teeth' of those who saw their privileges threatened, but that was too bad. He found inspiration in an eclectic range of political heroes, ranging from Chairman Mao – 'who changed the fortunes of China and perhaps the world' – to the former president of Ghana, Jerry Rawlings. 'If you have conservatives they will leave things as they are and just let sleeping dogs lie,' he said, warming to his theme. 'No, no, no, we want radicals. We can be as good as England, even better, if we have a revolution; why not?'

In this way, perhaps, Isaac showed himself to be typically Nigerian. He had an enduring faith in the potential greatness of his country, no matter how faltering its actual progress. 'Nigeria's going to be a good place. We have the resources, we have the manpower, we have the brains. Go to America – you'll see Nigerian doctors, scores of them, practising along with the white boys.' Rip the old structure down, he said, put the right people in charge, and just watch this country go.

In spite of everything, Nigeria is a country of optimists. It was not in Isaac's nature to be bitter about the past. Much better, he said, to carry on thinking positively about the future instead.

PART II

DEBT

13

INTO A RAVINE

||||||||||||||||||||||||||||||||||||||||||||||||||||||||||||||||||||||||||||||||||||||||||||||||||||||||||

The shining, beautiful car Nigeria inherited in 1960 had indeed crashed into a ravine. She will surely pull it out again and, re-fashioned, re-modelled, drive it forth once more into a surer future.

Sylvia Leith-Ross,
Stepping Stones

||||||||||||||||||||||||||||||||||||||||||||||||||||||||||||||||||||||||||||||||||||||||||||||||||||||||||

April 2011
Lagos, Nigeria

If Isaac regretted anything, he would say half in jest to his grand-children, it was that he'd never had the chance to become a great sportsman. 'World footballer of the year, undisputed heavyweight champion of the world, fastest man in the Olympics, four-hundred yards,' he mused, painting the scene with his hands. 'Isaac Fadoyebo, lane 1. I take off my tracksuit, I break the tape before any other boy in the world, the world will yell, "The boy is good!" The whole world will know me, respect me.' Then he laughed at his own foolishness. 'That has gone, gone for ever. I thought they would fix my leg in hospital, and I'd get my normal body. That didn't happen.'

Isaac didn't resent the British, who took him off to fight in a war the cause of which he barely understood, nor the Japanese, who nearly killed him and left him with a disability for the rest of his life. 'I take it to be my fate,' he'd say, 'I was destined to go to the battlefield, destined to be wounded. I can't blame myself, I didn't know what I was doing.' Besides, look at everything he'd achieved since. He was only nineteen when he'd returned from Burma, and he believed that, by and large, he'd overcome the challenges that he'd faced in the lifetime that followed. He would count his accomplishments on his fingers. One: 'I had to improve my education.' Two: 'I got O Levels.' Three, four, five: 'A levels, promotion, I got a car.' Six: 'I got coupled.' Seven: 'I trained my children.' He'd look at his extended fingers with clear pride and satisfaction. 'So, taking into account my humble beginnings, I am a successful man, and God help me.'

It can't have been easy for Isaac, being a Nigerian veteran of the Burma campaign. As the war receded into history, his experiences became less and less relevant to the concerns of his fellow Nigerians. That soldiers feel unappreciated when they come home is almost a truism of any time and any society. There were many British men who fought in the Second World War who afterwards said that those who had not been there could never truly understand what they had gone through. And, as Britain changed in the decades that followed, some felt that their sacrifices were not properly valued by younger generations. Some veterans struggled, with the passing of time, to even recognise the country they had fought for. But at least the Second World War is woven into the British national consciousness. Not just the course of its events, but also the belief that Britain was on the right side and that it was a 'good war', one worth fighting, a belief that still holds firm for most people even today.

Things were very different in Nigeria. The Second World War played almost no part in forming the independent country's self-identity. Many, perhaps most, Nigerians learnt nothing of the tens of thousands of their countrymen who fought in Burma. Today, Nigeria is a country of overwhelmingly young people; almost seventy percent of Nigerians are under thirty years old. Those aged over seventy represent less than two percent of the current population.

To the youthful majority, the Biafran War feels like ancient history, let alone the Second World War.

Forget history; making a life in Nigeria was struggle enough: to bring food home to children at the end of the day, to find enough money to pay for hospital fees, to escape the violence inflicted by ethnic, religious and criminal militias. Most people didn't have time to contemplate the past, and never had the chance to receive the sort of education that would help them to do so. But even those who knew something about the West African soldiers who went to Burma often felt ambivalent about the role these men had played. Why, after all, should they celebrate the defence of the British Empire? Ghana, Nigeria, Kenya and others achieved self-rule with a speed no one had anticipated in 1945, casting the contribution of Isaac and others in a less flattering light. New countries had new identities to forge and new myths to write as they struggled, not always successfully, to create a sense of national unity. From this perspective, the men who fought for the Empire could even be something of an embarrassment. Safer, perhaps, to concentrate on what they did *after* they came back from Burma, and their role in helping drive the British out, than remember the sacrifices they made in the war itself.

By the time Isaac reached his mid-eighties, he belonged to a fast-dwindling group of Burma veterans. The Nigerian Legion offices in Lagos were a couple of dank rooms, dilapidated brown paper files piled high against one wall, and a bare desk, no computer in sight. Captain John Adolie, a quiet and thoughtful man, ran this modest operation. He spent most of his time helping veterans of more recent conflicts – the Biafran War and Nigerian peacekeeping expeditions to the Congo, Liberia and Sierra Leone – rather than Second World War soldiers. But the Legion was still in touch with some 120 men who had fought in Burma. 'At least that was the number a couple of months ago, but they are dying very quickly now,' Adolie said. Many of the 'Burma Boys' were in a 'miserable condition, demobilised by the British with peanuts and no follow up'. The Legion had few means to help them, and relied on irregular handouts from a charity in London. The majority of the Burma veterans were living in Northern Nigeria. Their health varied, according to Adolie; ten were blind, but some were active, 'very strong', he called them. A handful were employed as security guards for the Legion's offices in the northern states of Bauchi and Kano. Given the fierce Islamist insurgency raging in Northern Nigeria at the time, in which thousands of people were killed and soldiers and policemen often targeted, this virtually constituted active service. It's hard to imagine that there were Second World War veterans anywhere else in the world who were not only still working, but also doing so in such dangerous conditions. What would the religious fanatics of Boko Haram, who carried explosives, machine guns and rocket-propelled grenades, have made of these venerable guards, dressed in khaki and armed only with sticks and *pangas*?

Isaac, at least in comparison with most other veterans, was comfortably off, but he too had had to adapt to bewildering changes. In his retirement, Surelere was unrecognisable from the neighbourhood to which he had moved. The trees and parks were long gone, and so was the orderly sense of progress. Isaac's house was typical, surrounded by high walls topped off with jagged glass shards, to keep out the dreaded armed robbers. There were heavy iron gates at the end of each street, painted black and gold. In the evening Isaac would watch the residents heave these gates shut. 'Surelere is a slum,' he would say matter-of-factly. Then he would chuckle, shake his head and retreat back into his compound.

When Isaac made one of his slow walks down his street, there were no birds to be heard, only the ugly roar of the generators that had become the ubiquitous background noise to modern Lagos. His neighbours tried to speak to him, but often he could not hear them above the din. Beyond his street, Surelere had grown into a collection of shabby concrete apartment blocks; traffic clogged the streets and the neighbourhood was trapped by a ring of raised motorways. 'Area Boys', gangs of unemployed youths, gathered on the dusty roundabouts, waiting to prey on passers-by who needed directions or whose cars broke down in the 'go-slows'. Walls were plastered in lurid posters for 'Nollywood' movies (*Baby Police, Dangerous Maiden 2*) or evangelical churches (The Mountain of Fires and Miracles Ministry, Deep Life Bible Church). These jostled for space with signs announcing cures for sexual ailments and unlikely educational opportunities abroad ('Gain Admission Into Universities in Ghana, Ukraine, Cyprus, Canada, Georgia etc').

Isaac's sense of dislocation between past and present was reinforced whenever one of his daughters drove him along the expressway to Lagos Island. Two concrete and steel white elephants rose above the monotonous urban landscape close to his house. One was the former national sports stadium; the other was the circular modernist design of the national theatre, once the setting for a grandiose arts festival. Both had been built in the oil-boom years of the 1970s, when Nigeria was flush with money, and both had since decayed and were all but abandoned. In their sad condition, they spoke of the disappointed hopes of an earlier time, and also of Nigeria's sometimes baffling indifference to its own history. This is a country, Isaac would say, where the best from the past is barely noticed, let alone maintained. When the Nigerian government moved the capital to Abuja, prestigious buildings in Lagos were left to rot. Build a new stadium, build a new theatre, think of the money that can be made from all those new contracts – that was the national ethos.

Then his daughter's car would cross Eko Bridge, and descend on to the Island. The old Lagos that Isaac knew, the port where Yoruba culture and handsome colonial buildings existed side by side, a place of cool breezes and *juju* music, had been swept away, replaced by something noisier, uglier and far less manageable. The little blue Brazilian house at 92 Tokunboh Street, the home where Isaac started his family, had been demolished in the 1980s and replaced by a three-storey concrete block. Tokunboh Street was full of such anonymous buildings, sprouting innumerable satellite dishes and air-conditioning units coated in dust. Shops and stalls encroached onto the narrow road, and the sky above was a tangled mess of telephone and electrical wiring, much of which had not worked for years. The old Marina, the tree-lined promenade that was once the pride of Lagos, survived in Isaac's memory but was buried under concrete and gravel, and overshadowed by an elevated expressway.

The decades of relentless population growth, the oil boom followed by bust, the corruption and misrule, had all swallowed up Lagos' history, and left snarling traffic jams and mountains of rubbish in their wake. By the beginning of the twentieth-first century, nobody seemed to have known how many people lived in Lagos, although everyone could see that the city never stopped growing. The British, at least, had tried to keep track of the changes. The 1921 census, shortly before Isaac was born, listed a population of 99,700. By 1931, this had risen to 126,100, and that number had more than doubled to 276,400 by 1951. At independence in 1960, there were more than 600,000 people in Lagos. From this point, population growth accelerated, and estimates as to how many people lived in the city started to diverge wildly. The United Nations said there were roughly 2 million people in Lagos in 1970. By 2025, it projected this number will be close to 19 million. Others put it much higher. In Isaac's lifetime, Lagos went from being a large town to a megacity, a monster that was out of control.

It's not that Lagos, or Surelere for that matter, had become a place without hope. Far from it. The city was bursting with creative and entrepreneurial energy, and was booming in its way. In the early 2000s, Nigeria's economy had picked up after a long slump, and that was particularly true in and around Lagos. Surelere became the home of Nollywood, the multi-million-pound Nigerian film industry. But, in the new, cut-throat Nigeria, those who thrived needed cunning and wits. Many of those who made fortunes were ruthless hustlers. A decent, hard-working man, a man like Isaac in fact, who played by the rules and expected the state to give back to him what was his due, was in danger of being left behind.

Through the decades, he never forgot his village. Emure-Ile, if anything, became more important to Isaac the older he got. As a young man, he had been determined not to 'rot away' there, but in his later years he was a generous benefactor on his regular visits to see those who had stayed behind. He was the most successful member of the family, and in his mind this brought with it responsibilities. He looked after his mother, Ogunmuyonwa, who died in 1981, but also his surviving sisters, and paid for any number of nephews and nieces to go to school. 'They are on his payroll,' Isaac's daughters would say, rolling their eyes, exasperated to discover that the money they had given him to look after himself in his old age had once again been divided up and handed on to a diverse group of villagers and relatives. He had pushed his own daughters to ensure they got a good education, and now he wanted to try to give the same opportunities to his extended family. His daughter Tayo, a doctor, liked to say that one of her cousins, a nurse, would 'be frying *gari* by the roadside if it was not for Isaac Fadoyebo'.

On the edge of Emure-Ile, beyond a little stream that runs through stands of bamboo, in a clearing hacked out of the scruffy bush, there is a large, modern bungalow set back from the dirt road. It's an incongruous building, at odds with the wooden Hezekiah African church immediately opposite, and with the older village houses up the hill, some of which have elegant framed doorways decorated with motifs of lions and crowns. Isaac built this house, in fits and starts, over the years, whenever he had a little bit of spare money. It was, he said, where he would enjoy the end of his retirement. There was, his daughters suspected, another unspoken motive. They had been raised as city girls, and Isaac worried, not entirely without reason, that they looked on village life somewhat unenthusiastically. By build-ing this house, he and his family would always have a comfortable place to stay in Emure-Ile. He was trying to tie his daughters, and their children, to the land of his ancestors. He liked to give visitors a guided tour of the house's bare concrete rooms, still without doors and windows. 'This will be the kitchen, and here we have a bedroom,' he would say, as he proceeded from room to room, pointing from right to left, before always ending in the large room in the middle.

'And this is the living room that I have named after my chief host in the Burma jungle. This is Shuyiman's room.'

It wasn't only the village that preoccupied Isaac as he reached old age. His memories of Burma had never left him. From the very day he had been discharged in 1945, he had wanted to put his experiences down in writing. It was a British colleague at the Department of Labour, Mr H.S. Smith, who pushed and nudged him to get started, sometime in the 1950s. Mr Smith introduced Isaac to Michael Crowder, a distinguished historian who was living in Lagos. Crowder visited Isaac at his house and together they drew up a structure for telling his tale. But it wasn't until Isaac retired many years later that he found the time to complete his work, sixty pages hammered out on an ancient typewriter. He called it *A Stroke of Unbelievable Luck*.

Tayo encouraged Isaac to look for a publisher, but by the late 1980s the book industry in Nigeria was in a sorry state. Publishers were interested in the autobiographies of wealthy politicians and businessmen, essentially subsidised vanity projects, not in the life of an unknown like Isaac Fadoyebo. Nobody would touch his manuscript, so he sent it to Britain. A few publishers wrote back, asking if Isaac had any photographs to accompany his account. He did not, and suspected that they thought his story was 'a sort of fairy tale'. The correspondence with the British publishers dried up, and *A Stroke of Unbelievable Luck* gathered dust on a shelf in his home.

In 1989, the BBC World Service marked the fiftieth anniversary of the start of the Second World War with a programme on Africa's involvement in the conflict. Isaac read an advertisement in a Nigerian newspaper in which the BBC appealed for contributions from any readers who might have interesting stories from the war years. In an act of enormous faith in Nigeria's creaking postal service, Isaac sent his one and only typed manuscript to London, where a producer recognised its significance and passed it on to a grateful British historian.

A Stroke of Unbelievable Luck was eventually published in the United States, as a university monograph in a low-key, academic sort of way. Isaac received a few copies to distribute to his daughters, but no money. It reads like the quintessential Isaac – understated, and is slightly dated in its language. He tells the story of his Burma adventure and concludes with a few idiosyncratic musings, on the folly of funding space exploration while so many still live in poverty on Earth, and on the need for the United Nations to enforce world peace. He dedicated it to his parents, 'who innocently passed through deplorable mental torture', to Shuyiman, 'alias "Gulasha Bap", who did more than any other person regarding my safety and welfare' and to all those, 'friend or foe…who fell in South East Asia during the Second World War'. Sadly, there are only a handful of written accounts by African soldiers from the entire war. None is as complete, as powerful and as elegant as *A Stroke of Unbelievable Luck*.

I stumbled across a copy in the library of the Imperial War Museum in London in 2009. I had lived for several years in Nigeria, where I was a reporter, and had become intrigued by the story of the African soldiers who fought in Burma. Although I had left Lagos in 2001, I had always wanted to learn more about this forgotten aspect of the Second World War. But, at least initially, the museum's library was something of a disappointment. There was plenty of material on the Burma campaign, and some even about African soldiers, but all of it written by British officers. Even the most colourful and perceptive accounts gave only a limited insight into the Africans' point of view. Why did they go to Burma? Were they forced to do so? Did they believe in the British cause? How did their experiences change them? These questions intrigued me, but answers were elusive. So I was surprised and delighted when I found Isaac's memoir on the library shelves. I had never heard of Isaac Fadoyebo, but after reading his story I knew that I had to try to track him down. Here was the man who could bring the Burma Boys to life, who could help me understand the thoughts and motivations of these African soldiers. Moreover, Isaac's unusual tale of tragedy and survival had already raised new questions in my mind about the war, Africa and Burma.

In truth, I was not hopeful that I would find him. The British academic who'd edited *A Stroke of Unbelievable Luck* had not heard from him in ten years. I knew that, even if Isaac were still alive, he would be an old man, and I wondered what sort of health he'd be in. But I managed to get hold of an address in Surelere, and asked a friend in Lagos to pass by there and see if there was, by any chance, a venerable Mr Fadoyebo at home. I heard nothing back for several weeks, and assumed the worst. Then I got an email from my friend: 'I went there. I found him! But his leg is bad, and he has difficulty moving. He says you should call him. I think you should do so quickly.' At the bottom of the email was a phone number.

I was living in Athens at the time. I went up to the rooftop terrace of my apartment, where the mobile phone signal was strongest. I remembered the capricious nature of Nigerian telecommunications; the rooftop would be a good place to shout if the line was weak. I looked over the domes and cupolas of the Byzantine chapels of our Plaka neighbourhood, to the Acropolis above, and mouthed a prayer. The ringing tone in Lagos was faint, but the voice that answered was strong, stronger than I had dared to hope. 'Mr Phillips,' it boomed, 'when are you coming?'

Isaac was eighty-five years old when I met him and he told me his story. We sat facing each other on a pair of the white, not-quite sturdy plastic chairs that are ubiquitous at any social occasion in Nigeria, our knees almost touching. I was leaning forward, holding a small digital recording machine. Isaac spoke methodically, and punctuated his sentences with the occasional deep, slow chuckle. 'Poor Essien whispered to me,' said Isaac, now whispering himself in a suddenly hoarse voice, '"Take me, God, take me home, O God."' He re-enacted Essien's dying gasps, just as he had heard them the first time, and then came to a sudden stop. When he was explaining how he nearly died crossing the paddy field, he said that, had the villagers not come to rescue him with a stretcher, his bones would still be lying in that field, 'turned over and over at yearly intervals by the ploughing implements of the local rice farmers'. He was silent for a long time, looking down and shaking his head, as if he could see his neglected bones jutting out of that damp soil and the enormity of his adventure was hitting him for the first time. 'At yearly intervals,' he repeated, with just a hint of relish.

When Isaac tried to explain why he'd joined the Army, he blamed it on 'youthful exuberance'. A particularly cruel British officer was a 'bad egg' and an ill-disciplined colleague was 'a miscreant'. The young thief with the knife in the jungle was guilty of great 'wickedness against my haggard and pathetic figure'. Each archaic turn of phrase gave me a little insight into his character. His self-effacing manner, his stoicism, was somehow familiar. I realised that Isaac reminded me of my grandparents' generation at home in England, of their emotional restraint, and how they would talk about the war when I was a small boy. Or, in fact, *not* talk about it very much, unless prompted. My grandfather would mention his experiences on D-Day in an off-hand way, but only if I badgered him. Isaac had some of the same mannerisms. In a peculiar way, he was very 'British'.

We talked in the bare courtyard of his home in Surelere. Blue lizards, with bobbing red heads and fat tails of a faded orange colour, ran along the tops of the walls that hemmed us in. There was no breeze, and we had to shift our chairs to catch the retreating shade. Isaac lived alone, not in the main house of the compound, which was a small bungalow that he was now renting out, but in an even more modest, two-room house, at the back of the property, with sun-bleached yellow walls streaked with grey smears. Inside, his possessions were piled chaotically in the dark living room, and the windows were covered in dust. 'Forgive the mess,' he would say, embarrassed, before adding, by way of explanation, 'when I move back to the village, I'll be taking all this with me.'

There had been no electricity in his neighbourhood for a week. Each time Isaac wanted to watch football on television, he had to turn on the noisy generator. Still, he did his best to be an attentive host. I sipped a warm Coca-Cola, and, when I had finished, a small boy loitering on the street outside was brusquely dispatched to bring another bottle.

The first day that I visited happened to coincide with Nigeria's presidential election. After we had spoken for some time, Isaac and I made our way to the polling station at the end of his little cul-de-sac. Isaac's movements were slow. It took him some time to get out of his chair and onto his feet, getting into position by manoeuvring his weight onto his good leg, and then heaving himself up with trembling arms. He walked stiffly, with a limp. But, when he was upright, he was still a tall, impressive man. Isaac maintained a steady, dignified pace as he walked down the street. Everybody greeted him, and he seemed to know who they were without turning his head, greeting everyone back by name. At the polling station, he was ushered to the front. 'Make way for Pa, make way for Pa,' urged the electoral officials. They didn't need to; the long line of voters, some of whom had been waiting for hours, had already moved aside for him. 'Thank you, Sistah,' Isaac said to a female official, before dropping his neatly folded voting slip into the ballot box.

Nearly all of Isaac's daughters and many grandchildren lived somewhere in the vast sprawl of Lagos. They visited him regularly, bringing food and checking on his health. They gave him lifts around the city, and at weekends accompanied him to the innumerable weddings, baptisms, birthday parties, chieftaincy ceremonies and funerals that are the essence of every Lagosian's social life. He was clearly a much-loved man, yet he struck me as being lonely. Who is not, really, at the age of eighty-five? I sensed he had not spoken about all of his memories for some time. His family knew the outline of his experiences in Burma, but it had been many years since he had shared them in their entirety. He was not one to volunteer too much if he felt he lacked an enthusiastic audience. He only really got going with me after he saw my interest. Maybe it was the very intensity of Isaac's recollections that was the basis of his loneliness.

It would be tempting to say that Isaac was haunted by his months in the jungle, but that's not quite accurate. He looked back on his survival with a sense of wonder. *Was that really me? How did I come through it?* He remembered many details with extraordinary clarity; not just the dramatic moments such as when he was shot or rescued, but also the names of colleagues and officers and the words he'd picked up when trying to converse with Shuyiman and the other villagers. In all our conversations, I only ever noticed one major inaccuracy. Isaac had a recollection of seeing Gandhi in India, on the journey from Bombay to Calcutta. A stationmaster – he thought it was at Nagpur – needed help controlling the crowds who had come to see the hero of India's independence struggle. 'Otherwise they would have mobbed him to death,' Isaac said. 'People thought that if you had any problems, and you touched him, everything would be solved, if you were sick you'd be healed…they saw him as a saint.' So the African soldiers were asked to guard Gandhi. 'We soldiers saw him, very small fellow, in his loin-cloth, very small frame,' said Isaac, 'and we protected him. I didn't hear him talk, I just saw him.' Later, as I read more about Gandhi's life, I realised this encounter could not have taken place. At least it could not have been in November 1943, when Isaac was travelling to Calcutta, because Gandhi was in prison from August 1942 to May 1944. Perhaps it happened on Isaac's return journey to Bombay, in early 1945, but by then he was recuperating from his injuries, and moving on crutches with some difficulty. He would not have been asked to police a political rally. Still, Nagpur is on the railway line from Bombay to Calcutta. Maybe another African soldier helped guard Gandhi there, and told Isaac about it. Memories can slip away from us, but they can also be preserved in a distorted form that calcifies over time. Perhaps Isaac, at some subconscious level, wished he had seen Gandhi.

Isaac often talked about David Kargbo. And yet, after the day they said goodbye in Freetown harbour, the two men never wrote or spoke to each other again. Isaac struggled to answer my question as to why they had not swapped addresses and written in subsequent years. 'It was not something that occurred to me' was all he said, but he seemed perplexed and saddened by his own answer. By the time

Isaac had wanted to get in touch, he did not know how to even start looking for David. It could be that, in the years immediately after the war, they had both associated letter-writing with being in the Army. Or that Isaac, always conscious of David's seniority in rank and age, had felt somewhat inhibited from maintaining a friendship. Or perhaps, as they set out on new lives in Africa, each of them intent on finding work and starting a family, they did not want to dwell on what they had endured together.

Captain Brown was also in Isaac's thoughts these many years later. Sometimes he speculated that the Captain had survived Japanese captivity after all. He would rerun in his mind those last moments he had seen him. 'He gave me tea, I took it to be my Last Supper,' he said, 'then the Japanese took him away. I thought he would make it. He had no scratch on him.' A few hours later, he'd recall, with sadness, that Captain Brown had never been seen again. I think Isaac sensed that he was drawing closer to the end of his life. He was thinking of those who had helped him on the previous occasion when he had confronted death. Maybe he expected to be reunited with them one day soon. In his old age, Isaac only went to church on rare occasions, but it seemed that his faith never wavered.

Isaac wanted to show me something that he kept in a box under his bed. He brought out a yellowed piece of paper, carefully folded but thin and brittle after all these years. It was a certificate, from 4 February 1946, signed by a British officer, Major General R.L. Bond, thanking 'NA/46573 Private Isaac Fadoyebo' for 'Loyal Service' with the Royal West African Frontier Force. Then he produced a little grey booklet, his Service Record from his time in the British Army. Under 'Campaigns Fought', a civil servant with a neat hand had written 'Burma'. Under the next column, entitled 'Medals', the same hand had written 'Not Yet Decided'. I read the words and looked at Isaac. Not yet decided? That was six-and-a-half decades ago, since when Isaac had heard nothing more. How long did the British Army need to make up its mind, and how much courage did a man need to show to merit a medal? There was a long and awkward silence, broken by

Isaac, as if he could see my embarrassment. 'Medals? Why would I want medals? These are enough, they show I was there.' These documents mattered to him, I realised, because they were incontrovertible proof that he was entitled to his military pension. He did not keep them for sentimental reasons.

Winston Churchill once wrote that there is nothing more exhilarating in war than being shot at by the enemy but the bullets missing. Isaac wouldn't have known; the only time he had been shot at, he was hit. In that sense, his taste of 'real war' had lasted only a matter of minutes. But it was what happened to him in the weeks and months that followed that was so extraordinary.

Isaac knew that he was sharing his old age with his family only because of the courage and generosity of a man with whom he had had no contact for sixty-seven years. He said, 'Not a day goes by without me thinking of my debt of gratitude to Shuyiman. How I would love to see him again.'

14

HERE YOU LEFT US

||||||||||||||||||||||||||||||||||||||||||||||||||||||||||||||||||||||||||||||||||||||||||||||||||||||||||||||||||

Wait and look at this sight, you people who are passing by
From West Africa, from the cold parts of Europe,
from the hottest parts of India
and from faraway Australia
We came to lay down our lives
Six feet under the ground
Our bones rest
When you get home, help us tell those people
that we won't have the chance to
Meet in this world again, that
Here you left us
Inscription on makeshift grave in Burma

||||||||||||||||||||||||||||||||||||||||||||||||||||||||||||||||||||||||||||||||||||||||||||||||||||||||||||||||||

April 2011
Lagos

Isaac's words stuck in my head: 'How I wish I could see Shuyiman and his people again. Himself, his wife Khatoun, his daughter Gulasha, and the baby. They were wonderful, they were sent by God to take care of me.' The reality, which neither of us voiced but which I think we both understood, was that he would not see Shuyiman again. Isaac was frail and his world was shrinking. He was in no condition to make the journey back to a remote part of Burma, even if his daughters allowed him to go. As for Shuyiman, he had not been a young man in 1944; surely he would have died many years ago. And yet I knew Isaac was still troubled by the fact that he had never said goodbye to Shuyiman. He had never thanked him for everything he'd done to save his life.

Over the course of my trips to Nigeria, and as Isaac shared more of his memories with me, I had warmed to his modesty, integrity and gentle humour. He had become my friend. I was growing close to Isaac's family as well; his children and grandchildren represented a snapshot of the vitality and ingenuity of Lagos that I had always enjoyed. I wanted to help Isaac. When I suggested that I should try to find Shuyiman's family, he leapt at the idea. He would write a letter that I could carry to Burma.

The further I delved into Isaac's story – in long conversations with him and other British and African veterans – the more I understood that it revealed another, far greater debt, the one between Britain and Africa. The African men who volunteered to fight for Britain, and who did so in a system that gave them scant reward, are among the least celebrated of all the soldiers of the Second World War. A West African contingent took part in the Victory Parade through the streets of London in June 1946, but thereafter their contribution quickly faded from memory. More than half a century would pass before the British authorities would put up a monument, on Constitution Hill, honouring the millions of Indian, Caribbean and African troops who fought in the two World Wars. There is a pavilion beside the monument, which records the names of seventy-four soldiers from the Empire who were awarded the highest medals for valour and gallantry – the George Cross and the Victoria Cross. Not a single one of them is a black African. I was in no position to atone for all the crimes and mistakes of Empire, nor, in fact, was I oblivious to the sincere intentions of some of those who helped run the colonies. I was not even sure in what form the debt to the African soldiers who went to Burma could ever be repaid. But I had the strong conviction that remembering them was a good place to start.

I found myself in a dispiriting correspondence with an official at the British Ministry of Defence, trying to find out what could be done about Isaac's medals. The official, whose job it was specifically to deal with such historic cases, bafflingly said that the British did not issue medals 'to overseas personnel as it was the responsibility of their own nation'. It was difficult to know whether he wrote these words out of ignorance, or just plain indifference to the claim of an old man living in faraway Nigeria. I explained that Isaac was a subject of the British Crown at the time of the war, and, secondly, that in 1945 even those who did envisage a self-governing Nigeria had no idea when it would achieve that status. Was every African who fought in Burma supposed to wait for a notional independence date before finding out whether he would get a medal? And why should this have been the responsibility of African countries anyway, rather than the British for whom these men had fought? In fact, the British did give medals to some African soldiers immediately after the war, so it seemed that Isaac had been the victim of some sort of oversight at that time. According to my reading of the regulations, he was at least eligible for the 'Burma Star', awarded to all those who fought for the British in the Burma campaign. The official at the Ministry of Defence promised to look into the matter, but, despite my repeated enquiries, I never heard from him again. Later, I learnt that Captain Brown, who served alongside Isaac and died in the Burmese jungle, received four posthumous, and fully deserved, medals. Isaac was not treated with similar decency. 'Not Yet Decided' were destined to be the final words on his military decorations.

On my last morning in Lagos, I went to Isaac's house in Surelere to say goodbye. He had not heard me enter the compound. I found him in the yard, hunched over a table, half-dressed in shorts and an old vest, but writing intently. For the first time, I saw Isaac's misshapen right leg. He had no right knee as such, just a long dark scar underneath where his kneecap had once been. He was absorbed in composing the letter that he wanted me to deliver to Shuyiman's family.

In it, he confessed that Suleman and Dauda Ali were actually named Isaac and David, that they had pretended to be Muslims because of their desperate need for help. He felt it was important for the villagers to know this. He folded up the sheet and told me to take it away. 'There must be remnants of Shuyiman's village still standing,' he said unreassuringly. 'It's a farm in a rural area,' he added, waving his hand dismissively, 'completely rural.' I took the letter, and said my farewell.

I chose not to share with Isaac my fears as to how difficult it would be to find Mairong, or track down Shuyiman's family.

Taukkyan Cemetery is twenty miles north of Rangoon, set back from a busy road. The forest around the cemetery is thick and tangled, but inside the grounds the gravestones are set in regimented rows, the grass neatly cut, the bushes symmetrically shaped. A grey stone cenotaph with a central rotunda stands in the middle of the cleared land, a sort of temple dedicated to those soldiers whose bodies were never recovered. On each of its multiple faces are the names of the men who died fighting for Britain. There are no dates or ages for these men, and they have no epitaphs; just desolate rows of British, Indian and African names, inscribed side by side, regiment by regiment, the fallen of the Burma campaign, 26,380 in all. Whatever people think of the British Empire, it is meticulous in recording its dead.

The British got their victory in Burma, but it came at a heavy price. Rangoon fell in May 1945, as the monsoon rains began again and as Russian tanks were fighting their way into Berlin. The Japanese army evacuated the Burmese capital without a shot being fired, just as the British had done some three years earlier. It felt like an anti-climax. The Japanese left behind a devastated city, its streets buried under mud, rubbish and filth, as well as piles of now worthless Japanese occupation banknotes. There were no trams or buses. Shops and offices had been comprehensively looted in the anarchic period between the Japanese withdrawal and the arrival of the first British soldiers. Allied bombing raids had destroyed many buildings. There was no

232 Another Man's War

electricity or sanitation. Somehow, the 2,500-year-old Shwedagon Pagoda had stood undamaged through it all, and it rose majestically above the stinking wreckage of the city, its golden Buddhas retaining their perpetual calm.

The last weeks of war were fought in heavy rain as the British, now with Aung San's Burmese forces on their side, did their utmost to prevent the Japanese from escaping to the south and east. Although it still numbered some 70,000 men at this point, the Japanese army was, in General Slim's words, 'broken and scattered'. Many units had lost their artillery and transport. The soldiers caught in the Arakan made frantic efforts to rejoin their comrades further east, but many drowned on river crossings, or were killed by British artillery or Burmese guerrillas. For the first time, Japanese soldiers surrendered in their hundreds. Japanese casualties were appalling. Overall, some 185,000 Japanese soldiers were killed in battle or died of starvation or disease in Burma, more than half the total invasion force of 300,000 men.

By now, British generals were looking ahead, to the invasion of Malaya, and they pushed forward with all their might. Only the dropping of the atomic bombs on Hiroshima and Nagasaki brought the horror to an end, and even then isolated groups of Japanese soldiers fought on for weeks, apparently believing that reports of the Emperor's surrender were Allied propaganda. It was the longest campaign fought by the British Army in the Second World War, some three years and eight months of toil and bloodshed.

The diaries and memoirs of the British officials who struggled to re-impose their authority in Burma after the Japanese surrender make for dismal reading. It wasn't just Rangoon that was in ruins. Towns like Prome, Myitkyina and Meiktila had been flattened. Railways, mines, oil refineries, pipelines and river barges across the country had been destroyed, by the departing British in 1942 and their subsequent bombing raids, as well as by the retreating Japanese in 1945. Of some 1,200 passenger railcars in service before the war, only 12 remained. *Dacoits*, or bandits, roamed the countryside, armed with weapons that the Japanese had left behind.

The British would discover that their ability to rule faced another challenge, which was less tangible but ultimately more significant than all the physical destruction had been. Before the war, the Burmese had acquiesced in British rule, even if only under duress. Now, many no longer accepted it. Those British officials who expected that the majority of Burmese would be delighted to see them again after the chastening experience of Japanese rule were to be sorely disappointed. With the benefit of hindsight, all the sacrifices of the Burma campaign look strangely futile. Only three years would pass before Burma gained its independence, and, in a painful snub to Britain, it chose not to become a member of the Commonwealth.

Balwant Singh, a civil servant of Indian origin working in the British administration, had survived the Japanese occupation. He immediately sensed when the British returned after the war that it was impossible to put the clock back. Nobody could forget how the colonial masters had run away in 1942. General Slim's brilliant campaign had ensured an eventual victory on the field of battle, but 'the rules of the game had changed…the old aura of power and prestige was gone'. In 1945, Singh went to the installation in Mandalay of a British district commissioner. He watched the attendants in white robes and traditional headdresses, standing stiffly by the Sidaw, the 'Royal Drum' once used by Burman kings. The commissioner, in blue shorts, a white shirt and knee stockings, made an awkward speech about British plans for the future. 'The speech done, he gave away the awards and the ceremony was over,' Singh wrote in his diary. 'The Commissioner marched away grinning. I could almost believe that he saw the charade – the vain attempt of the British Raj to reestablish its prewar prestige.' Singh was posted to the countryside south of Mandalay, but his attempts to collect taxes were thwarted by *dacoits* and the growing separatist and Communist insurgencies. He and a dedicated group of policemen risked their lives several times to try to maintain order, but eventually lost all contact with the central government in Rangoon.

Similarly, Robert Mole, the deputy commissioner who had been so upset with the behaviour of West African troops in the Arakan during the war, was posted to the Irrawaddy Delta in late 1945. The delta had never been a popular posting among British officials – the climate was hot and humid and the mosquitoes unforgiving – but Mole seemed to have a particularly unhappy time. He was a fluent Burmese speaker with an astute understanding of the country but he soon discovered that the respect he had enjoyed before the war as a member of the civil service had simply vanished. The police, instead of helping him fight the endemic banditry, were involved in it themselves. Each month, he received reports of some one hundred violent crimes, including robbery, murder and rape, in the surrounding countryside. Mole's junior staff were 'almost without exception, lazy, uninterested, and very much involved in politics', in his account. The local politicians were 'dismal and sordid'; they did not bother to turn up to meetings, and generally refused to co-operate with him.

At least this time Mole was grateful for the presence of West African soldiers. The 82nd Division was still in Burma, guarding railways, escorting Japanese prisoners of war and patrolling through towns and villages to deter bandits. Some British officers reassured themselves with the idea that the Africans' impressive physiques would intimidate would-be troublemakers among the local population. A brigade from the Gold Coast was sent to help Mole, and he was pleased to see how well they got on with the Burmese. Sometimes, very well. One day, an African soldier and a Burmese girl came to him and asked if he could preside over their marriage. Mole tried to dissuade them, on the basis that 'the African could speak no Burmese and the girl had no English or African tongue, and how they managed to communicate their affection to each other was a mystery'.

There were other West Africans who got into romantic difficulties after the war. An intelligence officer for the 82nd Division wrote in November 1945 that several men had paid expensive dowries to Burmese families, with a view to taking a bride home. Unfortunately for these men, in many cases, the romance was not to last. The women ran away before embarkation, leaving the men feeling cheated. 'The Africans have been officially warned against this practice,' wrote the officer, 'but being as a race accustomed to fair dealing, they view these occasions with some resentment.'

Thousands of men from the British Army remained in Burma into 1946. On 22 April, many of them gathered in Rangoon for a two-day athletics meeting. The West African soldiers gave a dazzling performance on the track, sweeping the awards in the sprints, hurdles and high jump. Later in the festivities, the West Africans' massed bands, led by an elderly bandmaster and drummers draped in leopard skins, brought the spectators in the packed grandstands to their feet. But some of the more prescient officers who were there on those rousing days understood the poignancy of the event, at least as far as the British were concerned. John McEnery, a young lieutenant in the 82nd Division, knew that he was witnessing nothing less than 'the last great manifestation of the British Empire overseas. Never again would there be such a mixed gathering of British, Indian, Burma Army and West African troops.' At dusk at the end of the second day, the crowd hushed as the buglers played 'Retreat' and the Union Jack came down.

The Nigerians were the last West African soldiers to leave Rangoon, in October 1946. They held a torchlight farewell tattoo through the streets. British power in Burma was draining away.

The Attlee government in London began negotiating Britain's departure from India shortly after it won the election in 1945. Once Britain had made the decision to quit India, its position in Burma also became untenable. Its authority over Indian soldiers, who comprised the majority of men on the ground in Burma, was greatly diminished. Without the means to send other troops from further afield, the British lost their military power at precisely the moment when they needed it most. The nationalists, led by the uncompromising Aung San, sensed that Britain had no stomach, and not enough resources, for a fight. The Burmese police went on strike, forcing matters further. Even the assassination of Aung San by a political rival in July 1947 could not derail the movement for independence.

The last British governor, Sir Herbert Rance, presided over the independence ceremony at 4.20am on 4 January 1948. It was an inconvenient time of day for him but one deemed auspicious by Burmese astrologers. It was, oddly, the second time Burma had won its independence in the space of five years, but there was never any doubt that the British, unlike the Japanese before them, were sincere in handing over power. British officials wondered what their legacy in Burma would be. Some gloomily suggested it would not extend further than a passion for football. Unlike Indians, the Burmese had never taken to cricket, the quintessentially English game.

Burma had always been an unhappy colony, long before the Japanese tore away the fabric of imperial authority. 'The Burmese had been a proud people, unused to living in subjection to an alien race, and throughout their history had generally been the conquerors rather than the conquered,' wrote Mole. The unceremonious ousting of the last Burman king in 1885, the incorporation of Burma into British India's administration and the disruption of traditional land ownership structures had created deep resentments. But, just as in Africa, it was the Second World War that was the catalyst for change, and which hastened the end of the Empire. There was one important difference, however. In Nigeria, the war raised the colonial subjects up. In Burma, it dragged the colonial masters down. The result was a swifter, less dignified British departure from Burma.

Some Burmese argue that there has been no real peace in their country since the day the Japanese began their bombing raids over Rangoon in December 1941. Indeed, the historian Thant Myint-U has written, 'In a way Burma is a place where the Second World War never really stopped.' And, throughout the turbulent post-war decades, Burma has struggled with the most basic questions: what is this country, and who belongs to it?

Just as in Nigeria, the British created and then hurriedly pulled out of an inherently unstable country. With their departure, the minority populations – the Karens, the Kachins, the Shans and so on – could not help but view independence with trepidation, fearing it meant inevitable domination by the Bamar majority. They had been excluded from the talks between the British government and Aung San that set the timetable for an independent Burma. Although they were promised autonomy and equal rights, the agreements quickly unravelled following Aung San's assassination. The departing British were berated by all sides. On the one hand, the new Burmese government accused them of 'divide and rule', the charge so familiar from Nigeria and many other colonies; on the other hand, the ethnic minorities said they had been betrayed by the imperial master, which many had served with loyalty, even during the bleakest days of the war.

In the immediate aftermath of the British departure, Burma was on the verge of breaking apart completely. Communists, ethnic rebels and mutinous soldiers took over most of the country. Gradually, through the 1950s, the Burmese army fought back, retaking territory and establishing control beyond Rangoon. Britain, at that time still hoping for a close relationship with its former colony, played a vital part in the government's survival, supplying ten thousand rifles to replace those taken by mutineers, as well as Dakota aircraft and emergency aid.

In Rangoon, the British maintained a cultural foothold. Wendy Law-Yone was part of the small Anglicised elite, growing up in 1950s Burma. She read the classics of English literature at home, and shopped at the Rowe and Co. emporium in an imposing Edwardian building in downtown Rangoon. It was a time of some optimism in the country, at least for the educated classes in the capital. The new Burma was a democracy, and under Prime Minister U Nu there were regular elections, an opposition and a free press. Wendy's father, Edward Law-Yone, a courageous and outspoken man, was founder and editor of *The Nation*, an independent English-language newspaper. He was both a Burmese nationalist and a committed Anglophile, proud of his command of the English language. Indeed, when Edward Law-Yone was in full flow, it was difficult for anyone else to compete.

He once returned from lunch with Somerset Maugham, complaining that the famous wit and raconteur was 'a man of few words'; on another occasion, he publicly reprimanded the British ambassador for misquoting Shakespeare. He enjoyed going to the races and mixing with the cosmopolitan crowd that lived in Rangoon in the early years of independence. Their house, said Wendy, was often full of British embassy friends and 'old Burma hands'.

The intellectuals at the top of Burmese society revelled in their new freedoms, even as they sometimes looked back with nostalgia to the days of Empire. When the British were here, they liked to say, things worked in an orderly way, and there was none of the chaos and corruption that they blamed on the local officials who'd taken their place. Wendy had a nagging sense that both Burma and her family were living on borrowed time, that something would eventually give way. The danger signs were there. 'Even to a child,' she said, 'the adult conversations were peppered with *dacoits* and rebels and insurgents.' Everyone had guns, including Wendy's teenage brothers. Elections turned violent. Prime Minister U Nu lost his grip over his own party. Secessionist wars were also having an impact on Burma's army – it had become a larger, more autonomous force as it fought to keep down the rebellious ethnic minorities. As the generals grew more powerful, they also grew more acquisitive, buying up commercial interests, including Rowe and Co.

The turning point came in 1962, when General Ne Win seized power in a coup d'état. Wendy remembered the sudden chill that descended over Rangoon in the days that followed. 'The most frightening thing was the number of people who were jailed,' she said. 'There would just be rumours: "My god, he's disappeared, nobody knows where he's gone and nobody knows why." It changed dramatically.'

Inevitably, the soldiers came for her father, arresting him at the family home in the middle of the night. Edward spent five years in prison, much of it in solitary confinement. *The Nation* was shut down.

The new regime was determined to reshape society on puritanical lines. People became afraid of being seen or even talking to outsiders. Most foreigners were forced to leave Burma and visitors were restricted to twenty-four-hour visas. Horseracing and beauty contests were banned; nightclubs were closed. A few cinemas stayed open, repeatedly playing the handful of movies that survived the censors. Wendy and her brothers, starved of any other entertainment, could recite the screenplays of entire Bing Crosby films, verbatim. Hundreds of businesses and industries were nationalised, and soon the shops were empty. This was Ne Win's 'Burmese Way To Socialism'.

Of this time, Thant Myint-U wrote, 'it was as if someone had just turned off the lights on a chaotic and often corrupt but nevertheless vibrant and competitive society'. When Wendy tried to flee the country, she too was imprisoned. She was eventually released and allowed to go into exile in Thailand. Like many Burmese intellectuals who left in those years, she would never live in her country again. Edward was also released, and promptly got involved in a somewhat farcical attempt to organise an armed revolution against the military regime. When this failed, he moved to the United States where he died in exile.

Two weeks after Isaac gave me his letter, I looked up and down the grey slabs of stone of the cenotaph at Taukkyan Cemetery. Some of the names evoked the mud-walled cities of northern Nigeria – *Musa Gaya, Musa Sheriff, Musa Sokoto* – while others spoke of fishing villages on the Gold Coast – *Kofi Manu (38311), Kofi Manu (59904), Kofi Mensa, Kofi Osoedi, Kofi Sam*. Then I found the section entitled 'West African Army Medical Corps', traced with my finger downwards and my heart missed a beat. For here was Company Sergeant Major Archibong Bassey Duke, who fell beside Isaac clutching his red enamel cup of tea. And here was David Essien, who gasped, 'Take me, O God, take me, O God' as he lay dying. And Daniel Adeniran, who was also killed on that riverbank that same morning; and Felix Okoro who drowned in the Kaladan a few days before the attack; and even poor Moses Lamina, who suffered a slow and lingering death some weeks later, and whose corpse was eaten by jackals. They were all obscure men, but each of their names cried out to me. To find them here was a validation of Isaac Fadoyebo's memory.

He had never had access to an official casualty list, and he did not know these men's families back in Nigeria or Sierra Leone. But their fates were seared onto his conscience, and he still wondered why he had lived and they had died. The answer, he was sure, was Shuyiman.

15

NATIVES OF ARAKAN

IIIIIIIIIIIIIIIIIIIIIIIIIIIIIIIIIIIIIIIIIIIIIIIIIIIIIIIIIIIIIIIIIIIIIIIIIIIIIIIIIIIIIIIIIIIIIIIIIIIIIIIIIIIIIIII

Mohammedans, who have long been settled in Arakan, and who call themselves Rooinga, or natives of Arakan...

Francis Buchanan-Hamilton, *Asiatick Reseaches*

IIIIIIIIIIIIIIIIIIIIIIIIIIIIIIIIIIIIIIIIIIIIIIIIIIIIIIIIIIIIIIIIIIIIIIIIIIIIIIIIIIIIIIIIIIIIIIIIIIIIIIIIIIIIIIII

19 June 2011
Rangoon

Under General Ne Win, Burma turned inwards. His xenophobic and repressive regime was to become one of the longest-running military dictatorships in the world, driven, it seemed, as much by the memory of the humiliation of colonial rule as by an acute sense of threat to his country's unity. British-trained civil servants were sacked en masse, and British-trained officers were weeded out of the national army.

The regime was also vehemently opposed to giving ethnic minorities greater autonomy. The Burmese army tried to cut off the insurgency areas from the rest of the country. Whole towns and villages were destroyed, and residents were forced to move into mass relocation camps, whether or not they themselves had any connection with the rebels. But the fighting dragged on, fuelled in part by the heroin trade, from which the army and various rebel militias were earning huge profits.

Burma's soldiers, like their Nigerian counterparts, had grabbed power because they believed they were the only ones who could hold their country together. But Nigeria's generals ultimately lacked the ability, and possibly even the desire, to build an enduring military state. Instead, they contented themselves with looting oil revenues from the national treasury, with disastrous results for ordinary Nigerians. In Burma, the dictatorship was more complete, more perfect in a sense. The military seized control of much of the economy – gemstones, logging and oil – but also asserted its power over society as a whole. The generals saw themselves as the protectors and promoters of the nation's traditional Buddhist culture. They changed Burma's name, to Myanmar, ostensibly a more inclusive word for the non-Bamar population but also one that marked a clear break with the colonial past. Christianity and Islam, the religions of the ethnic minorities, were marginalised. The army continued to grow and consume an ever-larger portion of the government's budget. Over the decades, the military and the state became one.

I had flown into Rangoon, now known as Yangon, on an evening of glowering skies in June 2011. I had reported from Africa for fifteen years, but this was my first visit to South East Asia and I had little idea of what to expect. The monsoon rains had begun and much of the lowland of the Irrawaddy Delta was underwater. From the plane, it was impossible to say where the sea ended and the land began; there was no coastline as such, just a merging of grey waters as the Bay of Bengal met the paddy fields and fishponds of the delta. Palm trees, wind-lashed and sodden, stood like sentinels over this drowned landscape.

The city streets were dark at night, long avenues lined with mango and frangipani trees but few streetlights. I caught glimpses of elegant couples passing in and out of the shadows. In the hotel lobbies, there were many more Chinese businessmen than tourists. In downtown Rangoon, heavy old colonial buildings – government offices, banks and law courts, mostly – sat dark and brooding behind Doric columns. Many were stained green and black from damp and decades of neglect. They exuded sadness.

I had entered Burma pretending to be a tourist, because foreign journalists and writers were not welcome. The country was in a state of transition, and nobody seemed sure in which direction it was heading. A few weeks before my arrival, the military regime had surprised its critics by appearing to step aside. An elected, civilian government had, at least notionally, taken its place. But many opposition politicians had been prevented from taking part in the elections, or had chosen to boycott them, unconvinced that the regime was sincere about loosening its control over the country. It was not easy to read the generals' minds. They seemed keen to end Burma's isolation, and they certainly wanted more investment to revive the moribund economy. But there were also good reasons to be sceptical of their intentions.

Burma had known false dawns in the past, moments when it seemed the military might give way. Yet, brutal and tenacious, it had always clung on. There had been the great uprising of 1988, the annulled election of 1990 and, as recently as 2007, the 'Saffron Revolution', when Buddhist monks had protested and soldiers had used live ammunition to break up the crowds. The latest elections had taken place in November 2010, under a new constitution drawn up by the military twenty years after it had dissolved the last one. The constitution specified that a quarter of the seats in parliament were reserved for the military. The new president, Thein Sein, was a former general, and he appointed fellow officers to almost all the positions of power. If this really was a revolution, it was a carefully controlled, top-down one.

Hundreds of political prisoners were still in jail. The opposition leader, Aung San Suu Kyi, had been released from house arrest six days after the 2010 elections, but she remained non-committal about whether she would engage in the political process. She was a Nobel Peace Prize recipient, but her image was banned, her party illegal. Despite these restrictions, or perhaps in part because of them, she had attained an almost mythical status. She was admired at home and abroad, a resolute and morally courageous woman who had sacrificed her freedom in order to save her country. And, as the daughter of Aung San, the man who had charmed first the Japanese and then General Slim before becoming the martyred hero of the independence struggle, she had a legitimacy that subsequent military regimes could only envy. To many Burmese, Aung San Suu Kyi was simply 'The Lady'.

I had arrived in Burma just days before her birthday, and the authorities feared there would be demonstrations in her honour. Groups of soldiers and policemen – a Burmese friend referred to them disparagingly as 'green monkeys and blue monkeys' – stood on the wet street corners. The patrols watched passers-by with impassive faces, machine guns jutting from their ponchos. Their presence was unusual; the security forces in Burma tended to keep a discreet profile and were rarely seen on Rangoon's streets. But, if the armed men intended to deter any protests, they seemed to have succeeded. The crowds scurried past, heads bowed.

Rangoon was a city of strange, stilted conversations. People seemed to talk to me in riddles, hinting at fear and frustration rather than explicitly spelling it out, only to abruptly shut up whenever a stranger approached. The regime's spies, I was warned, were everywhere, and wearing plain clothes.

The newspapers, still rigidly censored, were a curious mixture of anodyne reports on ministerial workshops or road-construction projects, and shrill warnings of the dangers of foreign interference. The *New Light of Myanmar* printed a large notice on its back page every day, denouncing the Voice of America and the BBC for 'sowing hatred among the people' with their 'killer broadcasts designed to cause troubles'. Under the title 'People's Desire', it listed the objectives to which patriotic readers should aspire. They should 'oppose those relying on external elements, acting as stooges, holding negative views… wipe out those inciting unrest and violence' and 'crush all internal and external destructive elements as the common enemy'. The people should strive, above all, to become 'polite and disciplined citizens'.

In subsequent months, the situation in Rangoon would change

dramatically. Aung San Suu Kyi met President Thein Sein, and afterwards announced that her party, the National League for Democracy, would rejoin the political process and contest future elections. Many political prisoners were released, and Thein Sein enacted new laws that allowed workers to form unions and recognised the right to peaceful protest. American and European leaders arrived, promising an end to Burma's political and economic isolation from the West. Posters of Aung San Suu Kyi began to appear on walls and in shops all over the city, and the *New Light of Myanmar* stopped printing its daily denunciations of evil foreigners and their domestic stooges. Rangoon's days of fear were over.

On a city junction, behind wrought-iron gates and an overgrown garden is what remains of the Pegu Club, once the preserve of senior British Army officers and civil servants. It is now derelict. George Orwell, who was born in India and worked in Burma for five years as a policeman, understood the significance of the racially exclusive club in the Empire. In his novel *Burmese Days*, he wrote, 'In any town in India the European Club is the spiritual citadel, the real seat of the British power, the Nirvana for which native officials and millionaires pine in vain.' The club gave the Englishman a chance to play billiards and bridge, or share complaints about the natives with his colleagues. It emphasised his separateness and superiority. In the last years of British rule, the colonial government tried to make such clubs open up their membership to the Burmese, and the tensions around this process are central to Orwell's story in *Burmese Days*.

After independence, when most of the British went home, it turned out there were not so many Burmese who had been pining to join these prestigious institutions after all. Edward Law-Yone, in a 1951 editorial for *The Nation*, urged his fellow countrymen to put aside old resentments, and take up positions in the Rangoon clubs that were now rightfully theirs. He wrote that he had it on good authority that they would be welcome, whatever their misgivings. The problem, as he saw it, was that the Burmese still suffered from an inferiority complex: 'we should like to see less veiled hostility, less shyness in consorting, or just being together with Europeans'. If only the Burmese could understand that 'there is very little snobbishness left on the part of Westerners in Burma, because the pukka sahib tradition has been broken, and they realise they are here on sufferance'. Law-Yone's pleas fell on deaf ears. Membership to the British clubs withered in the 1950s, and finally collapsed after General Ne Win's 1962 coup.

The difference with Nigeria is striking. The clubs of colonial Lagos were just as important to the British, but most of them are still thriving today. Once the likes of Aduke Alakija had forced their way into the Ikoyi Club, they never looked back. Another prominent Lagos club, the Island Club, was established in the 1940s specifically to promote inter-racial friendship. Today, it occupies the former officers' mess of the Royal West African Frontier Force. In Nigeria, British snobbishness met its match in the local elite's own sense of entitlement. Nigerians cheerfully adapted colonial traditions they admired and discarded the rest.

The ruins of the Pegu Club looked as though they might not be standing for much longer. Skyscrapers of glass and steel were rising up all over Rangoon, and land in the city centre was becoming increasingly scarce and valuable. Like the country's politics, the city was in transition, only this outcome was more predictable. The new government was planning economic reforms to attract foreign investment. As Burma gradually opened up to the world, as excited investors came in and as the population continued to grow, Rangoon's streets would become clogged with imported cars and much of its history would surely be swept away. A new city – blander, less distinctive – was taking shape.

Somehow, I had to find Shuyiman's village in the middle of the Arakan, now known as Rakhine State. The only person I knew who had been to Mairong was Isaac himself, but he was understandably vague as to its location. Isaac was never given a map in the Arakan; he went where his officers told him to go. So even before the attack, he did not have a precise sense of where he was. Afterwards, he and David

Kargbo had been traumatised and confused, barely able to communicate with the villagers who saved them. Many decades had passed since they'd been carried away from a rice farmer's *basha* in triumph.

I knew that Mairong was on the banks of the Kaladan River, but this runs through Burma for over a hundred miles before emptying into the Bay of Bengal. Isaac did not remember exactly where the 29th CCS had embarked on their raft journey, and was probably never told their intended destination. But there was one piece of information I had deduced from his account. Isaac had always said to me, 'When you are coming from India, Mairong is on the right side of the river, but, if you are returning, it is on your left side.' Just to make sure I had understood this point, he called me in London the day before I flew to Burma. 'Do you get me?!' he bellowed down the line from Lagos. 'Check the right side of the river. The right side. Is it clear?' Mairong, in other words, was on the west bank of the Kaladan. It wasn't much, but it was a start.

Slowly, by reading and crosschecking the accounts of British officers, I had managed to build up an idea of the geography of the Kaladan Valley. I knew that the 81st Division had passed through Paletwa, but had retreated from Kyauktaw after the defeat at Pagoda Hill. Mairong was somewhere between the two, which narrowed the search down to a stretch of some forty miles. It was the late John Hamilton, meticulous chronicler of the 81st Division, who came to the rescue. In his notes, he had estimated where the attack on the 29th CCS had taken place, to within a couple of miles. I had also found a large-scale American military map of the valley dating from the 1950s. This had all sorts of useful details, although, discouragingly, I could find no village on it by the name of Mairong.

There was another potential flaw in my plans. I might be able to find where the village had been, but there was no guarantee that the people who had lived in it in 1944 would still be there today. In fact, there was no guarantee the village would still be standing. The Japanese surrender had not signified the end of fighting in the Arakan, any more than it had in other parts of Burma. In 1945, the

Arakan's towns were in ruins and, as elsewhere in the country, there were large stocks of weapons available to anyone who knew how to use them. The Buddhist majority in the Arakan had largely turned against the Japanese by the end of the war, but that did not mean they were ready to welcome the returning British. In the immediate post-war chaos, a Buddhist monk, U Sein Da, rebelled against the British. His revolt was put down by force, but after independence Arakanese Buddhists continued to demand greater autonomy. They had always felt separate from the rest of Burma, and the war years had only increased their sense of isolation. Rival Communist factions also tried to align themselves to the cause of Arakanese separatism.

There was another reason for the Arakan's enduring instability, of course, and that was the discontent of its Muslim minority. The communal hatreds and fears that had helped bind Mairong to the British cause were not resolved in the years after the war. Muslim guerrillas, calling themselves Mujahid, had taken up arms in the brief period between the end of the war and independence. Some wanted an autonomous Muslim region on the border with the new neighbouring country of East Pakistan, citing alleged promises made to them by the British during the war. Just like the Karens and the Kachins, the Muslims in the Arakan had hoped that their loyalty to the Empire would be rewarded once the Japanese were driven out. Others even flirted with the idea of the northern part of the Arakan being incorporated into East Pakistan. In the confused and violent years around independence, the Mujahid co-operated not only with Communist guerrillas, but even with Arakanese Buddhists rebels; the groups spoke of dividing the region between them once they had defeated the central Burmese government. At one point, in June 1949, Rangoon lost control of all of Arakan except for the port of Akyab and its immediate surroundings.

The Mujahid never numbered more than a few thousand men, and, in the 1950s, as the Burmese army grew stronger, the guerrillas were beaten back to the jungles of the northern Arakan. There they sought refuge in the same border hills that Isaac and the West

Africans had marched across on their way into the Kaladan Valley. The insurgency spluttered on, small groups of men looting from villages and making money by smuggling rice across the border to East Pakistan.

The Mujahid guerrillas spoke of themselves as being 'Rohingya' people, a fiercely contested term. They traced the word back through the generations, as proof that Muslims are indigenes of the Arakan, descendants of Arab, Moorish and Bengali traders who arrived hundreds of years ago. But the majority Buddhist population maintained that most of the Muslims were descended from more recent immigrants who had entered Burma from India when they were both under British rule, especially in the last years of the nineteenth century. The word 'Rohingya', the Buddhists said, had only come into widespread use since the Second World War, in an attempt to lend credibility to an ethnicity that was essentially invented.

In Rangoon, successive governments regarded claims coming from any minority group as a threat to Burma's unity. Although some Arakanese Muslim leaders professed loyalty to Burma, the government gradually forced Muslims out of the civil service and police force, and excluded them from the army. But it wasn't until 1962, and the military coup, that Muslims in Arakan learnt that even their right to remain in Burma was in question.

When he took power, General Ne Win immediately decided that Burma needed to get rid of those he saw as foreigners. He ordered the confiscation of Indian property and the expulsion of hundreds of thousands of people of Indian origin from Rangoon and other cities. Many of them had only returned to their homes in Burma after the war, following the exodus as the Japanese invaded in 1942. Mira Kamdar's family had lived in Burma since the turn of the century. Her grandfather, Prabhudas Kamdar, was forced to abandon his livelihood and leave Rangoon in the early 1960s. 'All valuables were confiscated, jewelry of course; watches; cameras; radios; banknotes of more than fifty rupees,' Mira wrote of her grandfather's experience. There were also humiliations. 'Women and men alike were thoroughly searched,' she said. General Ne Win was tapping into a rich vein of Burmese prejudice; the Indians made an easy target, as the riots of the 1930s had already shown, and Indians in Rangoon were regularly called *Kalars*, a derogatory word for the dark-skinned. Wendy Law-Yone remembered the casual contempt with which poorer Indians were held at the time. 'It's awful when I look back at the routine degradation of Indians... It's amazing the number of epithets and proverbs and jokes.'

And so the Muslims of Arakan became the victims, not only of the general suspicion towards perceived outsiders, but also the specific hostility towards people of Indian appearance. They too were *Kalars*, although often the authorities spoke of them merely as 'Bengalis', a people clearly foreign to Burma's 'true' Buddhist identity. In 1978, the military regime launched *Naga Min*, or Operation Dragon King, a systematic attempt to document the population living inside Burma's borders and stop illegal immigration. About 250,000 Muslims fled across the Naf River into Bangladesh (the former East Pakistan), taking with them stories of alleged rapes and murders carried out by the Burmese military and Buddhist militias. Many of those who ran away insisted they were not immigrants from the colonial period, but a long-standing indigenous people, the Rohingyas. They said the army seemed determined to expel them from Burma.

In 1982, Ne Win's regime introduced a new Citizenship Act that excluded the Rohingya from a list of Burma's indigenous ethnicities. Existing citizens were not affected, but any new applicant needed to show 'conclusive evidence' that their ancestors had lived in the Arakan before independence in 1948. For a population of mainly subsistence farmers and fishermen, this was an almost impossible stipulation. Many of the Arakan Muslims, or Rohingyas, who could not comply were now de facto foreigners in Burma, but, as nobody else would recognise them either, they had become effectively stateless. Families that had not taken great time and effort to get citizenship papers during the years after independence often now lost the right to own land in Burma, and could no longer work in government health or education services. Their freedom of movement was restricted, even their right to marry and have as many children as they wished. They were persecuted in the country in which they had been born and lived their whole lives.

In the early 1990s, there were shadowy reports of new Mujahid guerrilla resistance groups, operating out of jungle enclaves in what was now Rakhine State. In 1991, following more allegations of persecution by the Burmese army, there was another mass exodus of Muslims into Bangladesh. But their refugee camps were disease-ridden and poorly built. Some Muslim families tried to scratch a living in Bangladesh by merging into the local population; others wandered voluntarily back across the border into Burma, or were forced to do so by the Bengali authorities. Some managed to flee further afield, to Thailand and Malaysia, Pakistan and Saudi Arabia. Today there are almost as many Muslims from the old Arakan living outside Burma as within its borders. Little wonder that in Asia they are known as the 'new Palestinians'.

I worried what had happened to the village of Mairong in the years since 1944, whether it had been caught up in these waves of unrest, and how Shuyiman's family might have been affected. Balwant Singh, describing the turmoil in central Burma in the late 1940s, said he was impressed by the resilience of many in the countryside as law and order broke down. 'No doubt they felt insecure but there was nothing to be done except mend the village defenses, keep a sharp vigil at night, stay alert and hope for the best,' he wrote. 'Meanwhile the land had to be cultivated, the cattle fed and the house fires tended.' I was assuming that this was how it had been in Mairong. The villagers would have done their best to keep their heads down, to survive.

But I couldn't be sure of anything. Perhaps Shuyiman's family had been killed by the Burmese army, a Buddhist militia or one of the various rebel groups. Or they might have fled during the upheavals of 1978 or the early '90s. Maybe they now lived in one of the miserable refugee camps in Bangladesh, or had scattered across Asia or the Muslim world. If that was the case, I would never find them and Isaac's letter of gratitude would never be passed on.

16

IMPREGNABLE

||||||||||||||||||||||||||||||||||||||||||||||||||||||||||||||||||||||||||||||||||||||||||||||||||||||

Arakan is a second Venice; its streets are rivers; its gardens, valleys; its ramparts, mountains. For, as the natives of the country are naturally weak and timid, they have chosen for their city a site fortified by nature, and impregnable by force of arms.

Father A. Farinha,
Jesuit Portuguese visitor to Mrauk U, 1639

||||||||||||||||||||||||||||||||||||||||||||||||||||||||||||||||||||||||||||||||||||||||||||||||||||||

June 2011
Rakhine State, Burma

I travelled up the Kaladan River on a wooden boat, some thirty feet long, with a stinking old diesel engine and no name. Between them, the busy crew of four steered, bailed water, repaired a flapping tarpaulin, prepared a fish curry and brewed cups of sweet milky tea to keep our spirits high. The boat was dhow-shaped, painted red and blue, with a prow and stern that rose high out of the water and a fussy, decorative balustrade along the sides. The crew had tied a glass vase full of white, daisy-like flowers to the prow, 'to bring us luck on our journey', they said.

We left the port of Sittwe and crossed the choppy sea at the mouth of the Kaladan, a distance of several miles. Black clouds gathered above us and the wind picked up. When the rain started to fall, heavier and heavier, louder and louder, there was no place to hide. The boat was tossed left and right, forwards and backwards, and the waves lashed across the small deck, soaking everything. I retreated to the back, held on to the flimsy balustrade, and wondered at the wisdom of delivering Isaac's letter at the height of the monsoon season.

The engine whined and strained as it fought against the waves. It belched black smoke, and whined a little more. It seemed only a matter of time before it would choke and die, but, obstinately, it kept going. Behind us was the sea, in front of us the Kaladan River, two currents colliding head on, and the boat somehow had to struggle through the middle. Maung, the captain, wearing a black *longyi* and shiny purple raincoat but barefoot, steered with one hand on the tiller, staring intently ahead into the foaming brown swirl, until the boat passed over a final ridge of waves and entered the Kaladan.

We were heading up the same river that Isaac had travelled down in 1944. The Kaladan was not beautiful; swollen by the rains, it was the colour of the crew's milky tea. It was some two miles across, much wider than Isaac would ever have seen it. But, of course, he never made it this far down the valley. The surrounding landscape, though, would have been very familiar to him. The floodplain had changed little over the decades. There were still no roads, no electricity pylons and no modern buildings: just vivid-green paddy fields, rows of scruffy palm trees and clusters of huts built from mud and bamboo. Much as the villagers of Mairong had done while Isaac was in hiding, farmers were wading through the fields, or checking fish traps in the mangrove swamps on the edge of the river, their faces sheltered from the pounding rain by conical woven hats. Herds of water buffalo, their bodies more angular, their horns thinner, than their more intimidating African cousins, were splashing through the shallows and grazing on top of muddy banks. The odd hill rose out of the floodplain, covered in jungle – the 'Hill of Five Hundred Ducks' on the west bank, then, a bit further on, the 'Hill That Reaches The Sky'. Beyond the hills, in the far distance, were the mountains, steep and forested. Very occasionally, the flash of a golden pagoda rose above the tree line.

Once, we passed a ferryboat coming downriver, an old rust bucket, its listing decks alarmingly crammed with passengers, bundles of firewood and wicker baskets full of pigs and ducks. The women, their faces covered in *thanakha*, protective white paste made from tree bark, watched in silence as we chugged past.

It felt ominous and a bit discouraging: the impenetrability of the landscape, the dark skies threatening endless rain, the vast, wide river. It had been one thing to trace the course of the Kaladan with my finger over a few inches of dry map in the living room of my flat, quite another to travel up the real thing. Each of the straggling villages that we passed resembled Isaac's description of Mairong in some way. How would I ever know whether I had found the right one? And, even if I did, what if the people who'd lived there had been dispersed long ago?

To answer my endless doubts, I clung to one consoling idea. Provided that the community of Mairong was intact, then surely the events surrounding Isaac and David's stay there would be part of local folklore – the legend would have endured.

There was a shoot-out on the riverbank just near the village. Several soldiers were killed. Afterwards, we brought food to two injured black-skinned men. They said they were soldiers from Africa fighting for the British. We helped them for many months; they even came and stayed in our house. They tried to learn our language. If they had been caught, the Japanese would have punished the whole village. But, praise be to Allah, the British came back to rescue them. We never heard from them again.

Somebody, I was convinced, would remember this story, or at least have been told about it.

It was after dark when we turned up a tributary and arrived at Mrauk U. It had taken us eight hours to travel twenty miles.

Mrauk U means 'first accomplishment' in old Arakanese. A Dutch visitor in the seventeenth century described 'the golden roofs of the palace, which shone magnificently...lakes, fishponds, orchards and country houses...indeed it would be difficult to imagine a more

entrancing landscape'. Another European visitor from that time estimated that at least 160,000 people lived in Mrauk U. But empires rise
and fall. The Arakan Kingdom, and its capital Mrauk U, was overrun
by the neighbouring Burmans at the end of the eighteenth century,
its treasures looted or destroyed. By the time the British arrived, in
1825, and moved the Arakan's capital to Akyab, on the coast, Mrauk
U had sunk into obscurity. In January 1945, when the West Africans
of the 81st and 82nd Divisions drove the Japanese out of Mrauk U,
their prize had been the ghostly remains of an abandoned city. Today,
the modern town is a small and unremarkable place, a handful of
shops and bungalows on a pot-holed grid of dirt roads; *tuk-tuks*,
cyclists and children scurry around under bright umbrellas. The town
is overshadowed by the crumbling palace walls and the old pagodas
and temples, many of which are in ruins.

I was travelling with a man called Moe Kyaw, a registered guide
who was authorised to accompany tourists and had led previous tours
to Mrauk U. Moe had been recommended to me by a foreign reporter
who had made many undercover trips into Burma during the years
of military rule. Moe was an astute person, and through hints in his
conversation I sensed that he had already guessed that it was not the
pagodas of Mrauk U that had brought me this far. That night, we
ate in the dining room of an almost-deserted hotel. After the waiter
brought our food and retired to the kitchen, I told Moe the reason
for my journey. I had no choice. I needed his help.

I told him everything, from the beginning: the African soldiers
who came to Burma to fight the Japanese, the medical unit that had
been attacked on the banks of the Kaladan, the young soldier – Isaac
Fadoyebo – who had been left for dead, the villager called Shuyiman
who had saved him and his companion and kept them alive, their
eventual rescue nine months later. I told Moe that Isaac was still
alive, and that I was carrying a letter from Lagos. He listened to all
this impassively. Then I came to the crux of the matter: I was asking
Moe to accompany me another thirty miles upriver. Although my
plan, to find Shuyiman's family, could hardly be judged threatening

to the Burmese state, I wanted Moe to travel with me to an area that the army considered sensitive and where he had been explicitly warned not to take any foreigners. We both knew that this was a much greater risk for him than it was for me. If we were caught, I would probably be bundled out of the country for violating the terms of my visa. Moe, at the very least, would have his tourist guide permit confiscated, which would have left him without a livelihood. It was very possible he would also be thrown in prison.

I had already noticed how cautious Moe was in our conversations. When I asked him what he thought of the monks' uprising of 2007, he said, enigmatically, that he knew why the monks had to stage protests, but he also understood why the regime had used force against them. At one point, he had discreetly pointed out someone sitting nearby whom he suspected was a spy; another time he had drawn my attention to what he believed was a piece of electronic surveillance equipment. And, within moments of our having arrived at the hotel in Mrauk U, a well-dressed man had turned up at the reception desk, and asked to see my passport. He looked at it for a long time, returned it to the receptionist and pulled Moe aside. They talked intently for some minutes before the man left without addressing a word to me. 'Military intelligence officer,' Moe said. 'He wants to know why you are here.' In Mrauk U, I was a plausible tourist, albeit a rather adventurous one to have come during the monsoon season. Now I wanted him to take me into forbidden territory.

Moe did not say anything for a long time. He frowned and looked confused. But when his frown turned to a smile, and he clutched my hand, I knew that he was on board. He went to speak to Maung, the captain of the boat, who knew the Kaladan, and who could suggest our best approach. Together, they hatched a plan, which they presented to me in the empty dining room.

Maung would ride a motorbike the following day to Kyauktaw, where he would hire a boat. He would then travel several miles further up the Kaladan and look for a village called Mairong on the west bank. If he found it, he would try to get as much information as possible about its current inhabitants. Maung insisted on going alone. He said there was an army camp in that area, and, if I were seen there, as a white man, I would draw attention to all of us, with unpredictable but perhaps serious consequences. We would also have to contend with the fears and suspicions of the villagers themselves. Maung was a Rakhine Buddhist, not a Muslim. This was not ideal, but at least he was a local man. Moe, on the other hand, coming from Rangoon, could easily be mistaken for a policeman or government spy. We agreed that, if Maung did make contact with Shuyiman's family, he'd arrange with them a time and place where we could all meet together safely.

I liked Maung, if only for the phlegmatic skill with which he had steered his old boat, but I wished I could talk to him directly. Moe did his best to translate for me, giving Maung every scrap of information that I possessed that might help locate Mairong, and telling him exactly what he should ask if he did find the village. I could sense Maung's frustration that I was not more precise about Mairong's location, and he could probably sense mine that its name meant nothing to him. 'Don't worry, many villages have changed their names,' Moe said, although he was starting to sound doubtful. I realised there was something else that I needed to explain to Moe and Maung; if anybody did remember Isaac and David, it would be under their adopted Muslim names of Suleman and Dauda Ali. So many complications, so much that could go wrong.

The more I thought about it, the more likely it seemed that Maung would return unsuccessful. My brave quest would die with a whimper, and an apologetic phone call to a disappointed Isaac in Lagos. But everything was out of my hands now. I could only trust Maung. He would leave at dawn the following day, and promised to telephone as soon as he had news and was able to make a call.

I spent the next day with Moe, wandering around the temples and pagodas of Mrauk U, thinking about what Maung might find. The rain came and went in a series of bursts interrupted by pale sunshine. A pair of small girls in bright dresses, their solemn little faces covered in *thanakha*, watched me as I made my way up the steps of the massive Koe-thoung temple, past rows of stoic stone Buddhas and hideous ogres. The girls carried big floppy leaves, which they used as improvised umbrellas whenever the rain resumed.

In the Sanda Muni monastery, a friendly monk took me up to the museum, a dark and chaotic attic room. He showed me dusty cabinets crammed full of miniature Buddhas: Buddha sitting, Buddha standing, Buddha walking, Buddha underneath a tree. 'These are fifteenth century and these are sixteenth century,' he said with an airy wave at one cabinet, and then pointing to another, 'and here is Buddha's molar tooth, only brought out on special occasions.' A sacred relic, it had been venerated for centuries for its perfect proportions, cleanliness and unique qualities of whiteness. Another display case was full of coins – 'Ancient,' said the monk. I peered inside the cabinet. I could just make out the profile of Queen Victoria on one, and George VI on another.

In the afternoon, Moe and I walked back to the hotel, hoping there would be a message from Maung. There was none. We looked at each other, but didn't say anything. The receptionist told us that, because of the rain, the authorities in Sittwe had closed the river to any further traffic. We had got to Mrauk U just in time. This was a relief, but the weather would make things difficult for Maung as he travelled upriver. Here was yet another reason to steel myself for disappointment, to prepare myself for the message I would have to deliver back to Isaac.

Moe suggested we walk to the Shitthaung temple, the 'Shrine of Eighty Thousand Buddhas' famous for its labyrinthine sandstone passages. The walls are elaborately decorated with reliefs, not only of the Buddha, but also of elephants and giants. By the time we reached the temple, it was pouring once again. The inner passages were barely lit. A British soldier who visited the temple in the 1920s reported that 'bats are numerous though mercifully there are no tigers or snakes as one might expect' and recommended examining the ground carefully with a torch for possible reptiles. Thankfully, we encountered no wildlife, but for the carvings of the famous *Byala*, the mythical animal of the Arakan that boasts the crest of a dragon, the horn of a rhinoceros and the tail of a peacock.

In the monastery outside, novice monks, boys in their early teens with cropped hair and wearing only a saffron cloth round their waists, slid on their backs and tummies along the glistening tiles of the courtyard, their screams and shouts of joy just audible over the cacophony of the rain beating down on the tin roof. I could only wonder at what the West African soldiers had made of this strange and magical place in 1945. They must have felt a long way from home.

Moe went to see a friend, so I walked back to the hotel alone in the dark, along puddle-pocked streets, passing small candlelit shops and darting children who shouted their goodbyes for the day. I replied 'goodbye, goodbye', but my mind was elsewhere, stuck on my hope that there would be word from Maung when I got to the hotel. At reception, I was handed a note. The man behind the desk explained that Maung had returned a short time ago and was resting in his room. I tore open the envelope, but the note was in Burmese script. I asked the receptionist to translate it for me.

He looked at it with a furrowed brow, carefully turning the words into English. He mouthed them silently to himself, then eventually took the plunge and read them out in a halting voice.

'I have found Shuyiman's family. They are ready to see us tomorrow. They are happy that you are here.'

17

FOR OUR CHILDREN TO BE FREE

||||||||||||||||||||||||||||||||||||||||||||||||||||||||||||||||||||||||||||||||||||||||||||||||||||||||||||||||||||||

If ever an army fought in a just cause we did. We coveted no man's country:
we wished to impose no form of government on any nation. We fought…
for the right to live our lives in our own way, as others could live theirs,
to worship God in what faith we chose, to be free in body and mind, and
for our children to be free…

William Slim,
Defeat into Victory

||||||||||||||||||||||||||||||||||||||||||||||||||||||||||||||||||||||||||||||||||||||||||||||||||||||||||||||||||||||

16 June 2011
Pagoda Hill, Burma

Maung sat in the hotel dining room, his face glowing with pride. He chased his curry down with two large whiskies, and his face glowed all the more. Then he shared his news. He had travelled up the Kaladan River from Kyauktaw and got off his boat after an hour and a half when he saw what he took to be a Muslim village on the west bank. He requested to speak to the oldest man there. An elderly gentleman was produced, but he looked at Maung blankly when asked if he knew anything about two injured Africans hiding during the war. The villagers suggested Maung talk to another, apparently even older man, who was out working on his farm. This man's face lit up with recognition when Maung asked him about a strange story involving

Africans and the war. 'I've heard about that, but you've come to the wrong place,' he said, 'you need to go on to the next village.' Maung, now encouraged, got back into his boat and headed further upriver.

He found another settlement, where a Muslim woman who seemed to be in her eighties was sitting in front of a *basha*, sheltering from the rain. Maung asked her if she had ever known a woman in the village called Gulasha.

'Yes,' replied the woman, 'but Gulasha died.'

'And did you know her father?'

'Yes, he was called Shuyiman.'

At this point, a young man who had been listening to the conversation drew closer. 'Shuyiman was my grandfather,' he said, and pointed to another *basha* closer to the Kaladan, 'and that was his house.'

A path ran next to it, parallel to the river.

Almost seven decades had passed. A war had ended, an empire had fallen, civil wars had started and stopped and started again, there had been a coup, years of repression and many natural disasters. But Shuyiman's house was still there.

Maung asked the grandson whether Shuyiman had ever spoken of the war.

'Yes, of course,' he said. 'He always spoke of how he hid two Africans in our house.'

Maung fought back his excitement, and asked if the grandson knew their names. This was the point that I had emphasised the night before, with Moe's dedicated efforts at translation. We had to be absolutely sure that we had found not just the right village, but also the right family. Maung needed to ask his questions carefully, without giving too much away. 'Their names,' said the grandson, without hesitation, 'were Suleman and Dauda Ali.'

Maung shared with us the bare facts he had learnt while he was in the village. Shuyiman was dead. He had passed away some fifteen years after the end of the war, by which time he might have been sixty years old. Poor Gulasha, the little girl who danced with joy on the day Isaac and David were rescued, had died some thirty years ago, when she would have been in her mid-forties. Her mother, Khatoun, who laughed and prayed on that day, had outlived her daughter by some ten years, but had died in the early 1990s. Even little Kalu, the boy who was born when Isaac and David were hiding in the jungle, and whose crying kept them awake when they moved into the house, had died.

But Shuyiman had two other children, born shortly after the war, who were still alive. Maung told them there was a visitor from England who wished to give them a letter from Africa. They had seemed, he said, both delighted and apprehensive at this turn of events. They had made one thing very clear: they were firmly against the idea of my coming to Mairong.

'The army is close, we are scared here. We are not free in this land, everyone is afraid,' they told Maung.

Whatever political changes were under way in Rangoon meant little here in the Kaladan Valley, where the military was still the real authority. The visit of a foreigner to this remote village would be highly unusual. If an intelligence officer caught wind of it, they said, he would certainly want to know why it had happened, and talk to those involved. That prospect made them afraid.

It was frustrating. I had come so far. Now I wanted to go just a little bit further, to Mairong itself, to see where Isaac and David had been shot on the riverbank, and where they'd hidden in the nearby jungle. I wanted to see Shuyiman's house, to climb the bamboo ladder to his *basha*. My mission seemed so innocuous, so wrapped up in the distant past, that there should be no good reason why it would upset anyone. But there was nothing I could do about it. I already knew of the potential risks for my guides, Moe and Maung. Now the very people whom I had come to see, and whom Isaac wanted me to thank, were urging me to stay away. I was learning that Burmese of all ethnicities feared their army, but the Muslims of Rakhine State felt especially vulnerable.

And yet my journey was not in vain. Shuyiman's family had suggested an alternative meeting place for the following morning. They said we should meet on Pagoda Hill, a few miles south of Mairong.

It was the same hill that the Japanese had captured from the British on that fateful day, 2 March 1944.

Maung, Moe and I climbed up a steep, covered staircase that twisted through the jungle to the golden pagoda on the summit of the hill. This pagoda was said to be built on the very spot where the 'Great Teacher', Buddha himself, arrived in 554 BC. He had come at the invitation of a local king, who waited for him there with his entire court and army. According to legend, Buddha travelled from India using levitation, and landed on top of the hill accompanied by five hundred followers. He spent seven days in the Kaladan Valley, a spiritual sojourn during which he inspired everyone who met him with his compassion. Ever since, Pagoda Hill has been venerated as a holy place.

In the wide sweep of the Second World War, the fighting between Japanese and African troops that took place on the ridges and jungles of this hill was of no great significance. Even in the histories of the Burma campaign, the Battle of Pagoda Hill in the Arakan merits only a passing mention; it is often confused with a more celebrated namesake, which also took place in Burma, far to the north, just eleven days later, involving the Chindits. But, for the West Africans who were forced out of the Kaladan Valley as a result of their defeat, Pagoda Hill mattered. It mattered, too, for the British officers whose careers were destroyed that day, some of whom would go to their graves decades later still blaming colleagues for the blunders they felt tarred not just their own reputations, but that of the entire 81st Division.

And, of course, the fall of Pagoda Hill mattered for Isaac and David, who were shot and lying in shock and pain a few miles upstream when the British officers gave the order to the Gambian battalion to retreat from the advancing Japanese. That ought to have been Isaac's and David's death sentence. That they survived another nine months was down to a mixture of luck and courage. The courage was theirs, but also that of the family I was now, incredibly, about to meet.

Rain pounded down noisily onto the tin roof over the staircase. A troop of grey monkeys squatted in the rafters, hugging themselves to keep dry. They seemed faintly irritated by our arrival. I could see why Shuyiman's family had suggested we meet on Pagoda Hill. Save for the monkeys, we were alone, hidden under the trees, and it was unlikely that anyone else would take the trouble of climbing up here in this wet weather. The chances of any policemen or soldiers stumbling across us were slim. Far below us, to the west, I could make out the milky waters of the Kaladan River through the trees.

By the time we got to the top of the hill, I was soaked from rain and sweat. The rain was growing heavier, and the trees were now groaning in the wind. I tried to imagine Isaac and David huddled in their makeshift shelter for an entire monsoon season, drenched day after day, waiting for food, waiting to be rescued.

I looked at my watch; they were late. Maybe, I worried, they had decided it was too dangerous for anyone to travel on the river in this stormy weather. Or the boatmen might have refused to make the trip. They could have been afraid of flooding, or strong currents. Or maybe the family had been stopped by a soldier who was suspicious of their movements. Perhaps, having had the night to reflect on it, they had decided this strange story of a foreigner with a letter from Africa was a set-up, some sort of trap. So they had decided not to come after all.

My doubts grew and began to harden into a dull conviction; this meeting was not going to happen. That was when I looked up and saw five people climbing the steps towards me. They picked their way on bare feet, *longyis* wrapped round their waists, and glanced up shyly every few steps or so. There were two men, in old shirts, and three women, simple shawls draped over their heads. The oldest man, maybe in his early sixties, had large worried eyes and a small moustache. Much later, when I showed a photograph of this man to Isaac, he would tell me that he was the spitting image of his father, Shuyiman. The man was saying something to me, but I could not hear him over the noise of the rain on the tin roof. Anyway, we had no language in common. Not knowing what else to do, I embraced him. Shuyiman's son was called Adu, and tears were streaming down his face.

We stood on those steps, and talked for one hour. 'We could not sleep last night, when we heard the news. To know that one of our Africans was still alive. There was so much to think about, and to talk about,' said Roshi, the youngest of the group. He was the son of Gulasha and a grandson of Shuyiman, the man who had met Maung the previous day, and he spoke a little English. 'Then we thought, wonderful news about Suleman [Isaac], but what can you tell us of Dauda Ali [David]?'

If there had been any tiny piece of scepticism within me, it left me at that moment. This was Shuyiman's family. The story of the wounded African soldiers was indeed part of their village's folklore. And within the family itself I saw that the rescue of those soldiers was a treasured memory, the details lovingly handed down from generation to generation.

All five of Shuyiman's relatives that I met that day had been born after the war. One of the three women, Nurasha, was his only surviving daughter, and the other two were his daughters-in-law. All of them were still living in Mairong, still working in the paddy fields on the banks of the Kaladan. They were astonished that a stranger had come from the other side of the world with knowledge of what had happened in their village in 1944. They never imagined the good deeds of Shuyiman and Khatoun were still celebrated so far away, just as I had never imagined I would hear Isaac's story one more time. Only this time I was not sitting in a front yard in Lagos, listening carefully as he strained to paint a picture of distant jungles. I was in those very jungles, sheltering from the rains on Pagoda Hill, and the story was being narrated in the dialect of the Muslims of the Arakan:

> It started like this, the British soldiers slept by
> the river…some died, some ran away, but we
> found two injured…One of them was nearly

dead when we found him, that was Suleman, the other was called Dauda Ali…He was stronger, but he never left. He could have gone, but he wanted to save his friend…They were here for months; after some time we moved them into our house…We helped to bathe them, and gave them food. Then the Indian soldiers came and took them away…Afterwards, British officers came on two separate occasions and gave Shuyiman some money.

I asked if Shuyiman ever explained why he took such risks for these African men, who came from the other side of the world and with whom he could only exchange a handful of words. Adu replied, 'Our parents said those men were in trouble; they needed help, otherwise they were going to die. That is our culture.'

I learnt new details too, of how suspicious Japanese soldiers came to the family door and asked questions, and of how Shuyiman and Khatoun would calmly lie and say there was nobody hiding with them.

I handed them photographs of Isaac in Lagos, and read out his letter. It was entitled 'To All the Good People of Mairong Village, in the Arakan part of Burma':

> My name is Isaac Fadoyebo. I would like to thank the entire family of Shuyiman and all the good people of Mairong village for taking care of me and my comrade in adversity, David Kargbo, when we were in hiding in the Burma jungle. I still remember a few names like Mahmud Ali, Ismail Abdul Subahan, the village teacher Lalu, to mention a few of those who were coming to see us in the bush. May God bless you all.

Now they were weeping, all of them. They touched the photographs of Isaac, clasping them to their tear-stained faces, trying to feel him. They clapped at his words. The raw intensity of their emotions caught me off balance. All their lives, the two African soldiers had been almost mythical figures to them, from far off in the past and from a world that they could not imagine, let alone visit. For the first time, they could put a face to one of the names, and they could see that he was still alive, very much flesh and blood. Moreover, they could hear, from the words I read, that Isaac cherished the memory of Shuyiman and Khatoun just as they did.

We stood in silence, our heads bowed, in honour of the memory of Shuyiman and Khatoun, giving thanks for this wonderful encounter. I imagine that Shuyiman's family put it down to the providence of Allah, just as Isaac and David always attributed their survival to the blessings of a Christian God. For myself, I'm not sure I'd ever felt the common bond of humanity as strongly as at that moment. We were celebrating courage and a friendship that transcended time and distance and race, and shone through the horror of a World War.

Afterwards, I would ask myself if this meeting with Shuyiman's family had really happened. Like Isaac's description of being rescued, it took on a dream-like quality. When I think back on it, I see myself floating above, observing the conversation, but not actually participating in it. It seemed so incredible, so improbable that, if not for the photos I had taken, I would have doubted my own memory that it had taken place. We had struggled to make ourselves heard, let alone understood, through the sound of the rain and the confusion of Moe's halting translation. At times, we had all been talking at once. It had been too brief. Moe and Maung were anxious that we should leave, before any unwelcome strangers came to the pagoda and asked what a foreigner was doing in an area where tourists were not allowed.

On the long and uncomfortable journey back down the Kaladan, I thought about Isaac and Shuyiman, why they had sided with the British in the war, and of how their families had fared since. It wasn't sentimentality, or loyalty to a distant king that made them risk their lives, but the simple calculation that a British victory would benefit them and their families. They could not have known it at the time, but they had placed their bets on a fading Empire.

For Isaac, in spite of everything, the decision to fight for the British proved a sound one in the long run. He made it back home from Burma. And although he carried a disability for the rest of his life, his Army service smoothed his passage into the colonial and later Nigerian civil service. He became a respected man, even by those who knew nothing of what had happened to him in the war. Isaac never amassed any great wealth or lived in luxury, but I sensed that was of no great concern to him. What he cared about most was giving his children and grandchildren opportunities that he had not enjoyed when he was young. In this, he succeeded, and his family prospered. They had left the village life of Emure-Ile far behind. In spite of all of Nigeria's political and economic problems, Isaac had progressed.

Shuyiman's family, on the other hand, was living much as Shuyiman himself had during the Second World War. The British rewarded him for his courage with some money, but, however much it was, it made no lasting impact. Shuyiman's children and grandchildren are poor farmers, living in exactly the same village where he lived and died. Maybe Shuyiman had seen the British as somehow kinder, more benevolent than the Japanese. Perhaps he also simply assumed that, because British rule was all he had ever known, they were the stronger and would eventually come out on top. If so, he was both right and wrong. Right, because the gamble of helping Isaac and David paid off, and the British went on to win. Wrong, because Burma would soon be independent, and Shuyiman's good deeds during the war would count for nothing thereafter.

The British quickly forgot their debts to the Muslims of the Arakan. In 1947, on the eve of their departure from Burma, they established a Frontier Areas Committee of Enquiry, to make recommendations on how the rights of minorities could be protected after independence. The committee did not even consider the peoples of the Arakan. The Muslims' support for the British in the war had incurred the resentment of the Buddhist majority, yet this history brought them no lasting gain. If the British feel any guilt about this, it is only hinted at in a handful of obscure memoirs of some of the soldiers and officials who served in the Arakan. Many years after the war, one such official wrote of the Muslims, 'I have greatest admiration for their tenacity, their toughness, their uncomplaining acceptance of hardship and suffering, their intense loyalty to their families and to their religion and – with few exceptions – to the British cause during the war. From this last they reaped very little ultimate advantage.'

Isaac had seen his sacrifices and contribution lose their relevance once the British gave up their colonies, but at least he was not part of a persecuted minority in a newly independent country. Isaac's war ended, definitively, in 1945; Shuyiman's people were not so lucky. For them, the Japanese surrender marked only a pause in the Arakan conflict.

Today, many of the Muslims living in Rakhine State have lost the right to call themselves Burmese. So too they have been written out of the history books. I had noticed that the official guidebooks at Mrauk U made no mention of the Muslim influence at the Arakan court, just as the government museum in Sittwe, which otherwise made a deliberate effort to celebrate Burma's ethnic diversity, did not so much as mention them. They have become invisible. I had carried a thank-you message from Africa for what Shuyiman's people had done in a war that ended two generations ago, only to discover that they still do not have peace in their own land.

Subsequent events would make my meeting with Shuyiman's family all the more poignant. At the end of May 2012, a long period of relative calm in relations between the groups now commonly known as Muslim Rohingyas and Buddhist Rakhines came to an abrupt and bloody end. The trouble started when a Rakhine woman was raped and killed in the town of Ramree, reportedly by three Muslim men. A few days later, a crowd of Rakhine villagers stopped a bus, pulled off ten Muslims and beat them to death. The effect of these crimes was electric across the old Arakan region. Mobs of Rakhines and Rohingyas, armed with swords, knives and iron rods, attacked each other's villages, burning and killing. They destroyed mosques and temples. The Burmese army and police watched as the violence unfolded, and, when they did choose to intervene, invariably took the side of the Rakhines. In Sittwe, Rakhines burnt most of the Rohingyas' homes, while the police turned their guns on those who tried to put the flames out. Many Rohingyas, and a smaller number of Rakhines, were forced into overcrowded camps, without adequate food, shelter or medical care.

Burma's president, Thein Sein, had few words of comfort for the Rohingya, whom he called 'Bengalis'. The only solution to the crisis, he said, was to expel them all, as Burma would be better off without them. 'We will send them away if any third country would accept them,' he said. His new and supposedly democratic government used exactly the same harsh and exclusionist language as the previous military regime.

Tens of thousands of Muslims decided to leave Burma in any case. They set out by sea for Bangladesh, Thailand and Malaysia. It was a dangerous journey, and several hundred drowned. Those who did manage to reach neighbouring countries discovered that they were not welcome.

I wondered what was happening to Shuyiman's family amid this turmoil. A few days after President Thein Sein spoke, I managed to get through to them on the telephone. They were using a mobile that seemed to be shared by several families in the village. Over a terrible line, with long delays and wild interrupting sounds and frequent cut-offs, we had a halting conversation, with an exiled Rohingya activist in London doing his best to translate for me. The family explained that Mairong had not been attacked, but it had become like a prison.

They were running out of food, sharing what they had among themselves, but had been explicitly prohibited by the army from trying to buy any supplies from neighbouring Rakhine villages. 'If we go there, we will be killed,' said Shuyiman's grandson Roshi. 'We have shown our great-grandfather's ID card to the authorities, but they are not interested,' he explained. 'They say it makes no difference, we are all illegal immigrants and eventually we will have to leave.' He said the family did not want to go anywhere. They were ready to die.

Several months later, in October, the violence erupted a second time. This time, the worst of it was much closer to Mairong. It appeared to be more organised, less spontaneous than before. Rakhine crowds, egged on by Buddhist monks and extremist politicians, attacked several Rohingya villages. Again, the army and police either looked the other way, or joined in, as Rohingyas were killed or forced to flee. In a village outside Mrauk U, a human rights group reported that dozens of Rohingyas were massacred, including many children who were hacked to death. The police had been warned of the impending attack, but the only action they took was to disarm Rohingya villagers. In the following days, there was fighting around Kyauktaw. One source told me that some 120 Rohingya homes were burnt down and three people had been killed near Mairong; others said that, for the first time, the security forces actually fired at the Rakhine crowds to try to control the situation.

Some 140,000 people were displaced in these two bouts of violence, most of them Rohingya Muslims. It wasn't the story the outside world had expected, or wanted to hear, from Burma in 2012. Western leaders had lifted sanctions, and were queuing up to visit. Aung San Suu Kyi had been elected to parliament, but, instead of using her new freedom and power to denounce the cruelty, she preferred not to talk about what was happening in Rakhine State. When pressed, she would only say that she would not take sides. In April 2013, a Burmese government commission recommended the rigid separation of Rakhine and Rohingya communities 'until the overt emotions subside'. But, in Mairong, the villagers told me that the security forces were acting more like their jailers than their protectors, not even allowing the sick to travel to hospital.

It was the worst violence in the Kaladan Valley since the Second World War. And, despite the long decades between the two conflicts, there were striking similarities between the outbursts of ethnic and religious hatred. Now, as then, gangs marched from village to village, brandishing whatever weapons they could find. There must have been village elders, Muslims and Buddhists, who witnessed this latest violence and were reminded of what they'd seen in their childhoods. But Rakhine State's present doesn't just resemble its past; it is also shaped by it. No doubt some of the families with the most traumatic memories of 1942 took satisfaction in exacting their revenge this time around, in seizing back land that was stolen from their parents or grandparents, and in killing those who resisted. Many who lost relatives, friends or property then would have carried a burning sense of injustice, even loathing, through the years, and many would have passed this on to their children.

In part, this is Britain's and Japan's legacy. Outside powers, both exploited murderous local divisions in the Arakan for their own immediate advantage. They armed and raised the hopes of those who fought alongside them, with little concern for the long-term consequences. There are few people in Britain today who would know that in areas of Burma there are people still suffering from the fall-out of the Second World War.

In Britain, the war is seen, at least in moral terms, as a relatively straightforward affair. It's remembered as a time when the British people showed courage and pluck in the face of overwhelming odds, decency in the face of brutality. For a short and glorious period, the mantra goes, Britain stood alone for freedom (until the Soviet Union and the United States joined the war). This stirring story – of Dunkirk, the Blitz and the Battle of Britain – is captured in Churchillian language. 'Never Surrender', 'Their Finest Hour', 'Blood, Toil, Tears and Sweat'. Britain's passage through the twentieth century may have been characterised by relentless decline, but at least its role in the Second World War is a source of near unequivocal pride. And, while the British people are open to reassessing and finding new moral ambiguities in other aspects of their past, the consensus around the Second World War has remained firmly intact. Politicians still draw on memories of it to try to bind the country together. Anniversaries are observed with, if anything, increasing pride and solemnity. It was a war fought, the British believe, for all the right reasons. Where there is debate and even regret, for example over the bombing campaign against German cities, it is the morality of the methods that are scrutinised, not the end objectives.

From Isaac's or Shuyiman's perspective, that of the colonised, things look very different. The events of the early 1940s are not cast in black and white, but in shades of grey. Seen from Nigeria or Burma, Britain is less heroic and far from selfless. It was a Great Power under attack, and it mobilised its imperial resources in order to protect its far-flung possessions against other, emerging empires. Standing alone? Hardly. Australians, New Zealanders, Canadians and white Southern Africans all played their part. But millions of the Empire's less favoured peoples were also co-opted into the British war effort. Basothos and Swazis were taken from the mountains of Southern Africa to fight in the deserts of North Africa and on the long slog up the Italian peninsula. The Caribbean regiment also fought in Italy. East and West Africans fought first in Somalia and Abyssinia, and then travelled across the Indian Ocean, where they joined Punjabis, Baluchis and Gurkhas to play their part in the recapture of Burma from the Japanese. So on and so on. Were the British really fighting for freedom? In Europe, perhaps, but, when it comes to Asia, that seems a generous interpretation of their motives. The Burmese would discover that British rule was more humane than that of Japan, but they made it clear they preferred to live under neither. General Slim wrote that the Japanese army had to be destroyed and smashed as 'an evil thing'. However, the war in Burma was less a struggle of good against evil than it was one for wealth and influence. And, in waging this struggle, Britain depended to a large extent on the sacrifice and courage of others, of men like Isaac and Shuyiman. Once these others had served their purpose, they were forgotten.

I spent two days in Sittwe, waiting for the rain to stop so that I could catch a flight back to Rangoon. During the war, this city had been Akyab, the town on the coast with the airfield that the 81st Division had always coveted. On the evening of the second day, the weather brightened, and I took a long walk along the coastal road to the lighthouse on the rocky point that juts out into the Bay of Bengal. On one side, the beaches face the ocean, but, on the other, the coastline turns sharply inwards, marking the beginning of the estuary of the Kaladan. The seawater was brown, stained by the soil carried down the river from the highlands, past Mairong and Pagoda Hill and Mrauk U. The tide was out and Sittwe's wide grey beaches shimmered in the evening sun. Clusters of children played football on the flat sands, fishermen pulled their nets in and gathered to examine and divide up the catch. Rusty old trawlers and wooden canoes bobbed side by side just beyond the surf.

This was where British and Indian troops had stormed ashore in January 1945. But the Japanese had already gone, leaving only their dead behind. The British discovered that their own bombs had destroyed most of the town.

I looked out to sea, and thought of an old man in Africa, whom I knew was waiting impatiently for my call.

EPILOGUE

19 January 2013
Emure-Ile, Nigeria

Isaac was rushed to hospital in Lagos in September 2012, suffering acute pain from a perforated duodenal ulcer. He was operated on, but afterwards there were several complications. His daughter, Tayo, the doctor, felt that he was beginning to lose the will to live. She and Isaac's other daughters and his grandchildren sat by his bed in shifts through several long days and nights, preparing themselves for the worst. Then Isaac made a recovery. He started talking again, and could shuffle up and down the ward, even climbing stairs. Tayo told me that his spirits seemed to be improving, and that she was making plans to look after him at her own house after he was discharged.

I'd spoken to Isaac many times on the phone over the previous two years. The most memorable occasion was just after I'd returned from delivering his letter in Burma. I'd made careful notes before calling him that day, so as to convey all the events I'd experienced and the people I'd met as distinctly as possible. I didn't want to confuse him. But when I got through to Isaac I couldn't help blurting out, 'I found Shuyiman's family. They are still thinking of you.' There was a long pause. Was he still there? Phone calls to Nigeria often drop out for no apparent reason, but this time I could still hear the hiss and crackle of the line from Lagos. I said it again, slowly, my voice wavering a little, 'I found them, Isaac, they're still thinking of you.' Now I could hear Isaac over the hiss, gasping at first, then whispering,

'Alleluia, Alleluia.' He repeated it louder and louder, until his shouts were vibrating down the line, 'Alleluia, Alleluia!' I held the phone away from my ear. I could picture Isaac, in his little yard in Surelere, struggling to his feet and reaching for the sky.

I think my news was an affirmation for Isaac. Through the decades, he had dwelled on the experience that had defined his life, in all its horror and wonder. Now, right at the end, he had the satisfaction of learning that he had indeed remembered it the way it was. He'd been forgotten by those he'd fought for, but not by the strangers who'd saved his life.

We spoke often in the weeks that followed. Isaac would call me out of the blue, and ask me to go over this or that detail, to explain once more how I had found the village, what Shuyiman's son and grandson had said, even to describe the Kaladan in the monsoon rain. A few months later, I made another trip to Lagos. I gave Isaac the photographs I'd taken in Burma, and he made me go through every aspect of my adventure once more. He seemed buoyant and at peace.

That was then. Now, when I called Isaac in the hospital ward, he sounded weak and depressed. When I talked about planning to visit him once more in Lagos in the coming months, he said he hoped this would happen, but I could hear the doubt in his voice, which trailed off into silence. I put the phone down, and I had the cold and clear feeling that we would not talk to each other again. Isaac had decided to go. The following morning, 9 November, he suffered a massive blood clot to the lung, and collapsed. Despite Tayo's best efforts to revive him, Isaac died shortly afterwards. He was one month short of his eighty-seventh birthday.

My journey to Burma had rekindled Isaac's desire to find out what had happened to David Kargbo after the war. Of course, I shared Isaac's curiosity. David's version of events in Burma – and the tale of his subsequent life in Sierra Leone – were the most significant loose ends to the whole story. Isaac died before I was able to track down David's family, but I pushed on with my research nonetheless.

It felt like unfinished business that I needed to resolve. Eventually, it was an enterprising lieutenant colonel in the Sierra Leonean army, Fatorma Gottor, who helped me put the pieces together. He made contact with John Abdul Kargbo, David's eldest son, who in turn told me his father's story.

When David Kargbo returned home in April 1945, he too was mistaken for a ghost. His parents, just like Isaac's, had assumed their son had died when they were told he had been missing for months behind enemy lines. They had performed traditional funeral rites for him. David arrived in the village of Rogbin in the middle of the night after a long walk, and knocked on his parents' door. His father, Foday, and his mother, Kadday, looked outside and saw what they assumed to be an evil spirit disguised as their son. Terrified, they refused to let him in. But the spirit, who was wearing a British Army uniform, carried on knocking, and eventually lit a cigarette. This was what convinced Foday to open the door. Within moments, all of Rogbin was woken by his excited cries, and the celebrations began. David stood there, surrounded by weeping brothers, sisters and cousins.

David got a job in the colonial civil service, as a native administration clerk. He married and, just like Isaac, had six children. In the 1950s, the family moved to the southern town of Bo, where David was a school bursar. He seems to have been a much-loved figure, with friends all over the town, including many former soldiers who had fought in Burma. He liked to sing, not just hymns, but also the lovers' laments he had learnt en route to the war when he saw women from Nigeria and the Cameroons saying goodbye to the men who were boarding the ships. In the evenings, children and friends used to gather to hear David's Burma stories. He had a reputation as a raconteur, and with the passing of years his tales lost nothing in the telling. With a gleam in his eye, his memory perhaps lubricated by a beer or two, he would take his enthralled audience into the dark jungles of the upper Kaladan. Always outnumbered by the dastardly Japanese, David and his fellow West Africans fought bravely to the last bullet. When they ran out of ammunition, they swam across rivers, were captured, but managed to escape from a prisoner-of-war camp. An injured colleague begged David to put him out of his misery and kill him with a bullet to the head. Reluctantly, David complied. Eventually, after months of derring-do, the unit was rescued by British helicopters, and whisked back to India. 'I thought they were fairy tales,' said one boy, little knowing that the truth was scarcely less credible.

In fact, others did hear a more accurate version of David's Burma adventure. A nephew, Almamy Tom Kanu, was a pupil at the school in Bo, and remembered David talking about 'a Nigerian fellow' who had been stranded in the jungle with him, and who had been shot in the leg. 'He said he was always thinking of this fellow, always hoping to hear from him.'

David Kargbo never lost his slight limp. He would point to his ankle, and tell children that in Burma he had pulled maggots out of his wound with his own fingers. But it was his lungs that would kill him. In June 1962, he was admitted to Bo Government Hospital with severe respiratory problems, and died a week later. He was in his late forties. His school held a special assembly in his honour, where the pupils sang his favourite hymn, 'Amazing Grace'.

In the hills to the east of Freetown, a woman sits on the porch of her simple two-roomed house, and enjoys the view over the peninsula mountains and the city far below. She is a great-grandmother, in her late eighties, but she's still a striking woman, with a fierce and proud stare. Her name is Ya Marie, and she is David Kargbo's widow.

Ya Marie says her husband died so young 'because of the mysterious things that had happened to him in the war'. She never remarried. She cannot read or write, and has little to remember him by now. There were not many people in Sierra Leone who were left untouched by what is called the 'Rebel War', the murderous insurgency of the 1990s. In 1999, the rebels attacked Freetown. They raped, looted and murdered their way through the eastern suburbs, hacking the limbs off many civilians. Ya Marie's house was burnt down, and all her photos of David and the records of his war service were destroyed.

As far as I can tell, there is only one picture of David Kargbo that survives, and it belongs to a grandson living in the United States. It was taken in Bo, probably shortly before David died, and is in black and white. It shows a small man standing in a garden, his hair neatly combed. He's wearing slacks and a shirt and tie. I would imagine this is what he wore at church on a Sunday. He is holding a cigarette by his side. The beginning of a smile plays across his face. Maybe I've looked at that photo a little too long, but I see a hint of mischief. David Kargbo looks like a man with stories to tell.

David and Isaac shared a bond that no one else could understand – they had clung to life, and cheated death, together. Now neither is alive to tell his story, but they are not entirely forgotten – not among their families, and not in a village in Burma.

I managed to speak to Shuyiman's family one more time, after Isaac died. They asked for news of him, and, when I explained what had happened, their voices dropped and I sensed their sadness down the line. They also sounded frightened. They said soldiers had handed out a paper in Mairong telling everyone they would be killed or arrested if they tried to go to Kyauktaw to buy or sell food. Gangs of Rakhines had stolen their cows, and prevented them from fishing on the Kaladan. 'Maybe it would be better if we left this country,' Roshi admitted plainly.

He passed the phone to a man called Mohammed, who spoke some English. He said that he had been a student in Sittwe, but had abandoned his studies because of the violence. He had come back to Mairong and now he was trapped there.

'Nobody but God can help us now,' he said. 'Please don't forget us.' Then the line went dead.

Isaac's funeral ceremonies lasted for a whole week. At a service in the Anglican church in Surelere, half a mile from his Lagos home, friends and family sang 'Abide With Me'. It was the same hymn that Isaac and David Kargbo had sung every evening in the jungle, at the time when they thought they were all alone in the world. The priest asked everyone to remember the Muslim in a distant land, Shuyiman, who had given Isaac the chance to rebuild his life in Africa after the war. Then the coffin was loaded onto a hearse, its windows decorated with posters showing Isaac's face beneath the slogan 'Triumphant Exit'. We drove in a convoy out of Lagos, past belching trucks, snaking fuel queues and police roadblocks. We navigated our way along the treacherous highways of Southern Nigeria, swerving to avoid potholes and street hawkers, through the hazy, scrubby hills of Yorubaland. Isaac was returning to Emure-Ile for the last time. It was the village he had once run away from but which was always close to his heart.

In Emure-Ile, Isaac's coffin was paraded through the streets for an entire day. The pallbearers, in matching uniforms and jester-like hats, danced on and on, despite the clammy heat and their heavy load. The trumpeters and drummers, in the same uniforms, barely paused for breath. A school band marched ahead with more drums and twirling batons, traditional hunters fired their muskets in a series of jolting explosions, and even the motorbike taxi boys, the *okada* riders, performed stunts as they raced up and down, saluting in mock solemnity. Isaac's daughters, in matching lace and brocade dresses and sweeping *gele* headwraps, performed the *ajebure*, the traditional funeral dance, behind the coffin.

The procession stopped outside the various homes of Isaac's cousins, nephews and nieces, before eventually arriving at the new house he had been building on the edge of Emure-Ile, the sweeping modern bungalow that always struck me as so out of character with the rest of the village. Here the pallbearers opened the coffin, revealing Isaac's waxy, preserved body, resting on a bed of frilly white material and surrounded by flowers. He was dressed in fine beige and cream robes, a white skullcap on his head, and he gazed upwards with a glassy stare. Throughout that night, hundreds of people gathered around the house and filed in and out of the room where he lay, to pay their last respects. Outside, they danced and ate and drank. Isaac had always said that nobody from the village should be turned away from his funeral. Many people wore T-shirts that said '*Baba Sun re ooo!*' 'Daddy, sleep well'.

A final service was held the following day, at Our Saviours, the church that Isaac's father, Joshua, had helped to establish one hundred years before, when he was one of the first to bring Christianity to Emure-Ile. Then we watched Isaac's coffin being lowered into the dry baked earth. His daughters swayed and then steadied each other by the graveside, and filled their shovels with red soil. The other mourners bent down and picked up fistfuls from the ground. I thought of that day in August 1945 when the villagers threw dust at Isaac to see if he was a ghost. He did not disappear then, but this time his coffin was being covered by the slowly mounting piles of soil. Isaac, my dear friend, was vanishing from view. That's how we kept busy, under the fierce sun, shovelling dirt over Isaac. People had stopped crying. The Yorubas say the end of a long life well lived is a time for celebration, not mourning. Death is not the end, just a transition to another place. The spirit endures.

APPENDIX: KEY DATES

Colonial period

Mar 1824–Feb 1826	First Anglo-Burmese War
24 Feb 1826	Treaty of Yandabo; Burma cedes Arakan to the British
1827	Royal Navy establishes permanent defence station at Fernando Po (West African coast)
1850s	British establish presence around Lagos, after quinine is discovered as a treatment against malaria
Apr–Dec 1852	Second Anglo-Burmese War; British annex Lower Burma, including Rangoon
6 Aug 1861	Treaty of Cession; Lagos becomes British colony
1884	Oil Rivers Protectorate established (later renamed Niger Coast Protectorate); British occupation of larger Niger Delta area
Nov 1885	Third Anglo-Burmese War; British capture Mandalay and Upper Burma, taking control of the entire country
1886	Royal Niger Company granted charter by British government; sets up headquarters inland at Lokoja
1897	British conquer Benin; occupy south-western Nigeria
31 Dec 1899	Royal Niger Company's charter terminated
1908	Initial search for oil in Nigeria
1914	British amalgamate Northern and Southern Nigeria into the Protectorate of Nigeria
1916	Nigerian Council established; membership includes sultan of Sokoto, emir of Kano, alaafin of Oyo and other traditional leaders

1937	Shell and British Petroleum renew search for oil in Nigeria
1 Apr 1937	Burma granted separate administration from India under British colonial rule
1938	Burma Road, connecting Rangoon with Yunnan Province, China, opens

Second World War

3 Sep 1939	Britain declares war on Germany
Jun 1940–Nov 1941	British defeat Italians in the East African Campaign in Abyssinia; many African soldiers fight for both armies
8 Dec 1941	Japan attacks Malaya and Hong Kong; declares war on Britain
26 Dec 1941	Aung San founds Burma Independence Army
18 Jan 1942	Japan attacks Tavoy airfield, Burma; by end of January, Indian brigades retreat across Sittang Bridge
15 Feb 1942	British generals surrender to Japanese Imperial Army at Singapore
7 Mar 1942	British evacuate Rangoon
May 1942	British Army retreats into India; monsoon begins
Aug 1942	'Quit India' movement launched
Dec 1942–May 1943	First Arakan campaign; British defeated
30 Dec 1942	British Chiefs of Staff Committee decides to send African soldiers to Burma
1943–1944	Bengal famine
Jul 1943	First West African troops embark from Lagos to Burma
1 Aug 1943	Japan establishes nominally independent Burma with Ba Maw as prime minister and Aung San as war minister
Dec 1943	West African troops from 81st Division cross frontier from India into Burma
17 Jan 1944	'West African Way' jeep track opens, allowing soldiers from 81st Division to advance into the Kaladan Valley
5–23 Feb 1944	Battle of the 'Admin Box' (the Arakan); first significant British victory in Burma
2 Mar 1944	29th Casualty Clearing Station ambushed on Kaladan River
1–3 Mar 1944	Fighting at Pagoda Hill; withdrawal of 81st Division from Kaladan Valley
8 Mar 1944	Japan invades India, crossing Chindwin River

5 Apr–15 May 1944	Battle of Kohima (Nagaland, India)
16 May–22 Jun 1944	Japanese retreat with British in pursuit
8 Mar–3 Jul 1944	Battle of Imphal (Manipur, India); Japanese retreat into Burma, with British in pursuit
Dec 1944	West African soldiers advance down the Kaladan Valley again
31 Dec 1944	Japanese abandon Akyab (the Arakan port)
3 Jan 1945	British retake Akyab
23 Jan 1945	Battle of Myohaung (Mrauk U); Japanese in Arakan defeated by West Africans; afterwards, 81st Division withdraws from Burma, but 82nd Division fights there until the end of the war
20 Mar 1945	British capture Mandalay; Japanese burn portions of the city to the ground before retreat
27 Mar 1945	Burmese National Army revolts against Japanese
22 Apr 1945	Japanese abandon Rangoon
6 May 1945	British capture Rangoon
6 Aug 1945	US drops atomic bomb on Hiroshima
9 Aug 1945	US drops atomic bomb on Nagasaki
15 Aug 1945	Japanese surrender (VJ Day)

Independence and post-war period

Oct 1946	Last West African soldiers (a Nigerian contingent) leave Burma.
19 Jul 1947	Aung San assassinated
4 Jan 1948	Burmese independence from Britain
1956	First commercial discovery of oil in Nigeria (Olobiri, Niger Delta)
1957–58	Conference on independence and constitution for Nigeria (London)
1 Oct 1960	Nigerian independence from Britain
2 Mar 1962	Burma's elected government overthrown in military coup; 'Burmese Way to Socialism' begins (1962–74)
15 Jan 1966	Nigeria's elected government overthrown in military coup; soldiers rule Nigeria until 1999 (with the exception of a single civilian government, the 'Second Republic', which lasted from 1979 to 1983)

30 May 1967	Republic of Biafra declares independence from Nigeria
6 Jul 1967–15 Jan 1970	Nigerian Civil War
8 Aug 1988	Height of 8888 Uprising in Burma (pro-democracy movement)
18 Jun 1989	Junta changes Burma's name to Myanmar
27 Feb 1999	Democratic elections held in Nigeria
Aug–Oct 2007	Saffron Revolution in Burma (anti-government protests)
10 May 2008	Burmese constitutional referendum
7 Nov 2010	Burmese general elections
13 Nov 2010	Burmese opposition leader Aung San Suu Kyi released from house arrest
30 Mar 2011	Thein Sein becomes president of Myanmar
16 Apr 2011	Goodluck Jonathan elected president of Nigeria
2 May 2012	Aung San Suu Kyi becomes member of Burmese parliament
8–14 Jun 2012	Sectarian clashes erupt in Rakhine State (formerly Arakan)
Oct 2012	More sectarian clashes in Rakhine State, with reports of entire villages being burnt down

ACKNOWLEDGEMENTS

Many people have inspired and guided me as I wrote *Another Man's War*, but of course my greatest debt is to Isaac Fadoyebo.

I met Isaac while he was still in good health and able to share his memories with me. He was a gentleman. After he passed away, his memoir, *A Stroke of Unbelievable Luck*, was my most important source of information. I hope that this book does justice to Isaac's bravery and humility, but also to the wider significance of his story. He opened a door for me, and cast light on some of the most neglected aspects of recent African and British history. He made me think about the Second World War in a different way. Isaac was an exceptional man, but he was not unique. My wish is that this book will help Nigerians to see and acknowledge the many other Isaac Fadoyebos that surround them in their daily lives.

I relied on the co-operation and support of Isaac's six daughters: Nike, Jaiye, Omoniyi, Tayo, Toun and Shomi. They welcomed me warmly into their family, not least during the busy and fraught days around Isaac's funeral. They answered my many queries with candour, patience and humour, yet they never sought to interfere or steer my writing in any given direction. The same is true of Isaac's sons-in-law, including Shex, Gbenga and Ladi, and his grandchildren: Ayo, Yinka, Lekan, Olumide, Seni, Temi, Tosin, Ronke, Ganiyu, Lolu, Boye, Akin, Seun, Funlayo and Moyo. They gave generously of their time. It was a delight to get to know them and hear their perspectives on Isaac's life and Nigeria today.

Robin and Hugh Campbell were wonderful hosts in Lagos. They

provided me with a base that was not only comfortable and convenient but also full of stimulating conversation and friendship. Sam Olukoya was a resourceful and patient guide. Mayowa Adebola negotiated the potholes and go-slows, all the while keeping me entertained with his analysis of just where Nigeria, and Arsenal FC, have gone wrong. Ayoola Kassim, thank you for your help with the Yoruba language, and your friendship over the years. Yinka Oke also helped me with Yoruba. An old colleague from BBC days, Abdullahi Tasiu Abubakar, corrected my Hausa. Ahmed Idris in Abuja facilitated my various Nigerian visa requests with great patience.

Moe and Maung were the Burmese guides who took me up the Kaladan River, maybe just that little bit further than we had permission to travel. I have changed their names to protect their identity, but they can be sure of my gratitude. In London, Tun Khin was my accommodating Rohingya translator.

In Sierra Leone, Lieutenant Colonel Fatorma Gottor of the Sierra Leone Ex-Servicemen's Association went the extra mile to track down David Kargbo's family. John Abdul Kargbo then took over, and enthusiastically helped me fill in the missing years of his father's life. My thanks also to Colonel Paul Davis and Lieutenant Colonel Chris Warren at the Royal Commonwealth Ex-Services League (RCEL) in London, who put me in touch with Lieutenant Colonel Gottor. The RCEL is a charity that assists Commonwealth war veterans. It has a dedicated staff, but works with a small budget. Although this book is in part a tale of British neglect, the RCEL is very much the honourable exception.

Major Robert Murphy's niece Veronica Brennan helped me with information about his family. Robert Murphy has other descendants in Australia whom I was not able to trace. I hope a copy of this book somehow finds its way to them. I also hope that there is a surviving relative of Captain Richard Brown out there who might read it. I feel sad at the possibility that no one in Captain Brown's family will ever know the story of how his courage cost him his life.

*

A number of people read my early manuscript and made invaluable suggestions for its improvement. I benefitted from Peter Cunliffe-Jones' and Andrew Marshall's expertise on Nigeria and Burma respectively. Julian Thompson's military mind guided me through the strategy and tactics of the Burma campaign. Adam Roberts and Simon Robinson are not only good friends but also fine writers and I'm appreciative of the time they made in their busy lives to offer me their cogent thoughts and encouragement.

Conversations with Professor Ian Brown at SOAS, University of London, and Wendy Law-Yone gave me insights into some of the complexities of recent Burmese history. I drew on many sources for my understanding of Britain's African army, but Professor David Killingray's scholarship in this field is outstanding. It was Professor Killingray, as well as Martin Plaut of the BBC, who recognised the importance of Isaac's story when Isaac sent his manuscript to the BBC in the late 1980s, and it was Professor Killingray who dug out Isaac's Surelere address for me. Fidelis Mbah kindly went round to Surelere in early 2010, and made contact with Isaac.

In 2011, I made a film about Isaac Fadoyebo for Al Jazeera, *The Burma Boy*, which was the genesis of this book. Farid Barsoum saw the potential in the story and commissioned the film (it is easy to find on YouTube). Producer Ian 'Butch' Stuttard helped me turn it into reality, travelling with me from Nigeria to Japan to Burma. Cameraman Nick Porter captured our journey in beautiful pictures. Adrian Billing worked his magic in the edit suite. The Imperial War Museum in London allowed us to use their superb film archive. The result was an award-winning documentary that evoked a warm response from all over the world. I would also like to thank Salah Negm and Al Anstey at Al Jazeera, who subsequently gave me time off to write.

My agent Karolina Sutton patiently helped me shape my proposal and found a publisher prepared to take a chance. Robin Dennis at Oneworld has been everything this novice writer could have hoped for from an editor: critical but constructive, encouraging and thorough. Under her experienced eye, my rough early drafts were knocked into shape. Sam Carter made valuable contributions at the end, and Henry Jeffreys and Lamorna Elmer have done great work in publicising *Another Man's War*. Thank you also to Mary Tobin, the copy-editor, whose diligence has spared my blushes.

The interpretation of the past is a very subjective exercise; for all the help and guidance I've received in writing *Another Man's War*, the conclusions I've reached are, of course, ultimately my own. Likewise, any errors or mistakes are my responsibility alone.

My wife, Nicole, has, as ever, been full of patience, love and support. And while I was writing this book she brought me the greatest gift of all. So here's to a new generation; may their spirits soar far and wide.

NOTES

1. One big man

p. 3, *"All they knew...one big man"*: Jolasanmi Olaleye Falore, *Omo Ayeko: The Life and Times of Moses Oni Ayeko-Falore* (Ibadan: Hiswill Books, 1996), p. 71.

p. 4, *the posters screamed*: For examples of British propaganda posters used in Nigeria during the Second World War, see Peter B. Clarke, *West Africans at War 1914–18, 1939–45: Colonial Propaganda and its Cultural Aftermath* (London: Ethnographica, 1986).

p. 5, *'Adolf Hitler ma ṣẹ o'*: Sung to me by Mrs Bisola Williams in Lagos, 14 January 2013. Aged seventy-five, she remembered it perfectly from her childhood.

p. 7, *'the town burnt famously'*: *Illustrated London News*, 13 March 1852, quoted in Richard Huzzey, *Freedom Burning, Anti-Slavery and Empire in Victorian Britain* (Ithaca: Cornell University Press, 2012), p. 145.

p. 7, *'the final act in the long struggle'*: Bryan Sharwood Smith, *But Always As Friends* (London: George Allen and Unwin, 1967), p. 4.

p. 8, *'formerly we stole Africans'*: *Hansard*, 4th ser., xxv, 243–244, quoted in Huzzey, *Freedom Burning*, p. 169

p. 9, *first British person...in Owo*: Dates and details on the arrival of the British in Owo and subsequent developments come from Chief Adedokun Joseph Aralepo, official historian to the court of the *Olowo*. I met Chief Aralepo in Owo in January 2013, when he said he was 103 years old. He has kept a meticulous record of key dates in Owo's past, which he is determined to write up into a formal history. He says the secret to his longevity is his abstention from alcohol and womanising.

p. 9, *'detestable, abhorrent, disgraceful'*: Olatunji Ojo, 'Slavery and Human Sacrifice in Yorubaland: Ondo 1870–94', *Journal of African History*, vol. 46, no. 3, (November 2005): 379–404.

p. 13, *'a good African band'*: I visited St George's Primary School in January 2013. I found more than eighty pupils crowded into some classrooms. One block had been abandoned because the roof had been destroyed in a storm. Teachers crowded round me, pleading for donations towards a laptop or generator. Fortunately, the headmistress was able to find the school records from the 1930s, including the brown leather book, at the bottom of a wooden cupboard in the corner of her office.

p. 13, *'flowers were trimmed'*: Anthony Enahoro, *Fugitive Offender* (London: Cassell, 1965), p. 35.

p. 13, *'as familiar with...London'*: Ibid., p. 43.

p. 14, *'most modern and civilised town'*: 'Coaster', *Coast and Bush Life in West Africa* (London: Gay and Hancock, 1924), p. 13.

p. 15, *'Eton of Nigeria'*: Enahoro, *Fugitive Offender*, p. 51.

2. Let this bayonet drink my blood

p. 18, *'largely because no other party'*: John Hamilton, private papers, Rhodes House Library, Oxford University. Part of a collection of papers of British officers who led African soldiers, compiled in the early 1980s, and listed as RHL, MSS.Afr.s 1734. Hamilton's papers are (168) in this collection.

p. 20, *'What war?'*: J. Allen Bull, *Palm Oil Chop* (private memoirs, Pietermaritzburg: 1987), p. 65.

p. 20, *the boy...had been signed up*: Mario Kolk, *Can You Tell Me Why I Went To War?* (Zomba: Kachere, 2008), p. 16.

p. 20, *'packed...like firewood'*: Martin Plaut, *Africa and the Second World War*, BBC World Service for Africa, 3 September 1989.

p. 20, *former inmates of Kano jail*: Jack Osborne, interview, 5 May 2011. Jack was 101 years old at the time, and still fond of reading Russian and Portuguese literature in the vernacular. He died on 15 August 2012, aged 103. The *Daily Telegraph* ran this obituary: http://www.telegraph.co.uk/news/obituaries/9531609/Jack-Osborne.html.

p. 21, *kosa-ankobifour*: Cameron Duodo, 'Good Night, Good Knight: Profile of Major Seth Anthony', *New African Magazine*, 1 March 2009.

p. 21, *'vast numbers of men came forward'*: Philip van Straubenzee, *Desert, Jungle and Dale* (Durham: Pentland Press, 1991), p. 16.

p. 21, *'An African Soldier Speaks'*: Robert Kakembo, *An African Soldier Speaks* (London: Edinburgh House Press, 1946), p. 7.

p. 21, *'We thought that the Germans'*: Esther Salawu, interview, Lagos, 22 January 2013. Esther was in her late eighties at the time.

p. 22, *'It...would put any black man's back up'*: Plaut, *Africa and the Second World War*.

p. 23, *one in every hundred African soldiers...could read and write*: Trevor Clark, *Good Second Class: Memoirs of a Generalist Overseas Administrator* (Stanhope: The Memoir Club, 2004), p. 66.

p. 23, *'even if not particularly sophisticated'*: John A.L. Hamilton, *War Bush: 81 (West African) Division in Burma 1943–45* (Norwich: Michael Russell, 2001), p. 32.

p. 24, *'of pure European descent'*: David Killingray, *Fighting for Britain, African Soldiers in the Second World War* (Woodbridge: James Currey, 2010), p. 85.

p. 24, *never addressed a single word*: David Killingray, Rhodes House collection of officers' papers. RHL, MSS.Afr.s 1734 (243).

p. 25, *'Everything had to be portable'*: Lieutenant Colonel John Filmer-Bennett, Rhodes House collection of officers' papers. RHL, MSS.Afr.s 1734 (139).

p. 25, *'we took an enormous amount of exercise'*: van Straubenzee, *Desert, Jungle and Dale*, p. 15.

p. 26, *'silly munts'*: Major Ernest Lanning, Rhodes House collection of officers' papers. RHL, MSS.Afr.s 1734 (258).

p. 26, *never even seen a black person*: Ruairi Fallon, *My Father and the Forgotten Army*, BBC2, television programme, 7 July 2013.

p. 27, *'avoid too easy fraternisation'*: 'A Brief Introduction for HM's Forces about to serve in British West Africa', National Army Museum Archives, accession no. 2007-10-09.

p. 27, *'We were one army firmly divided by colour'*: Arthur Moss, *A Piece of War* (n.p.: Vajra Press, 2011), p. 49.

p. 27, *'One bloody African'*: Private correspondence shown to me.

p. 28, *'the men and women who had lived...in that jungle'*: Fred Clarke, *The Road to Spiderdore* (Taunton: Rocket, 1995), p. 64.

p. 28, 'echoed Rawalpindi and Dar-es-Salaam': Charles Carfrae, *Chindit Column* (London: William Kimber, 1985), p. 35.

p. 29, 'we regarded the troops as our children': R.R. Ryder, Rhodes House collection of officers' papers. RHL, MSS.Afr.s 1734, Box X.

p. 29, 'I'd been sent to pick up cannon fodder': Hugh Lawrence, interview, April 2013.

p. 30, a bishop's mitre and a duke's coronet: May Mott-Smith, *Africa From Port to Port* (London: Hutchinson and Co., 1931), p. 189.

p. 30, 'For to them he is more important than King': Arnold Mayard, Private Papers of A.A. Mayard, Imperial War Museum documents no. 1254.

p. 31, 'the usual dreary drinking session': Ibid.

p. 31, a dingy brothel: Inspiration for a Lagos brothel scene from Carfrae, *Chindit Column*, p. 64.

p. 32, 'Me-no likee English sold-ier': James Shaw, *The March Out* (London: Panther Books, 1956), p. 16.

p. 32, 'an unfortunate phase': Major Ernest Lanning, Rhodes House collection of officers' papers. RHL, MS.Afr.s 1734 (258).

p. 34, known by the soldiers as Werewere: Description of the bullying sergeant at Enugu, nicknamed Werewere, taken from J.O. Ariyo, *Oju Mi Ri Ni India* (London: Longmans Green, 1957), p. 27; in Yoruba and translated by Yinka Oke.

p. 37, fantastic names like Venus Bonaparte Smith: Creole women's names taken from Lawrence Green, *White Man's Grave* (London: Stanley Paul and Co., 1954), p. 191.

p. 38, 'our chaps place the Japs': Alan Warren, *Singapore 1942: Britain's Greatest Defeat* (New York: Hambledon, 2002), p. 46.

p. 39, 'The Japanese did not expect': Ronald Blythe, *Private Words: Letters and Diaries from the Second World War* (London: Penguin, 1991), p. 284.

p. 40, 'I have been considering use of African troops': General Archibald Wavell's correspondence with the War Office is in the Public Record Office at Kew. PRO WO 193/91.

p. 40, 'be in accordance with…Colonial Office policy': Ibid.

p. 41, 'that these resources released from West Africa': Ibid.

p. 41, In January 1943, the War Office: Colonel A. Haywood and Brigadier F.A.S. Clarke, *The History of the Royal West African Frontier Force* (Aldershot: Gale and Polden, 1964), p. 373.

p. 41, 'the virtually naked': Clark, *Good Second Class*, p. 68.

p. 42, 'jungle-reared or not': Hamilton, *War Bush*, p. 30.

3. A calabash in the wind

p. 44, 'Since the day we left…a calabash': Kenneth Gandar Dower, *Abyssinian Patchwork: An Anthology* (London: Frederick Muller, 1949), p. 33.

p. 46, 'known to his peers as "Kit" ': Hamilton, *War Bush*, p. 352.

p. 47, 'really does fight to the last man': Major General Christopher Woolner wrote a sixty-page report on the formation, training and performance of the 81st Division in July 1944, just as he was about to be relieved of his position. It can be found in the Rhodes House collection of officers' papers. RHL, MSS. Afr.s 1734 (403).

p. 48, 'Sir. Which time dis war done finish?': Richard Terrell, *Civilians in Uniform* (London: Radcliffe Press, 1998), p. 53.

p. 49, men were worried that the wells…were nearly empty: Alf W. Gardner, *Na Godé* (Brighton: Pen Press, 2003), p. 111.

p. 50, *as dark as the indigo of aro*: Aro is a famous Yoruba black-indigo dye, used for fabrics and skin decoration.

p. 50, *'dis place ebe Englan, nobbe Blackman country'*: 'This must be England, it is not a black man's country.' Letter from a Nigerian soldier quoted in Dower, *Abyssinian Patchwork*, p. 36.

p. 51, *'But you don't arm these monkeys'*: Bull, *Palm Oil Chop*, p. 78.

p. 51, *so few black faces on the streets*: Ronald W. Graham, *There was a Soldier: The Life of Hama Kim* (Africana Marburgensia, 1985), p. 10.

p. 51, *'I for one have never forgotten its delights'*: Carfrae, *Chindit Column*, p. 76.

p. 51, *'a city of well-stocked shops and lovely weather'*: Moss, *A Piece of War*, p. 79.

p. 51, *'the undernourished and ill-dressed native blacks'*: Ibid., p. 78.

p. 51, *an older white woman intervened*: Ibid., p. 79.

p. 52, *'I cannot leave my homeland'*: Major Ernest Lanning, Rhodes House collection of officers' papers. RHL, MSS.Afr.s 1734 (258).

p. 52, *'like a huge sheet of glass'*: Clarke, *The Road to Spiderdore*, p. 90.

p. 52, *'One would see them huddled'*: Bull, *Palm Oil Chop*, p. 77.

p. 52, *'E i lo dee E i lo dee'*: Ariyo, *Oju Mi Ri Ni India*, p. 40; in Yoruba and translated by Yinka Oke.

p. 53, *'No be say all people where de for house'*: Ibid., p. 36.

p. 53, *'as the weather grew warmer, the drums beat'*: Captain Richard Ryder, Rhodes House collection of officers' papers. RHL, MSS.Afr.s 1734, Box X.

p. 54, *'sat glumly waiting to be dismissed'*: Terrell, *Civilians in Uniform*, p. 61.

p. 54, *'the King of England's enemies'*: Carfrae, *Chindit Column*, p. 75.

p. 54, *'One thing doubt me, sah'*: David M. Cookson, *With Africans in Arakan*, National Army Museum, accession no. 2007-10-9.

p. 55, *'were utterly bewildered'*: Brian Crabb, *Passage to Destiny: The Sinking of the SS Khedive Ismail* (Stamford: Paul Watkins, 1997), p. 77.

p. 55, *'the sufferers became frightened'*: Carfrae, *Chindit Column*, p. 76.

p. 56, *'dying almost like flies'*: Jack Osborne, interview, 5 May 2011.

4. The generals are met

p. 57, *'The Generals are met'*: David M. Cookson, *De Bello Kaladano: An Unfinished Epic*, verse 2, National Army Museum, accession no. 2007-10-9.

p. 59, *'starched and pressed'*: John Hamilton, Rhodes House collection of officers' papers. RHL, MSS.Afr.s 1734 (168).

p. 59, *'With my rifle hot in my hands'*: Moss, *A Piece of War*, p. 81.

p. 60, *'India woman like angel'*: Terrell, *Civilians in Uniform*, p. 64.

p. 60, *'Is it not madness to worship what is good to chop?'*: 'Chop' means food in West African 'pidgin'.

p. 61, *'useless to try and stage'*: Private papers of General Noel Irwin, Imperial War Museum documents no. 10516.

p. 61, *about 100,000 soldiers*: Julian Thompson, *Forgotten Voices of Burma* (London: Ebury, 2010), p. x. Thompson estimates that the Indian contribution to the 14th Army was 340,000 men, with 100,000 Britons and 90,000 Africans (as well as 66,000 Chinese and 60,000 Americans, who were under separate command). David Killingray, *Fighting for Britain* (James Currey, 2010) estimates that 120,000 Africans, including various support units, served in the Burma campaign. In addition to the two West African divisions that fought in the Arakan, East African soldiers from the King's African Rifles fought with the 11th Division, mainly in the Kabaw Valley.

p. 62, 'well-to-do West Country farmer': Frank Owen, 'General Bill Slim', *Phoenix: South East Asia Command Magazine*, 1945, reproduced at the Burma Star Association, http://www.burmastar.org.uk/slim.htm

p. 62, 'more obviously at home': William Slim, *Defeat Into Victory* (London: Pan Macmillan, 1999), p. 165.

p. 64, J.O. Ariyo...struck by the similarities: Ariyo, *Oju Mi Ri Ni India*, p. 63; in Yoruba and translated by Yinka Oke.

p. 64, 'seeing is believing': Captain Melvin Crapp's papers in the Rhodes House collection include a fascinating batch of letters by West African soldiers recording their impressions of Calcutta in December 1943, the same month that Isaac was there. RHL, MSS.Afr.s 1734 (108).

p. 65, 'Please Miss, this be welfare?': Major Ernest Lanning, Rhodes House collection of officers' papers. RHL, MSS.Afr.s 1734 (258).

p. 65, twenty times the size of Lagos: I have used an estimated population for Calcutta in 1947 of four million, taken from the Asian Urban Information Centre of Kobe (http://www.auick.org/database/ids/ids01/ids01-04.htm) and a contemporary New York Times report (http://www.nytimes.com/1997/09/03/opinion/03iht-edold.t_5.html).

p. 66, 'widespread distress and suffering': Penderel Moon, ed., *Wavell: The Viceroy's Journal* (Oxford: Oxford University Press, 1997), p. 35.

p. 66, Calcutta in those last weeks of 1943: For more information on the experience of British officers commanding West African troops in Calcutta during the Bengal famine, see Moss, *A Piece of War*, p. 90; and Clark, *Good Second Class*, p. 77.

p. 69, 'but in many small outposts': Cookson, *With Africans in Arakan*.

p. 69, 'Dis not a better Kismuss': Bull, *Palm Oil Chop*, p. 101.

5. Black men held the gate

p. 70, 'All hail...black men held the gate': Cookson, *De Bello Kaladano*, verse 44.

p. 71, 'we would be like microbes': Clark, *Good Second Class*, p. 79.

p. 72, 'Our troops were either exhausted': Private papers of General Noel Irwin, Imperial War Museum documents no. 10516.

p. 73, If the West African division could take the valley: Slim, *Defeat Into Victory*, p. 223.

p. 75, 'They were small men': Hamilton, *War Bush*, p. 64.

p. 77, Good juju: John Rayment *Temporary Gentlemen* (Maidstone: George Mann, 2003), p. 53.

p. 78, 'Not a few men, who have survived the worst': Anthony Irwin, *Burmese Outpost* (London: Collins, 1945), p. 140.

p. 78, the airdrops to include kola nuts: Bull, *Palm Oil Chop*, p. 89.

p. 79, 'capable of operating for months': Hamilton, *War Bush*, p. 28.

p. 82, 'Can't somebody help me?': John Cattanach, *The Jeep Track: The Story of the 81st West African Division Fighting on the Arakan Front in Burma* (London & New York: Regency Press, 1990), p. 48.

p. 82, 'He good man': Clark, *Good Second Class*, p. 84.

p. 82, 'They would let us move forward': Ibid., p. 84.

p. 85, 'at a loss to understand...paradoxical wish': Carfrae, *Chindit Column*, p. 118.

p. 85, 'they didn't spare our people': Plaut, *Africa and the Second World War*.

p. 85, 'When we found the sort of thing they were doing': Christopher Somerville, *Our War: British Commonwealth and the Second World War* (London: Weidenfeld & Nicolson, 1998), p. 223.

p. 85, 'Only way you can identify them': Ibid., p. 230.

p. 86, 'The soldiers knew who had these powers': Ibid., p. 231.

p. 86, 'they were fighting against cannibals': Plaut, *Africa and the Second World War*.

p. 87, 'the Jap was farther down the human scale': George MacDonald Fraser, *Quartered Safe Out Here: A Recollection of the War in Burma* (London: Harville, 1992), p. 125.

p. 87, 'This may seem quick work': Irwin, *Burmese Outpost*, p. 140.

p. 87, 'part of an insect horde': Frank Owen, 'General Bill Slim', *Phoenix: South East Asia Command Magazine*, 1945, reproduced at the Burma Star Association, http://www.burmastar.org.uk/slim.htm.

p. 87, 'minute compared to the misery': Rayment, *Temporary Gentlemen*, p. 99.

p. 87, 'quarter was neither asked': Slim, *Defeat Into Victory*, p. 188.

p. 87, 'dangerous vermin': Carfrae, *Chindit Column*, p. 180.

p. 88, 'They scared the Japs': Jack Osborne, interview, 5 May 2011.

p. 88, 'the Japanese consider [the Africans]': Hamilton, *War Bush*, p. 346.

6. Full of loneliness

p. 90, 'The jungle is eerie...full of loneliness': Private Papers of General Noel Irwin, Imperial War Museum documents no. 10516.

p. 90, 'great dash': Slim, *Defeat Into Victory*, p. 224.

p. 91, 'the whole area was turning into a graveyard': Irwin, *Burmese Outpost*, p. 109.

p. 92, 'It was a victory': Ibid., p. 127.

p. 92, huts full of personal belongings: Terrell, *Civilians in Uniform*, p. 126.

p. 92, 'They showed none of the joyous symptoms': Cookson, *With Africans in Arakan*.

p. 93, 'An isolated whale-back hump': Hamilton, *War Bush*, p. 88.

p. 93, 'Burmese': The Buddhists living in the Arakan, today called Rakhine State, are in fact a distinct people with their own dialect, although they share a religion and bear a resemblance to many other Burmese.

p. 94, 'Salaam aleikum': Hamilton, *War Bush*, p. 88.

p. 96, 'among the shells and bullets there had been no pride': Waruhiu Itote, *'Mau Mau' General* (East African Publishing House, 1967), p. 27.

p. 97, 'colour and other racial differences signified little': Carfrae, *Chindit Column*, p. 168.

p. 97, 'difficult to see how you could not like men': John Hamilton, Rhodes House collection of officers' papers. RHL, MSS.Afr.s 1734 (168).

p. 97, 'was judged on his merits': Slim, *Defeat Into Victory*, p. 195.

p. 97, 'the percentage of Africans possessing consciences': Shaw, *The March Out*, p. 92.

p. 98, 'found themselves in a forbidding country': Carfrae, *Chindit Column*, p. 168.

p. 98, 'I never for one moment questioned': Clark, *Good Second Class*, p. 85.

p. 100, Mairong: The village's name has been changed to protect the identity of those who live there.

7. Juju on the River Kaladan

p. 101, 'Some of the Africans think there is a juju on the River Kaladan': Captain Stephen De Glanville was a civilian affairs officer, attempting to restore some sort of administration in those parts of the Arakan that were controlled by the British. Some of his letters are in the Public Records Office in Kew. PRO WO 203/209.

p. 106, 'a disaster': Major General Woolner's Report, Rhodes House collection of officers' papers, RHL, MSS.Afr.s 1734 (403), July 1944.

p. 106, 'grave dilemma': Ibid.

p. 107, 'had been too quick for us': Ibid.

p. 107, 'not only a dud': A private letter of Major General Woolner, RHL, MSS.Afr.s 1734 (403), 1960.

p. 108, arrived safely back at Paletwa: The War Diary of the 7/16 Punjab Regiment is in the Public Record Office. PRO WO 172/5000, War Diary 7/16 Punjab Regt.

p. 108, 'Every unit and sub-unit': Slim, *Defeat Into Victory*, p. 143.

p. 109, 'unable to understand why their long and victorious advance': Major General Woolner's Report, RHL, MSS.Afr.s 1734 (403), July 1944.

p. 109, 'a dramatic change came over the situation': Major General Woolner's Report, RHL, MSS.Afr.s 1734 (403), March 1944.

p. 109, 'A completely erroneous impression': Major General Woolner's Report, RHL, MSS. Afr.s 1734 (403), July 1944.

p. 110, 'impossible to express': Ibid.

p. 114, a dialect of Bengali: The Muslims in the Kaladan Valley are today usually called Rohingyas and speak a language derived from the Chittagonian dialect of Bengali, with Urdu and Arabic influences. I use words and phrases (transliterated into the Roman alphabet) exactly as Isaac told them to me some sixty-seven years after he first learnt them. My intention was to catch the essence of his memory, rather than to provide a translation into a precise Rohingya word or phrase.

p. 115, 'He just disappeared': The quote from Richard Brown's sister comes to me from George Fraser, another Aberdeen veteran of the Burma campaign. Fraser's mother was a friend of Miss Brown and a neighbour on Great Western Road. When Fraser returned from the war, he met Miss Brown, and recalls that she frequently lamented the loss of her brother. I spoke to George Fraser in February 2013, when he was ninety-three years old. All my efforts to trace any living descendants of Richard Brown have, so far, been in vain.

p. 115, the War Office issued a death certificate: Captain Richard Brown's Army Record, Army Personnel Centre, Historical Disclosures.

p. 120, 'After twelve days hunger': A three-page report written by David Kargbo, and approved by Isaac Fadoyebo, after their rescue (see Chapter 10 for more details), is in the papers of Richard Ryder, an intelligence officer with the Sierra Leone regiment, in Rhodes House. RHL, MSS.Afr.s 1734, R. Ryder.

8. Cover me, Lord

p. 121, 'Let this world...Cover me, Lord': Ralph Nixon Currey and Ronald V. Gibson, ed., *Poems from India, by Members of the Forces* (Oxford: G. Cumberlege, Oxford University Press, 1945), p. 27.

p. 127, the capture of Imphal's huge airfields: For a discussion of the Japanese objectives at Imphal, see Julian Thompson, *The Imperial War Museum Book of the War in Burma 1942–1945* (London: Pan Macmillan, 2012), p. 142.

p. 127, 'change the course of the World War': Slim, *Defeat Into Victory*, p. 285.

p. 128, 'I was saved from the consequences': Ibid., p. 308.

p. 128, 'Glossy black scalps': John Nunneley, *Tales from the King's African Rifles: A Last Flourish of Empire* (London: Cassell, 2001), p. 127.

p. 129, 'For three weeks you are not taking off': Somerville, *Our War*, p. 222.

p. 129, 'a soggy, bloody mess': Moss, *A Piece of War*, p. 122.

p. 130, annual rate of malaria: Slim, *Defeat Into Victory*, p. 177.

p. 130, 'dashing and brilliant': National Army Museum Archive, newspapers on the Burma campaign, accession no. 2007-10-09.

p. 131, The Chindit campaigns: The term 'chindit' is a corruption of the Burmese word

298 *Another Man's War*

chinthe, a mythical beast, half-lion and half-dragon, that guards Buddhist temples. It was the emblem of the Chindit units.

p. 131, 'When the sick and wounded were so exhausted': Quoted in Julian Thompson, *The Imperial War Museum Book of War Behind Enemy Lines: Special Forces in Action, 1940–45* (London: Pan Macmillan, 1999), p. 237.

p. 132, 'Rain was absorbed by...packs': Carfrae, *Chindit Column*, p. 142.

p. 132, 'We didn't even keep a record': Jack Osborne, interview, 5 May 2011.

p. 132, 'the sun wholly deserting us': Carfrae, *Chindit Column*, p. 165.

9. Loyalty and patience

p. 136, 'I have come to love and respect these Mussulmen...loyalty and patience': Irwin, *Burmese Outpost*, p. 23.

p. 139, At night, the village was quiet: Inspiration for the sounds of a Muslim village in the Arakan at night comes from Irwin, *Burmese Outpost*, p. 55.

p. 141, 'They stripped him': Ibid., p. 148.

p. 144, 'Dobama! Dobama!': Izumiya Tatsuro, *The Minami Organ* transl. by Tun Aung Chain (Rangoon: Translation and Publications Department, Higher Education Department, 1981), p. 125.

p. 144, 'over exploiters and blood suckers': Typescript by an unnamed Arakanese on the Japanese occupation, from the Clague Papers. Sir John Clague (1882–1958) was a civil servant involved in the British administration of Burma during the war (he was based in India after the Japanese invasion). His papers, held in the British Library, include letters sent to him from Burmese contacts, describing life under the Japanese. Clague Papers MDD Eur E252/44 F143.

p. 144, 'information of our every movement': John Smyth, *Before the Dawn* (London: Cassell, 1957), p. 139.

p. 144, The majority ethnic Bamar: 'Burman' is most often used as an ethnic term that refers specifically to the Bamar people. 'Burmese' is most often used as a general political term, denoting the nationality of all people who come from Burma, regardless of ethnicity. But, in order to avoid any confusion for the general reader, I have tended to use 'Bamar' instead of 'Burman' here.

p. 145, Indians outnumbered Burmese: Nalini Ranjan Chakravarti, *The Indian Minority in Burma* (Oxford: Oxford University Press, 1971), p. 19.

p. 145, Indian landlords...and Indian shopkeepers and traders: Mira Kamdar, *Motiba's Tattoos: A Granddaughter's Journey into Her Indian Family's Past* (New York: Public Affairs, 2000), p. 86.

p. 145, to learn not only English, but also Hindi: Derek Tonkin, 'A Fresh Perspective on the Muslims of Myanmar', http://www.networkmyanmar.org/images/stories/PDF14/The-Muslims-of-Myanmar.pdf, July 2013.

p. 146, Tens of thousands of Indians died: Thant Myint-U, *The River of Lost Footsteps: A Personal History of Burma* (London: Faber and Faber, 2007), p. 226.

p. 146, 'Akyab reads Indian...newspapers': C.M. Enriquez, *A Burmese Wonderland: A Tale of Travel and Upper and Lower Burma* (Calcutta: Thacker Spink and Co., 1922), p. 58.

p. 147, 'Whilst it lasted it was a pretty bloody affair': Irwin, *Burmese Outpost*, p. 23.

p. 147, 'If they see a British soldier lying wounded': Ibid., p. 36.

p. 147, 'A considerable number were massacred': Peter Murray, 'The British Military Administration of North Arakan 1942–43', p. 7, http://www.networkmyanmar.com/images/stories/PDF13/peter-murray-1980.pdf.

p. 147, 'large numbers of Mohamedans bent on loot': This letter, marked 'Secret', is in the Public Record Office in Kew, part of a collection of documents from officials involved in trying to restore administration in those parts of the Arakan that were controlled by the British. PRO WO 203/309, Arakan Administration, 16 July 1943, Letter to Colonel Lindop.

p. 147, *'related lively stories of their adventures'*: This letter is by an informer for the British, writing to General Irwin, who led the failed Arakan offensive of 1942–43. It can be found in Irwin's papers in the Imperial War Museum. Zainuddin, 'Confidential Account of My Experiences prior to and during the Re-occupation of the Kyauktaw Area by the British', Private Papers of General Noel Irwin, Imperial War Museum documents no. 10516.

p. 148, *'the Indians in the Kaladan'*: This letter is part of the collection of documents from officials involved in trying to restore British administration in the Arakan. It can be found in the Public Record Office in Kew. PRO WO 203/309, Arakan Administration, Letter from Major P. Burnside, 2 March 1944.

p. 148, *the nous to further strengthen their bond with Shuyiman*: In analysing Shuyiman's motivations, I have had to resort to some conjecture. This is based on a conversation with his family, extensive conversations with Isaac, and my own reading of the situation in the Kaladan Valley in 1944, as laid out in this chapter. I believe that Shuyiman helped Isaac and David for four reasons: because he felt pity for them; because he wanted the British to win the war; because he hoped to be rewarded; and because he had a (mistaken) feeling of religious solidarity. I would imagine that the relative importance of each of these reasons varied over time, but together they provided Shuyiman and Khatoun with sufficient incentive, and courage, to take the extraordinary risks that they did.

p. 148, *accounts of how Muslim families went to great lengths*: Peter Haining, *The Banzai Hunters* (London: Conway, 2007), p. 144.

p. 149, *'I am glad for the people who died'*: Khin Myo Chit, *Three Years Under the Japs* (Rangoon: self-published, 1945), p. 1.

p. 149, *'This was regarded by the Burmese people as the greatest humiliation'*: Ibid., p. 4.

p. 149, *'the British sucked Burman blood'*: Quoted in Piers Brendon, *The Decline and Fall of the British Empire* (London: Jonathan Cape, 2007), p. 433.

p. 150, *'The people here are very poor'*: Dorman-Smith Papers, E251/23, Oriental and India Office Collection, British Library. Sir Reginald Dorman-Smith (1899–1977) was Governor of Burma for a troubled period, during 1941–46. After the Japanese invasion, he was in exile in Simla, India, from where he received intelligence reports, such as this letter, on the situation in Burma.

p. 151, *' "Go on Aung San" '*: Slim, *Defeat Into Victory*, p. 518.

10. Home again

p. 154, *'The most famous ballad…"Home Again" '*: D.F. Mackenzie, 'Songs of the "Happy Warriors"', *Victory*, 23 July 1945, p. 10.

p. 155, *'In the month of December the 6'*: From the report written by David Kargbo, and approved by Isaac Fadoyebo, after their rescue, in the papers of Richard Ryder, an intelligence officer with the Sierra Leone regiment, in Rhodes House. RHL, MSS, Afr.s 1734, R. Ryder.

p. 160, *During the screenings in the cinema*: Ernest Lanning's papers in the Rhodes House collection of officers' papers. RHL, MSS.Afr.s 1734 (258) Ernest Lanning.

p. 160, *'more letters from their friends'*: The Emir of Katsina quoted in *Sierra Leone Daily Mail*, 8 March 1945.

p. 163, 'Oh my African brother, do not forget': David Kargbo/Isaac Fadoyebo report in Richard Ryder's papers, Rhodes House. RHL, MSS.Afr.s 1734, R. Ryder.

p. 165, 'despite the Jap mortar fire': van Straubenzee, *Desert, Jungle and Dale*, p. 80.

p. 166, 'I estimate that about 98 percent': F.S.V. Donnison, *British Military Administration in the Far East, 1943–46* (HMSO, 1956), p. 107.

p. 166, 'the battle that might have been fought': General Oliver Leese quoted in Hamilton, *War Bush*, p. 243.

p. 166, the historic city of Mrauk U: Mrauk U was then known by its Burmese name of Myohaung. It has since reverted to its Arakanese, or Rakhine, name.

p. 167, 'forgotten flank': John Hamilton, Rhodes House collection of officers' papers. RHL MSS.Afr.s 1743 (168).

p. 167, 'Only Indian, American and English troops': Original letter in David Killingray's papers in the Rhodes House Collection. RI IL, MSS.Afr.s 1734 (243), and quoted in Killingray, *Fighting for Britain*, p. 210.

p. 168, 'went in anonymously': Sidney Butterworth writing in 1957, quoted in Hamilton, *War Bush*, p. 21.

p. 168, 'To the African, singing': D.F. Mackenzie, 'Songs of the "Happy Warriors"', *Victory*, 23 July 1945, p. 9.

p. 168, 'High spirited, gay, fond of joking': Howard Jardine, 'Introducing the West African', *Madras War Review*, 15 June 1945.

p. 168, 'there have been three cases of rape': Letter from Captain S. De Glanville CAO Arakan Hill Tracts, 26 February 1944, 'My Dear Brigadier'. This letter is part of the collection of documents from British officials involved in trying to restore British administration in the Arakan during the war. It is kept in the Public Records Office in Kew. PRO WO 203/309.

p. 169, They killed three people: Robert Mole, *The Temple Bells Are Calling: Memories of Burma* (Pentland Books, 2001), p. 199.

p. 170, 'the pungent scent of the West Africa Coast': Inspiration for the smell of the West Africa Coast from Bull, *Palm Oil Chop*.

p. 170, 'He came to me, shook my hand': Isaac Fadoyebo, *A Stroke of Unbelievable Luck* (Madison: University of Wisconsin–Madison, African Studies Program, 1999), p. 57.

11. Great awakening

p. 172, 'This war has brought about a great awakening': Kakembo, *An African Soldier Speaks*, p. 20.

p. 173, 'The men were in high spirits': n.a., 'Wounded Nigerians From Far Eastern Theatre', *Nigerian Daily Times*, 25 April 1945.

p. 173, 'appreciate the grimness of the ordeals': n.a., 'Heroes from Burma', *Nigerian Daily Times*, 25 April 1945.

p. 173, 'various stages of deformity': n.a., 'Sir Gerald Whiteley Welcomes Nigeria's War Wounded From Burma Front', *West African Pilot*, 25 April 1945.

p. 173, 'he read as much as he ate': n.a., 'Tough-Talking Chief Enahoro', *Drum* magazine, August 1959, quoted in Sally Dyson, ed., *Nigeria: The Birth of Africa's Greatest Country* (Ibadan: Spectrum Books, 1998), p. 158.

p. 174, 'the angriest young man': Ibid., p. 157.

p. 175, 'So long as the British Empire remain steadfast': n.a., *Nigerian Daily Times*, 20 August 1945.

p. 176, 'the achievements of the West African soldiers': Lieutenant General Burrows quoted in *Nigerian Daily Times*, 20 August 1945.

p. 176, 'uphold the traditions of their fathers': Hugh Stockwell, *Arakan Assignment; The Story of The 82nd West African Division* (New Delhi: Roxy Press, c. 1946), p. 2.

p. 176, *'felt an intrinsic pride'*: n.a., 'Welcome Heroes!', *West African Pilot*, 25 April 1945.

p. 177, *'an electric shock'*: Sylvia Leith-Ross, *Stepping-Stones: Memoirs of Colonial Nigeria 1907–1960* (London: Peter Owen, 1983), p. 119.

p. 178, *'Having fought for liberty'*: Kakembo, *An African Soldier Speaks*, p. 46.

p. 178, *'we could only imagine as the worst monsters'*: Waruhiu Itote, *'Mau Mau' General* (Nairobi: East African Publishing House, 1967), p. 14.

p. 179, *' "At least if I die in this war" '*: Ibid., p. 10.

p. 179, *'a good looking young man, diligent'*: John Nunneley, interview, 20 December 2009. When I met Nunneley in his home in Richmond, he was eighty-seven years old and still sprightly. I had sought him out after reading his haunting account of the Japanese retreat after the battles of Kohima and Imphal in his book *Tales From the King's African Rifles*. After the war, Nunneley campaigned for reconciliation with Japan. He died on 27 July 2013, aged ninety. The *Daily Telegraph* ran this obituary: http://www.telegraph.co.uk/news/obituaries/10331623/John-Nunneley.html.

p. 180, *'Gandhi taught us'*: Plaut, *Africa and The Second World War*.

p. 181, *'The whole area appeared under-populated'*: Hamilton, *War Bush*, p. 316.

p. 182, *'One cannot help but wonder'*: Ibid., p. 318.

p. 182, *'Man will kill himself'*: Ariyo, *Oju Mi Ri Ni India*, p. 88; in Yoruba and translated by Yinka Oke.

p. 182, *'a devastating blow'*: Richard Ryder's papers in the Rhodes House collection of officers' papers. RHL, MSS.Afr.s 1734, Box X, R. Ryder.

p. 183, *One policeman was stabbed*: Private diary of Headley Vinall, courtesy of daughter Margaret Scord.

p. 183, *'they started being less punctilious'*: Hugh Lawrence, interview, April 2013.

p. 184, *'given up all hope of being employed'*: The letters to Hamilton from his former soldiers are in his private papers in the Rhodes House collection of officers' papers. RHL, MSS.Afr.s 1734 (168).

p. 184, *'Our World War II veterans must be made to enjoy'*: n.a *West African Pilot*, 10 July 1945 quoted in G.O. Olusanya, 'The Role of Ex-Servicemen in Nigerian Politics', *Journal of Modern African Studies*, vol. 6, no. 2 (August 1968), p. 227.

p. 185, *'every white man we saw'*: Somerville, *Our War*, p. 319.

p. 185, *'looking back…in comparison with the tumults'*: Basil Davidson quoted in Plaut, *Africa and the Second World War*.

p. 185, *'I am opposed as there is always a danger'*: Private diary of Hugo Marshall, 1 March 1948, courtesy of his grandson Peter Cunliffe-Jones.

p. 186, *the same tactics, and often the very same personnel*: Wendell Holbrook, 'British Propaganda in the Gold Coast, 1939 1945', *Journal of African History*, vol. 26, no. 4 (1985), p. 360.

p. 186, *'every soldier who went to India got new ideas'*: Plaut, *Africa and the Second World War*.

p. 189, *'It was as if a dead man was back'*: Fadoyebo, *A Stroke of Unbelievable Luck*, p. 60.

12. The cries turn to laughter

p. 191,'Your son went…The cries turn to laughter': Quoted in Ariyo, *Oji Mi Ri Ni India*, p. 96; in Yoruba, translated by Yinka Oke. The original text reads:

> Omo nyin re Soja
> E mi sunkun
> Abode soja
> Ekun d'erin o.

p. 192, *'He was shot with another soldier'*: Adedeji Onafade, interview, Emure-Ile, Nigeria, 16 January 2013. She estimated her age to be eighty-four.

p. 192, *'There was joy on everyone's face'*: Thomas Olajide Adegbola, interview, Lagos, 24 January 2013.

p. 192, *'Let us just thank god that I'm alive'*: Isaac Fadoyebo, interview, Lagos, 29 November 2011.

p. 192, *'I was not prepared to have my leg further mutilated'*: Fadoyebo, *A Stroke of Unbelievable Luck*, p. 61.

p. 193, *'unexpected and premature departure'*: Ibid., p. 61.

p. 194, *'careless and fond of going out'*: Ibid., p. 5.

p. 194, *O Levels, and then A Levels*: In the British system of education, pupils typically took up to a dozen subjects at O Level at the age of fifteen or sixteen. They still take A Levels at the end of secondary school, typically in three or four subjects, and A Level results tend to determine whether and where a pupil goes to university.

p. 195, *'The town was very quiet'*: Esther Salawu, interview, Lagos, 22 January 2013.

p. 196, *'the tumble of houses'*: Leith-Ross, *Stepping-Stones*, p. 165.

p. 196, *small-time gangsters known as jagudas*: n.a., 'In Praise of Lagos', *Drum* magazine, December 1960, quoted in Sally Dyson, ed., *Nigeria*, p. 272.

p. 196, *Aduke Alakija*: All Aduke Alakija quotes come from an interview in London, 30 April 2013. She had just celebrated her ninety-second birthday.

p. 198, *'inter-racial bonhomie'*: Elspeth Huxley, *Four Guineas: A Journey Through West Africa* (London: Chatto and Windus, 1954), p. 188.

p. 198, *'utterly different...a proud assertive people'*: Margery Perham, *West African Passage: A Journey through Nigeria, Chad, and the Cameroons, 1931–1932* (London: Peter Owen, 1983), p. 25.

p. 199, *starting to feel out of place*: Leith-Ross, *Stepping-Stones*, p. 167.

p. 200, *'created and fostered by our own politicians'*: Nelson Ottah, 'Tribalism Is Nigeria's Deadliest Enemy', *Drum* magazine, February 1960, in Dyson, ed., *Nigeria*, p. 191.

p. 200, *'Never has there been such a delirium'*: Bayode Rotibi, 'It's Our Last Lap to Freedom', *Drum* magazine, September 1960, in Dyson, ed., *Nigeria*, p. 238.

p. 201, *'Nigeria, we hail thee'*: 'Nigeria We Hail Thee' was Nigeria's national anthem from 1960 to 1978, when it was replaced by 'Arise O Compatriots'. Both anthems are in English.

p. 201, *'genius'*: n.a., 'Lumumba's Offensive Speech in King's Presence', *Guardian*, 1 July 1960, http://www.theguardian.com/world/1960/jul/01/congo.

p. 201, *'Nigerians, in their hour of triumph'*: n.a., 'How We Celebrated Independence', *Drum* magazine, January 1961, in Dyson, ed., *Nigeria*, p. 278.

p. 202, *'I think we rushed independence'*: Aduke Alakija, interview, London, 30 April 2013.

p. 203, *'Officers began to retire'*: Chinua Achebe, *There Was A Country* (London: Allen Lane, 2012), p. 48.

p. 204, *'comrade in adversity...big hearts'*: Fadoyebo, *A Stroke of Unbelievable Luck*, p. 37; Isaac also used these phrases to describe the Japanese in conversations with me in Lagos and Emure-Ile, Nigeria, in April 2011.

p. 205, *'We would picnic under the trees'*: Nike Ajayi, interview, Emure-Ile, Nigeria, 16 January 2013.

p. 206, *'alive with girls, cars'*: Sam Uba, 'Irrepressible Lagos', *Drum* magazine, July 1967, in Dyson, ed., *Nigeria*, p. 169.

p. 207, *'He's a human being'*: Tayo Fadoyebo, interview, en route from Lagos to Emure-Ile, 15 January 2013.

p. 208, 'I live a simple and contented life': Fadoyebo, *A Stroke of Unbelievable Luck*, p. 5.

p. 209, 'If you build on a faulty foundation': The quotes from Isaac about the problems of Nigeria come from long conversations between us in Lagos on 29 November and 3 December 2011.

13. Into a ravine

p. 213, 'The shining, beautiful car...into the ravine': Leith-Ross, *Stepping-Stones*, p. 176.

p. 213,'I thought they would fix my leg in hospital': Isaac Fadoyebo, interview, Lagos, 29 November 2011.

p. 215, 'At least that was the number a couple of months ago': John Adolie, interview, London, January 2013.

p. 218, The 1921 census...The United Nations: Statistics from Alistair Sommerland, *Lagos Island: A Short History* (British Deputy High Commission, Lagos, 1998); Kaye Whiteman, *Lagos: Cities of the Imagination Series* (Oxford: Signal Books, 2012); and UN World Urbanization Project, 'World Urbanization Prospects: The 2011 Revision', p. 7, http://esa.un.org/unup/pdf/WUP2011_Highlights.pdf.

14. Here you left us

p. 228,'Wait and look...Here you left us': Quoted in Ariyo, *Oju Mi Ri Ni India*, p. 85; in Yoruba and translated by Yinka Oke. The original text reads:

> *E duro ke e wo ihin*
> *Enyin ero ti nkoja*
> *Lati iha iwo orun Afrika*
> *Lati ile tutu Yuropu*
> *Lati inu orun gangan India*
> *Lati ona jinjin Australia*
> *Ni a ti wa fie mi wa le'le*
> *Ni ese mefa sisale ile yi*
> *Ni egungun wa sun*
> *Bi e de'le, e ba wa wi fun*
> *Awon wonni ti a ko ba ni ipin*
> *mo laiye pe*
> *NIHIN NI E FI WA SILE SI.*

p. 232, some 185,000 Japanese soldiers were killed: Izumiya Tatsuro, *The Minami Organ*, transl. by Tun Aung Chain (Translation and Publications Department, Higher Education Department, Rangoon, 1981), p. 206.

p. 232, It wasn't just Rangoon that was in ruins: Details from Michael W. Charney, *A History of Modern Burma* (Cambridge: Cambridge University Press, 2009), p. 58.

p. 233, 'the rules of the game had changed': Balwant Singh, *Independence and Democracy in Burma, 1942–1952: The Turbulent Years* (University of Michigan Center for South and Southeast Asian Studies, 1993), p. 6.

p. 233, 'The speech done, he gave away the awards': Ibid., p. 22.

p. 234, 'almost without exception, lazy': Mole, *The Temple Bells Are Calling*, pp. 246, 250.

p. 234, 'the African could speak no Burmese': Ibid., p. 235.

p. 235, 'The Africans have been officially warned': John H. McEnery, *Epilogue in Burma 1945–1948: The Military Dimensions of British Withdrawal* (Staplehurst: Spellmount, 1990), p. 56.

p. 235, 'the last great manifestation': Ibid., p. 56.

p. 236, 'The Burmese had been a proud people': Mole, *The Temple Bells Are Calling*, p. 289.

p. 236, 'In a way...the Second World War never really stopped': Myint-U, *The River of Lost Footsteps*, p. 258.

p. 237, *supplying ten thousand rifles*: Ibid., and John F. Cady, *A History of Modern Burma* (Ithaca: Cornell University Press, 1958), p. 598.

p. 238, 'Even to a child': Wendy Law-Yone, interview, London, June 2013. See also Wendy Law-Yone, *The Golden Parasol: A Daughter's Memoir of Burma* (London: Chatto and Windus, 2013).

p. 239, 'it was as if someone had just turned off the lights': Myint-U, *River of Lost Footsteps*, p. 294.

15. Natives of Arakan

p. 241, 'Mohammedans...natives of Arakan': Francis Buchanan-Hamilton, *Asiatic Reseaches* (Asiatic Society Calcutta, 1801), vol. 5, p. 237.

p. 242, *Rangoon, now known as Yangon*: As explained at the front of the book, in 1989, when the military government renamed Burma as Myanmar, Rangoon became Yangon. Since then, governments, international organisations, human rights campaigners and journalists have agonised over which names to use. Myanmar and Yangon are now more widely used, but, for the sake of consistency with the rest of the book, I have stuck to the old names of Burma and Rangoon, and hope this does not cause offence.

p. 244, 'sowing hatred among the people': Back page of *New Light of Myanmar*, 18 June 2011.

p. 245, 'In any town in India the European Club': George Orwell, *Burmese Days* (London: Penguin, 2009), p. 14.

p. 246, 'we should like to see less veiled hostility': Edward Law-Yone, 'Not For Europeans Only', *The Nation*, 24 May 1951, courtesy of Wendy Law-Yone.

p. 247, *where the attack on the 29th CCS had taken place*: See IWM 03/787, notes by John Hamilton on Isaac Fadoyebo's *An Unbelievable Stroke of Luck*; and Hamilton, *War Bush*, p. 123.

p. 249, 'All valuables were confiscated': Kamdar, *Motiba's Tattoos*, p. 107. The Indians of Burma suffered a similar experience to that of Indians forced out of Idi Amin's Uganda in the early 1970s, only the expulsion from Burma was on a much larger scale and did not achieve the same degree of international notoriety.

p. 250, 'It's awful when I look back': Wendy Law-Yone, interview, London, June 2013.

p. 250, *About 250,000 Muslims fled*: Martin John Smith, *Burma: Insurgency and the Politics of Ethnicity* (London: Zed Books, 1991), p. 241.

p. 250, *new Citizenship Act*: For contrasting interpretations of the 1982 Citizenship Act, see Human Rights Watch, http://www.hrw.org/node/109177/section/8; and see Derek Tonkin, 'A Fresh Perspective on the Muslims of Myanmar', 7 July 2013, http://www.networkmyanmar.org/images/stories/PDF14/The-Muslims-of-Myanmar.pdf.

p. 251, *freedom of movement was restricted*: Chris Lewa, 'North Arakan: An Open Prison for the Rohingya in Burma', Forced Migration Review, a project of the University of Oxford Refugee Studies Centre, http://www.fmreview.org/en/FMRpdfs/FMR32/FMR32.pdf.

p. 251, 'new Palestinians': Smith, *Burma: Insurgency and the Politics of Ethnicity*, p. 241.

p. 251, 'No doubt they felt insecure': Singh, *Independence and Democracy in Burma*, p. 100.

16. Impregnable

p. 252, 'Arakan is a second Venice...impregnable': Letter from Father Farinha quoted in C. Eckford Luard with H. Hosten, ed., *Travels of Fray Sebastien Manrique 1629–1643*:

A Translation of the Itinerario de las Missiones Orientales (London: Hakluyt Society, 1926), p. 172.

p. 253, Maung: A pseudonym to protect his identity.

p. 255, 'the golden roofs of the palace': Willem Schouten, 'Voyages', quoted in ibid., p. 218.

p. 255, at least 160,000 people lived in Mrauk U: Ibid., p. 217.

p. 255, Moe Kyaw: Again, a pseudonym to protect his identity.

p. 258, 'bats are numerous': Enriquez, *A Burmese Wonderland*, p. 69.

17. For our children to be free

p. 260, 'If ever an army fought…for our children to be free': Slim, *Defeat Into Victory*, p. 183.

p. 263, Buddha travelled from India using levitation: Myar Aung, *Famous Monuments of Mrauk-U: Useful Reference for Tourists and Travellers*, transl. by Ah Lonn Maung (Yangon: Middle Line, 2007), p. 119.

p. 269, 'I have greatest admiration for their tenacity': Peter Murray, 'The British Military Administration of North Arakan 1942–43', p.4, http://www.networkmyanmar.org/images/stories/PDF13/peter-murray-1980.pdf.

p. 270, In Sittwe, Rakhines burnt most of the Rohingyas' homes: Human Rights Watch, 'The Government Could Have Stopped This', August 2012, http://www.hrw.org/reports/2012/08/01/government-could-have-stopped.

p. 271, the army and police either looked the other way: Human Rights Watch, 'All You Can Do is Pray', April 2013, http://www.hrw.org/reports/2013/04/22/all-you-can-do-pray.

Epilogue

p. 278, 'a Nigerian… he was always thinking of this fellow': Almamy Tom Kanu, interview, May 2013.

INDEX